# LONGMAN LINGUISTIC LIBRARY

# A HISTORY OF AMERICAN ENGLISH

# LONGMAN LINGUISTICS LIBRARY

# A History of American English

J. L. Dillard

Longman
London and New York

**Longman Group UK Limited**
Longman House, Burnt Mill, Harlow,
Essex CM20 2JE, England
*and Associated Companies throughout the world.*

*Published in the United States of America
by Longman Publishing, New York*

© Longman Group UK Limited 1992

First published 1992
Third impression 1993

**British Library Cataloguing-in-Publication Data**

A catalogue record for this book is available from the British Library

**Library of Congress Cataloguing-in-Publication Data**

Dillard, J. L. (Joey Lee), 1924–
A history of American English / J. L. Dillard.
p.   cm. — (Longman linguistics library)
Includes bibliographical references and indexes.
ISBN 0-582-05298-X — ISBN 0-582-05296-3 (pbk.)
1. English language—United States—History. I. Title.
II. Series.
PE2809.D543   1992            91-25675
427'.973–dc20                 CIP

Set in 10/11 Times Roman

Produced by Longman Singapore Publishers (Pte) Ltd
Printed in Singapore

To Mary, without whom this work would have been impossible – and not worth doing in the first place

# Contents

# Preface

The present book deals with something like the same subject as my *Toward a Social History of American English* (Dillard 1985), but it is only in the roughest sense a companion volume. I am not, however, rejecting the basic orientation of the other book. A few details – like the prominence of the Basques in the early language contact picture – amount to corrections. At the time of the other book, Bakker's researches were not available and I took the statements about Basques among the Northwestern coastal Indians as folk representations of 'Europeans' or 'Frenchmen'. That amounts to another lesson in taking sources seriously. That has been a major thrust of my earlier books, and I am in a sense only now beginning to learn my own lesson.

Many scholars have been helpful to me in the presentation of this work; I could not have begun to do it alone. Among these may be mentioned prominently Terry G. Jordan, Walter Prescott Webb Professor at the University of Texas, Austin, and Frederic G. Cassidy, chief editor of the Dictionary of American Regional English. Professor Cassidy deserves special thanks for his cooperation and help, providing me with many materials from DARE, while knowing that we are of basically different orientations insofar as American dialects are concerned. I may not have always understood what those experts had to say, and I did not always take their advice. Responsibility for mistakes remains entirely and exclusively my own.

In preparing the manuscript, especially in coping with the mysteries of computer technology, special thanks are due to Dr. Gene Beckett, Director of the Learning Centre at Shawnee State University, Portsmouth, Ohio, and to members of his staff.

J. L. Dillard

# Chapter 1

# On the background of American English

English came to North America and what eventually became the United States as a part of the general movement of European languages and their speakers not only to the one 'new' continent but to almost all parts of the world. The type of English spoken during the period of exploration and colonization was important to the history of American English. So were the languages spoken by other groups – immigrants and native Americans. The first point has received recognition from the beginning of the study of American English. The second has tended to be overlooked.

The first officially English-speaking group came to the Americas in the 1497 expedition of John Cabot under a patent from Henry VII. Its leader, Genoese-born Giovanni Caboto (whose name was also spelled Tabot and Chabot in various documents), had been in the spice trade in the Middle East before the expedition in which he 'discovered' and named Newfoundland. His son Sebastian, whose strengths and weaknesses as an explorer have been much discussed and debated, was as internationally oriented as the father. English came to the New World in a context of language contact, and language contact is the salient feature of its early history.

There are theories of European presence in the area preceding Cabot, and even Columbus, to complicate an already complex picture. At any rate, it was not long before that presence increased greatly. Axtell (1988: 145) reports that 'By 1517 "an hundred sail" could be found in Newfoundland's summer harbors. The discovery of the Great Banks in the 1530s only increased the traffic between Europe and America.'

The speculation about pre-Columbian exploration includes the possibility that early fishermen sailing from Breton or even from Bristol may have sought the rich catches of cod and other fish of which Sebastian Cabot is supposed to have reported that they were so thick as to impede the progress of his ships. The speculations themselves have little to do with the early history of American English; the fishermen, it now seems, a great deal.

It was an Englishman perhaps less complicated than either John or Sebastian Cabot, Sir Humphrey Gilbert, who, after at least one failure, founded the first relatively permanent settlement of what might simply be called English speakers. According to the *Dictionary of National Biography*, however, his 'mixed' colony consisted of 'raw adventurers, landsmen, and sailors'. The possibilities concerning this first English-speaking colony are fascinating, but documents do not seem to be available.

For all the European migrants to the New World there was a complex language contact situation presenting historical problems which are hardly solved by facile statements about communication by signs and chains of interpreters. (For the latter, the fascinating problem is still the first link in the chain.) When Verrazzano complained that in his last contact with North American 'natives', in 1524, he suffered because 'we could converse with the bad people (*mala gente*) only by signs' (Sauer 1971: 61), we might wonder how he had communicated with the presumably contrasting 'good people'. Considerations of maritime language history may cause one to wonder what language(s) Captain John Hawkins used in his voyages 'capturing negroes on the Guinea coast and [selling] them to the Spaniards at the point of his sword' (Lowery 1959: 89) as well as visiting the French in Florida on his second voyage in 1564.

Perhaps of even more linguistic significance, in view of Bakker (1987), is the early prominence of Basques. Fishing ships also engaged in trading for pelts, said to have visited the shores of Maine, included Basques who visited the Fagundes colony (Sauer 1971: 61). Whalers of that nationality have been reported as early as 1536 (Axtell 1988: 146) or even earlier according to some (see Bakker 1987: 2). L'Escarbot (1609: 172) reported:

> For to accommodate themselves with us, they [the native Americans] speake unto us in the language which is to us more familiar, wherein is much *Basque* mingled with it: not that they care greatly to speake our languages; for there be some of them which do sometimes say, that they come not to seek after

us: but by long frequentation they cannot but retain some word or another.

Bakker (1987: 4) theorizes that a 'Basque Nautical Pidgin may perhaps be a missing link between a Portuguese Proto-Pidgin (or the Lingua Franca) and creole languages all over the world'. The most important maritime contact languages of the exploration period, with a few changes, may have been involved in the early period.

At any rate, 'one of three Basque–Icelandic vocabularies preserved in manuscript' (Bakker 1987: 1) contains

> ser ju presenta for mi   'what do you give me?'

where the use of *for* seems to be a marker of an oblique ('beneficiary') case. The same text also contains another expression, *fenicha for you*, where *fenicha* represents an obscenity quite typical of frank sailor badinage, in which *for* seems to mark a direct object. In Schuchardt's (1909) Lingua Franca materials, *per*, a virtual Romance equivalent of *for*, may precede a pronoun in either direct or indirect object function (see also Harvey, Jones and Whinnom 1967). Schuchardt's examples include

> mi mirato per ti   'I have seen you'

> mi hablar per ti   'I say to you'

and there is a parallel, with a slight phonological change, in the contact variety of Italian used in Ethiopia (Bakker 1987: 27)

> non dire ber luy   'don't tell him'.

Holm (1989, II, 629) cites Afrikaans *vir* and Indo-Portuguese *per* in the same functions.

A directly parallel use of *for* seems to exist in English nautical pidgin of the same general period, here used in the African slaving trade, as attested by William Smith, *A Voyage to Guinea*:

> This fit Wife for you.

Although Smith (or his printer) capitalized *Wife* in accordance with the general usage of the time, when nouns were so capitalized, an analysis of this *wife* as a verb would fit better into Pidgin English structure – something about which neither Smith nor his printer may have known. The preceding sentence of the quoted African's discourse, *This no my wife*, clearly contains a

nounal use of *wife* in a negated zero copula predicate. A pidgin
context, at least, seems established.

Where Smith, and most English readers, quite probably
interpreted:

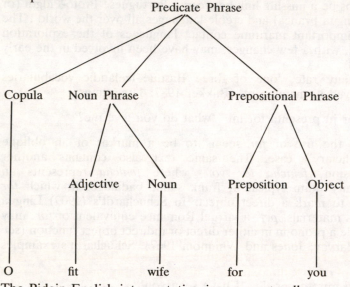

The Pidgin English interpretation is more naturally:

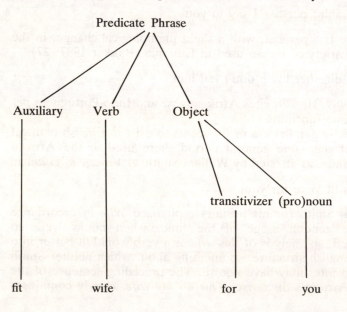

*Fit* replaces more ordinary English (the term is borrowed from Taniguchi 1972) *can* in certain West African English pidgins today and may have done so very early. By the time of P. Grade (1892) the usage seems to have been well established. Grade gives the examples:

> Me no fit for help me alone 'I cannot help myself alone'
> Me no fit lie  'I cannot lie'.

The first of Grade's citations is from *'ein eingeborener aus Bagida, Mensa'*; the second, from *'ein Kruneger, Friday'*.

The interpretation that a 'noun' or other part of speech may serve as 'verb' (or predicator) is at least possible in much of the pidgin literature of about the same time. The missionary periodical *The Religious Intelligencer*, published from the 1820s, has forms like

> O, how I sorry for him

where the description of *sorry* as a predicator, although not that favoured by an approach which tries to make the pidgin as close to ordinary English as possible, is at least feasible. The same page of the text contains a more probably adjectival use of *sorry*:

> (I am) only sorry 'cause can't read Bible

and two occurrences of the noun form:

> (I) love tell him [Jesus] all my sorrows
> He [Jesus] take away all my sorrows

Such variability, especially between Pidgin English forms and more standard forms, is commonplace in these texts.

Aside from its evidence about the origins of some Pidgin English structures, the Basque nautical pidgin seems to have had some significance for the total language picture of early North America, perhaps not only on the northern shores (see Chapter 5.) For the more northerly area, L'Escarbot (1609: 268) reported about 'our French-men, and chiefely the Basques who doe go euery yeare to the great riuer of *Canada* for the whales' with a 'confusion' of nationalities which only serves to emphasize the multinational (and multilingual) nature of the fishing and trading fleets. It was these Basques, apparently often identified with seagoing Frenchmen as 'Normans', about whom L'Escarbot reported (1609: 172):

> Whereof the [Canadian] Savages being astonied, did say in words borrowed from the Basques, Endia Chave Normandia, that is to say, that the Normans know many things. Now they call all Frenchmen Normands [*sic*] except the Basques, because the most part of the fishermen that goe fishing there, be of that nation

which a transmissionist would almost immediately take for a Lingua Franca-related text.[1]

Early contact with the Basque pidgin seems to have been extensive. A text presented in an unpublished (1986) paper by Bakker (quoted in Holm 1989, II, 629) is

> for you mala gissuna    'you are a bad man'.

Variant forms of Basque *gizon* ('man') occur in North American varieties, notably *kessona* in a Basque–Amerindian pidgin studied by Bakker (1987, ms.). Goldin, O'Leary and Lipsius (1950) have *gazoony*, said to be characteristic of 'mid-West prisons' and to mean 'a degenerate, especially a passive pederast; a *punk*'. Wentworth and Flexner (1975) have *gazooney, gazony* ('An ignoramus, *Maritime*') with no indication as to date. They also have 'A young hobo; an inexperienced or innocent youth. Hobo use'.[2]

*Mala*, in the text cited by Bakker, is obviously Romance. Another form cited in the same text, *gara*, seems likely to be from something like Spanish *guerra* (ultimately from Germanic), and the mixing of Romance forms (cf. *chave* above) from different languages is a commonplace feature of the maritime communication situation. (See Chapter 5, especially in the Gulf Corridor situation.)

Accretions to the vocabulary in the early contact area came from such sources. Scargill (1977: 25–6) specifies that 'a Portuguese farmer or *llavrador* in 1499 explored our [i.e. the Canadian] coast and gave the name of his trade to Labrador'.

The early fishing activities brought terms like *baccalaos* ('codfish) and *capelin*, (a small fish), named by French fishermen because of a fancied resemblance to the European *capelan*, and *penguin* from Welsh. The words referred to here probably came, however, more directly from maritime activity than from the languages cited as etymological sources, at least in any traditional sense of borrowing.

Terms not rated 'Americanisms' by the esoteric standards of the branch dictionaries were also heard along the coastline. *Barcalonga* for 'a large . . . fishing-boat . . . common to the Mediterranean' (*Oxford English Dictionary*, citing Falconere, *Dict. Marine*, I, 89) is first listed from 1682. The term is attested in the Americas, used in the Portobello/Bastamentos area, in a kind of journal (anonymous) of Bartholomew Sharp's privateering expedition quoted from a 1752 manuscript by Jameson (1970: 89). Pontillo (1975) lists uses of *barca* and congeners but not *barca longa*. *Barque longo* is attested as early as 1680; such non-Spanish (and non-Iberian) forms are considered Lingua Franca by Pontillo (1975) and by Harvey, Jones and Whinnom (1967). The *Dictionary of Americanisms* records *Barkentine* or *Barquantine* as 'a name applied in the great lakes of North America'. Maritime forms obviously went far in the Americas.

For the originally maritime variety Pidgin English, recognition has come late – and not necessarily from the most orthodox sources; Mario Pei, whose very name has tended to be opprobrious among linguists, has perhaps the most complete presentation (1967). Perhaps even less prestigious among linguists was Edgar Sheppard Sayer, whose *Pidgin English* (1939/43) attracted a scathing review from Hall (1944), ironically one of the most active linguists in discovering and publicizing the widespread existence of pidgin and creole languages. Sayer asserted, perhaps more from personal experience than as the result of professional analysis, that 'Thirty million people speak Pidgin English' (1939/43: 1).

Sayer also asserted the uniformity of Pidgin English: 'fundamentally Pidgin English does not change as it leaps from continent to continent, island to island. Local custom determines the slight variations in the words used and their meaning' (1939/43: 80). Any attempt to follow his contention that one who could speak the Pidgin English of Australia or the Pacific islands could also communicate with West Africans has tended to run afoul of the numerous local pride movements, most of which – moving away from an attitude of disparagement amounting almost to self-hate for the local non-traditional variety – have proceeded to a kind of supportive, patriotic attitude which takes pride in seeing the language variety as something locally unique.

Where even Pei and Sayer have hesitated to talk about the *historical* – as opposed to the geographic or demographic – spread of Pidgin English, works like that of Bakker (1987), which suggest a sixteenth-century origin, appear especially significant. Attestations, gleaned from a heterogeneous multitude of sources in which use of the pidgin is virtually accidental – where, in fact, it is often treated as 'funny' language used by a non-European – tend to show quite widespread distribution by the early nineteenth century, more sporadic but still geographically and demographically widespread use in the eighteenth, some evidence of use in the seventeenth (especially through comparison to the spread of historically analogous varieties like Pidgin French), and – as in Bakker's reconstruction – more than a little possibility of existence in the sixteenth century.

That something special was involved at sea, at least insofar as English was concerned, is made to appear likely by statements like this from Philip Ashton, who was taken by pirates on 15 June 1722 when out on the schooner *Milton* on the fishing grounds of Cape Sable. After Ashton had been for some time on the pirate ship, 'Low presently sent for me Aft, and according to the Pirates usual Custom, *and in their proper Dialect* asked me, if I would sign their Articles, and go along with them' (Barnard 1726, emphasis added). Ashton, who wrote his account for seafarers and especially for fishermen who might fall into the hands of the 'Sons of Violence', also includes (p. 31) forms like

. . . to have made a Boon Prize of him . . .

where *boon* functions more like a special maritime form of Romance *bon* ('good') than like the familiar English noun *boon* . (See the discussion on the phonology of Romance /o/ in English contact varieties in Chapter 5.) Ashton, who writes of the *Cape de Verde* [sic] *Islands*, quotes these pirates in quite ordinary English, but he uses the same variety to report the speech of Spaniards whom he encounters. In fact, the literary conventions of the time involve abstract reference to the 'dialects' or other language forms of groups such as sailors and pirates and accommodation to the reader in presentation through more ordinary literary English.

In a journal of an English seaman who lived and worked in the king's ships from 1659 to 1703, Lubbock (1934) consistently finds forms like *liver* ('deliver') and *unliver*, where the prefix *un-* apparently has the force of the more conventional *de-*: 'and two or three days afterward we began to "un-liver" out our sugars, and in eight or ten days we "livered" out all' (Lubbock 1934: 78).

An equally tantalizing report comes from 'Doctor' Willard, whose 'Inland trade with Mexico' was published in the *Western Monthly Review* in 1829 (Thwaites 1906, XVII, 327).

Into what nook of our globe can we penetrate, and not find our citizens with their 'trade and traffic'? We not long since read in a paper, that a Yankee captain was running a steam boat in the Yellow sea . . . . We delight to consort as a listener among the crowds of American tars. Their peculiar dress and step, walking the firm earth as if 'she' reeled; their frank, reckless, and manly port; their voice, formed to its tones and expression amidst the roars of the winds and the dash of the waves; their dialect, their outlandish phrase, all furnish food for imagination.

Language seemingly related in grammatical structure to Pidgin English characterizes the recorded speech of *un petit nègre* in New France in the early seventeenth century (LeJeune 1632: 39–40); actually, that *petit nègre* proves to have been six years old and therefore not beyond the fantastic creativity which the 'bioprogram' (Bickerton 1982) attributes to children. Not as early as the first reports of mixed ethnic and language groups but still quite early, reports of other pidgin varieties (including English) abound. See Dillard (1985) for Pidgin English in the early history (there 'pre-history') of English in the American colonies.

By the colonial period, pidginized varieties of French as well as some specialized varieties of Iberian are well attested in the general area which includes the Caribbean and North America. The Lingua Franca, of which Columbus himself was held to be a speaker by Pontillo (1975: 34), is at least reported for the port of St Augustine, Florida, as late as 1837 by historian John Lee Williams. Pidgin English is obviously the most relevant of such special varieties for the development of American English, although at least one of the others may have had a kind of indirect input. It was surely a maritime variety – if not a pidgin – that the first Indians to have real contacts with them spoke to the Puritans in 1621. The Puritans could understand the Indian's English, although they 'much marveled' at it. Squanto and his friend Samoset apparently learned whatever English they spoke from sailors. A pidgin used in these circumstances would be a 'ship's jargon' in the terms of Stefánsson (1909), or a 'reconnaissance language' in the terms of Naro (1978), or not an 'extended' pidgin.

At any rate, from the Indians who had been 'skulking about' the Puritans in 1621, a certain one came 'boldly amongst them' and spoke to them in this kind of English. This Indian, Samoset, proved not to be of 'ye parts' but from Maine or, in more contemporary terms, 'these eastern parts where some English ships came to fish, with whom he was acquainted and could name sundry of them by their names, amongst whom he had got his language' (Bradford 1647: 114).

As Bradford's *Of Plimouth Plantation* and other documents make abundantly clear, the Englishmen depended upon the Indians for many basic survival techniques such as acquiring food (see also Weatherford 1988). Although the European groups may have displayed chauvinistic feelings of superiority, their dependence upon and vulnerability to the Indians forced them into certain cultural (including linguistic) compromises. Especially among those charged with direct interaction with the Indians, relatively few of whom like Roger Williams and John Eliot learned the Indian languages, use of Pidgin English was a frequent necessity. That Samoset was succeeded by Tisquantum, whose name the Puritans treated according to their normal phonotactic pattern by making it Squanto – the first of a long line of such treatments – led to further revelations about maritime language and the coastal Indians. He was 'a native of this place, who had been in England and could speak better English than' Samoset. Squanto had been taken to sea by 'one *Hunt*, a m$^r$. of a ship' and had been in some danger of being sold as a slave in England. Whatever English Squanto learned in England – and there are no known surviving quotations – it may have been a pidgin that Hunt, 'who thought to sell them for slaves in Spain' in 1614, and his crew transmitted to the Indian(s). Mixtures of Pidgin and more ordinary English have been observed in many situations (Fayer, nd).

Tisquantum and Samoset may have been unusual in their experience – at least insofar as Tisquantum's actually going to England was concerned. Wood (1634: 63) comments: 'For when they change their bare *Indian* commons for the plenty of Englands fuller diet, it is so contrary to their stomachs, that death or a desperate sicknesse immediately accrewes, which makes so few of them desirous to see *England*.' It is not clear exactly what was the relationship between the English spoken by these two Indians and that used by others within the next fifty years or so, but it is certain that few of them would have been far removed from possible maritime contact.

According to Goddard (1977, 1978), Pidgin English was quite widely spoken by Indians in New England by the 1630s and 1640s. There is actually little direct evidence that Maritime Pidgin English was in existence any earlier, but it is reasonable to suppose that such a variety – which its early reporters tended to call 'debased' or worse – would be around for a while before anyone would call attention to it. As a matter of fact, the early reported examples can be recognized as pidgin even before it is referred to as 'broken' or 'bastard' or whatever other terms are used. Students of Atlantic Pidgin (Goodman 1985) have shown the very widespread maritime nature of the variety; pidgin varieties of Iberian, French and some other languages can be traced to roughly the late sixteenth century. That Pidgin English, however interacting with other varieties of English and with other languages, showed up in New England is only part of the kind of pattern observed for non-linguistic history, in which New England was only part of what was for England in general 'a sideshow, an epiphenomenon on the outer margins', no more important than the Caribbean and other areas (Cressy 1987: vii).

If the Pidgin English attested in New England from the early seventeenth century was brought in from elsewhere, some evidence points to West Africa, the earliest slaves having been brought into the area at just about that time. The Amerindians may have given us the first attestations, but Africans had had opportunities to develop a special variety of English since 1530 (Angogo and Hancock 1980: 67). Opinions are divided about many matters pertaining to this, but the documents indicate that American Indian Pidgin English was one of the earliest pidgin varieties at the very least.

The earliest attestations of pidgin among the East Coast Indians in the early seventeenth century (Goddard 1977, 1978) constitute a variety which it may be convenient to designate a 'non-extended' pidgin. Attestations include

> The Spaniard [sic, for plural] they say is all one *Aramouse* (viz. all one as a dog) the Frenchman hath a good tongue, but a false heart: The English man all one speake, all one heart . . .
> (William Wood, *New England's Prospect*, 1634, p.82)

> . . . they cried out, what much hoggery, so bigge walke, and so bigge speake; and by and by kill . . .
> (p.87)

> . . . they bade her good morrow, crying out, what cheere what cheer Englishmans squaw horse . . .
> (p. 99)

Wood makes it relatively clear that *what cheer* was an expression used by the English colonists which the Indians learned. *Squaw horse* for *mare*, on the other hand, follows a commonplace pattern of contact language usage. Other developments in Pidgin English, and in maritime contact language in general, seem to follow these attestations.

These materials precede the Pequot War of 1636–7. In 1645 two Indians, Josias and Cutshamakin, were apparently special to Bradford because they were 'acquainted with the English language'. Insofar as the evidence goes, the type of English they were familiar with was that indicated in the citations above. Rather noteworthily, the specific feature of the 'transitivizer' -*um* is not part of those attestations.

Around 1673 that structure does appear in speeches attributed to Waban, a 'Justice Peace' in one of the 'praying villages' of New England. Waban is quoted:

> You big[3] constable, quick you catch um, Jeremiah Offscow; strong you hold um; safe you bring um afore me.

The transitivizer is written separately in the quotations of Waban, but later analysis treats it as enclitic.

Apparently around 1670, a special change took place in some contact varieties in many parts of the world, the transitive marker in question. Opinions are divided about many matters pertaining to this, but some information concerning it is of obvious relevance. Todd (1987: 123) and Holm (1989, II, 534) report phonologically similar transitivizer at least for Cameroonian Pidgin English, Australian Pidgin English (Holm 1989, II, 540) and Tok Pisin of Papua, New Guinea.

This particular structure has no direct parallel in ordinary English, especially British, even though Flanigan (1985) attributes the form to borrowing from contemporary British -*em*, as found notably in Restoration drama. Very rapid transmission indeed from the language of the Restoration to distant maritime usage would be necessary, and an important syntactic difference argues against such an origin.

Farquhar's *Beaux' Strategem* (1707) has sequences like the following.

> I, i, 195: . . . we can't say that we have spent our fortunes, but that we have enjoyed 'em
> III, 3, 437: . . . can keep um [tempers] fast

The Restoration '*em*/'*um* is nothing more than the familiar derivative of the Old English *heo*/*heora*/*hem* with loss of /h-/ in unstressed position, surviving in informal styles and without stress even in some formal styles where the Norse-derived *they, their, them* had not taken over. Even if this did provide the surface representation for the Pidgin English transitivizer, restructuring had to take place before the Pidgin English form was produced. Among other things, it can occur with a following feminine singular object for which *him* would not readily substitute, as in the following quotation of a Nova Scotian Indian.

> Mr. Admiral, he one d–d rascal, he kissum my squaw . . . .
> (Thomas Chandler Halliburton, *The Old Judge, or, Life in a Colony*, 1849 p. 73)

The seventeenth-century English form could serve as object of a preposition –

> . . . at the head of 'em . . .
> (*Beaux ' Strategem*, I, 1, 227)

> . . . there must be secrets among 'em
> (III, 3, 32)

– whereas the pidgin form exists only in the environment /Vtrans ___ (object). Where the object has been optionally deleted, the transitivizer is still used with a verb of transitive force. Considering the grammatical mismatch, it might be well to consider Huttar's suggestion (ms. 7) of the possible origin of the use in some Surinam creoles, 'in specific Bantu languages . . . [including] Noni, a Grasslands Bantu language of Cameroon'.

Given the possibility that African influence may not have been necessarily characteristic of the earliest forms of the pidgins and creoles (Singler forthcoming a), it seems quite feasible that the maritime pidgin use of *per* and early Maritime Pidgin English use of *for* (see above) preceded the development of *-um* as a transitivizer. The most direct evidence, however, is that there was a certain amount of overlap. According to Bakker's evidence, *per* or *for* as a transitivizer would have occurred in the mid-seventeenth century; /-Vm/ in the same function seems to be first attested in the mid-seventeenth century (see below) in American Indian Pidgin English. If the above analysis of Smith's *fit wife for you* is accurate, the *per/for* transitivizer was in use in some varieties of Pidgin English during the same period. Such overlapping and 'relic' usage is of course by no means unusual in language history. Insofar as the chronological problem is concerned, maritime contact varieties appear to have a tran-sitivizer form at a time in which transmission from Restoration English forms would be barely possible even under optimal conditions. Valkhoff (1966: 218–21) has similar forms in South Africa from the period of the 1670s, from Cape documents dated a little later than the first American Indian use of the *-um* transitivizer. One of the two forms of 'creole' Dutch in use had the transitivizer in structures like:

> Gy dit beest fang*um* zoo, en nu dood maak*um* zoo. . .
> 'You caught the cow [beast] so, and you made it dead so. . .'

The other does not use it with transitive verbs:

> Ons soek kos hier. . . . 'We are looking for [seeking] food here. . .'

The variability itself has a striking parallel in American Indian Pidgin English texts. For American Indian Pidgin English (Leechman and Hall 1955; M.R. Miller 1968) there is an apparently irregular distribution in the use of the /-Vm/ transitivity marker. The text quoted from Leechman and Hall by Holm (1989,II,510) has it after *catch* (one of two occurrences) and *throw*, but not after zero copula, *got, savvy, walk, make, see, hear, know, stay, move, go* and *run*. Some of these would be [+transitive], although *move* is not here used in the transitive sense. Some of the same variability is observable in maritime texts off the coast of Africa. A text printed in Owen (1833) representing the speech of Africans from Kabenda Bay to Fernando Poo has:

> Dat nutting; by by you come back, lookum nudder (another) deck.
>
> (II, 178)

but also

> . . . e [fetiche] no catch house, e lib in dat wood . . .
>
> (II, 181)

> You go here, you go dere, you send boat every where. Gaboon man look um dat too much fear . . .
>
> (II, 182)

There are numerous other cases where the presence of the *um* 'transitivizer' seems to be a variable factor, with no evident distribution in terms of verb subclasses.

Many of the same features, including the transitivizer in variable distribution and forms like *suppose* or *spose* 'if' were reported by *The Religious Intelligencer* from Regent's Town, Sierra Leone, in 1820, where, according to the editor of the periodical, 'Natives of twenty-two nations live together . . . with no common medium of intercourse but a little broken English.'

Of course, a 'little' broken English can go a long way, especially if 'broken' means 'pidgin'.

Although John Eliot is known primarily as the learner, describer, preacher in and translater into the Algonquian language, the Waban who provided what may well be the first attestation of American Indian Pidgin English with the transitivizer was his follower. (In fact, it is earlier than the materials cited by Valkhoff and places even more strain on the theory of transmission from Restoration English.) Eliot had settled a group of converts at Natick in 1651 and then thirteen other colonies of 'Praying Indians', totalling more than 1500 (Commager and Morris 1958: 44). Since even Eliot was somewhat diffident about using the Indian language, at least in his early sermons, and since an Indian like Cockenoe who could 'speak English fluently' (Winslow 1968: 89) was rare enough to be worthy of special notice, Pidgin English was a likely medium of communication. Waban himself provides, in addition, an interesting case of Indian problems in acculturation to the British legal system as well as an indication of the language problems of the assimilating Indians:

> Tie um all up, and whip um plaintiff and whip um
> fendant, and whip um witness . . . .

Language matters were, of course, only part of the problems of those Indians being forced into assimilation – which may be why even the ethnically conscious historians of the past few decades have had little or nothing to say on the matter. The sad tale of money has its own part, a perhaps obvious conclusion supported by statements like this extract from Edward Randolph's Report to the Council of Trade of 1676:

> The Massachusetts government having made a law that every Indian being druncke should pay ten shillings or be whipped according to the discretion of the magistrate; many of these poor people willingly offered their backs to the lash, to save their money!
> (Documents Relative to the Colonial History of the State of New York, III, 242)

Such prevalence of whipping lends credence to the contents, at least, of Waban's warrants.

Conversion to the language system of the Englishmen was accompanied by (always partial) conversion to the religious system as well as to the monetary system. According to

statements like that of (Dutch) Ambassador van Gogh to the
Secretary of the States General, Chelsey, in November 1664:

> They [the colony of Massachusetts] convert Indians by hiring
> them not to obey their heathen Sachims, and by appointing
> rulers amongst them, over tenns, twenties, fifties, &c. The
> lives, manners, & habits of those whom [sic] they say are
> converted cannot be distinguished from those who are not
> except it be by being hired to hear sermons, which the more
> generous natives scorn.
> (Documents Relative to the Colonial History of the State of
> New York, III, 79)

Whether the 'generous natives' also scorned the language
assimilation process is not actually attested, but it would seem a
highly reasonable conclusion.

By the time of King Philip's War of 1676–7, however, the most
independent of the Indians had apparently absorbed something
of the Pidgin English tradition. The following is represented
(Tompson 1676: 53–4 ) as a speech from King Philip inciting his
people to attack the English:

> They ['our fathers'] sel our land to english man . . . This no
> wunnegin, so big matchit law, which our old fathers never
> saw . . . We drink we so big whipt, but english they go
> sleep, no more, or else a little pay. Me meddle Squaw me
> hang'd, our fathers kept what Squaws they would whither
> [sic] they wakt or slept.

Grammatical features (base-form verbs in a clear past tense
situation, subject form *me*), vocabulary (*wunnegin*, *matchit*) from
Indian languages, and special idiomatic phrases (*so big . . . law*,
*so big whipt*) are characteristic of the Indian English of the time
and are also pidgin features. Special use of English vocabulary
items like *meddle* ('commit adultery with, fornicate with') are
also found in other pidgin texts. The Jamaican Maroons (Dallas
1883, II, 226) are quoted:

> Massa parson say, no mus tief [steal], no mus meddle wid
> somebody wife . . .

*Matchit* was widely used by the Indians in New England and at
least known to the whites (Goddard 1977: 38). It was used,
without a gloss, in Mary Rowlandson's report of her captivity in
1682 (Lincoln 1913/156):

. . . they . . . said, it were some Matchit Indian that did it.

Words like *wunegan* or *wunnegin*, cited in King Philip's speech above, became equally familiar and should be considered part of the English of the area in the seventeenth century, even though they may not have survived into the twentieth. *Wunnegin* ('good'), with variants *weneikinne* ('handsome'), *wunnegin* ('welcome'), was familiar in the period. Bartlett (1877) reported it still in use, meaning 'fine or showy', around Norwich, Connecticut. Words like *sagamore* (cited by L'Escarbot 1609 in the form *sagamos*) and *Sachim*, for 'a Lord, a ruler, or a captaine', have remained familiar at least in historical contexts; *netop* ('friend'), while not so commonplace as *wigwam* or *squaw*, is in Wood's 1634 list and is also easy to find in seventeenth- and eighteenth-century American English texts. Knight (1818: 99) reports

 . . . two sanhops, two squaws, a young sanhop, and a pappoose [*sic*]

citing two Indian words which have become almost offensively familiar because of condescending white usage, and a third which is not so familiar. *Sanhop*, in this context, appears to mean 'warrior'. For other Indian borrowings, see below (*passim*).

American Indian Pidgin English spread rapidly. The notes of missionary David Brainerd, who had his troubles with the use of interpreters in his preaching, told how some of the Indians were beginning to learn some English and quoted a penitent Indian woman from Crossweeksung, 'a scattered Indian village eighty miles from the forks of the Delaware', in 1745 (Edwards 1884: 206) 'in her broken English':

 . . . by-by my heart be glad desperately. Den me tink, glad my heart Jesus Christ send me hell. Did not me care where He put me: me lobe him for all

*Bimeby* is the more widely reported form for the pidgin time adverbial *by-by*, which may have served instead of verbal auxiliaries in 'rudimentary' or non-extended pidgins. The undifferentiated subject pronoun *me* is paralleled in many pidgin contexts, as in

 Me so big naughty Heart, me heart all one stone.

Winslow (1968: 104) attributes this formula to Wequash, Roger Williams' friend. The sentence may have been a kind of evangelical religious formula in Pidgin English preaching. In *The Religious Intelligencer* from Liberia and Sierra Leone at a slightly later period, almost identical quotations occur. Col. James Smith, in 1799, reported a Delaware Indian in western Pennsylvania saying to him:

> shoot um down all one [the same as, just like] pigeon

and

> No, all one fool you, beal [bears] now elly [very] pool [poor]
> (quoted in Taylor 1981).

In most early varieties of Pidgin English (as distinct from creoles and partly decreolized varieties), the form *be glad* is somewhat unusual, one distinction being:

> be NP
> 0   Adj.

However, a development by which *be* with adjectives or verbs indicated some kind of special relationship (see Chapter 3 on Black English Vernacular) may already have been in progress. The 'repatriated' Africans in Sierra Leone quoted slightly after 1800 in *The Religious Intelligencer* show some tendency to produce

> be Adj

in the right discourse environment.

African slaves were certainly in the New England area in the early part of the seventeenth century, and they often had close social relationships with the Indians (Greene 1942). Whether they transmitted Pidgin English to the Indians, or the Indians transmitted it to them, or both got it from a third source remains a crux of language history. There is evidence, however, that African and Indian were differentiated. An officious 'Justice Jun'' of Madam Knight's Journal (1705) scornfully reports 'You speak negro to him' when 'Justice Sen'' interrogates an Indian who received a hogshead stolen by a 'negro Slave belonging to a man in ye Town' in this manner:

> You Indian why did You steal from this man? You sho'dn't do so – it's a Grandy wicked thing to steal.

Justice Jun' probably interprets *grandy*, from the Romance/Iberian contact variety which has some genetic relationship to Pidgin English, as the 'negro' form. Cotton Mather's quotation from an African in 'The Angel of Bethesda' (1721) uses the word in the same sense. The Indian's reply to the younger justice is still 'me no stomany', indicating a lack of understanding (cf. Drechsel

1976), utilizing still another probable American Indianism which, in a number of forms, is widely attested in the English of New England in the colonial period. Krapp (1925, I, 269) quotes *Ames's Almanac* for March 1730:

> '. . . what? you no Stommonee . . .'

Justice Jun[r] *all one* ('the same as'), characteristic of both African and American Indian Pidgin English of the period.

Against all these attestations – and there are many more – of American Indian Pidgin English, which were never attributed to all the Indians and about the representative nature of which we can only guess, there are conclusions like that formed by Read (1941) on the basis of newspaper advertisements for runaway Indian slaves of New England masters, in the period 1705–45, which apply the description 'very good' to the English of two Indians, 'good' to that of ten, 'speaks English well' to one, and 'pretty well' to another. The advertisements come from newspapers ranging from Boston (where one runaway is described as a 'Carolina Indian man') to Long Island (where it is specified that the Indian 'speaks no other language'), to Philadelphia and to Charleston. One from Boston is said to 'speak. . . indifferent good English' and another from the same city 'speaks French, English, and Spanish, but all bad'.

Wide-ranging pidgin-like attestations (from reporters who were probably indifferent users of the pidgin themselves) suggest a need to interpret these descriptions of the English of runaway Indians, and it is probably significant that degrees of English proficiency are reported. Under the circumstances it would be quite unexpected for a White to describe an Indian's variety of English as 'good pidgin'; in fact, the term *pidgin* itself does not seem to have been in general American use until the middle of the nineteenth century. Europeans in (for example ) West Africa today are certainly users, in many cases, of bad pidgin and are occasionally ridiculed by Africans for their efforts. Although Read writes of these as 'newspaper advertisements for runaways' (1941: 72), one of the Indians is said to be for sale. He is described as 'a Lusty Indian man Servant . . . fit for any Service' and the claim that he 'Speaks very good English' may well be an inducement to prospective buyers as much as a description. Hardly anything could be less relevant to the interpretation of 'good' in this context than the twentieth-century prescriptive use of the term *good English*.

During the colonial period, the same problem arises in the interpretation of equivalent statements made about Black slaves.

There is a conflict between one interpretation of the advertisments for runaways and the literary – including many non-fiction – attestations. Again, it seems significant that an occasional advertisement for a Black runaway slave refers to his 'speaking better English than most negroes' (Littlefield 1981: 157). Black runaway slaves were also fairly frequently referred to as polyglot.

In addition to the problem of imprecise data furnished by amateur observers, there is also the limitation that we have no way of knowing that the Indians or Africans advertised for or quoted were a good sample. Read assures us (1941: 72) that: 'The following series of miniature "case histories"' is typical of the many scores to be found in colonial newspapers, but provides no further data. The Indian group, like the African, was obviously not entirely consistent in its use of English. The runaway Indians were not only enslaved, which was atypical, but also urban – and therefore probably detribalized – and it may well be that running away in a White-dominated area was easier for those who mastered relatively standard English.

It may, in the long run, be necessary to accept both types of report as evidence, taking into account both chronological and geographical associations. That is, the East Coast Pidgin English which Goddard (1977, 1978) attests for about 1620–50 may have been giving way, in Boston, Philadelphia and even Charleston, to a more ordinary variety of English ('standard' or approaching the non-standard variety used by parts of the English-derived population). Somewhat farther west, where Brainerd was, pidgin would have been much more nearly the norm (Miller 1968) and would have been used, as the novels of James Fenimore Cooper among others suggest, even by White frontiersmen.

Consider freedman Austin Steward's (1857: 223) experience with Indians by whom he was often visited during his residence in Canada. He reports one 'tall, brawny Indian' as saying:

Me lost in the woods, and me come to stay all night.

The same 'old warrior' was taken, almost as a slave, to Virginia, where he was quoted (1857: 229)

Me must get a rifle.

Or consider this one from Granville Stuart, dated in his journal 30 April 1880 and written in the Wyoming area, concerning how 'an old Indian friend' sized up the difficulty in shooting white-tailed deer (Stuart 1880: 112):

Wild turkey hard to kill. Indian break some stick, turkey stop one second, say maybe Injin, Injin be good hunter.

Zero copula and simplification are observable even where the transitivizer, a variable feature, is lacking. Elements of Pidgin English like the transitivizer remained available for American jocular usage until at least as late as Sinclair Lewis's *Arrowsmith* (1935), in which a friend invites Martin Arrowsmith to *catchum little drink*.

Rather than with such contact phenomena, it has been customary since Schele de Vere (1872) to begin with the dialects – standard, non-standard, or other – of England. The accepted history of English immigration to North America seems to be that there were several waves of English speakers who immigrated, including those of the colonial period, such as the 20,000 or so Puritans who came to Massachusetts between 1621 and 1640, the smaller group of Royalist cavaliers arriving in Virginia between 1642 and 1675, the migrants to the Delaware Valley between 1675 and 1725, and those who went to the Appalachian back country between 1718 and 1775. After the colonial period, major groups – who seem to have been strongly influential in the forming of regional dialect patterns – came around 1816–18, around 1830 and around 1850. Numerous later immigrants, and the native Americans who were already there, are accorded little or no influence in the formation of the dialect pattern.

Where the immigrants of the colonial period are concerned, the first group has been treated much more than the others – in fact, almost to the exclusion of the others – and the discussion below follows many of the well-worn patterns. The third has most often been treated in terms of the settlement of William Penn's Quakers in the 1680s, with four dominant early groups: 'Quakers and other English and Welsh colonists . . . and German and Scotch–Irish settlers, who moved immediately into the back country' (Carver 1987: 183). See, however, the discussion of the Finnish and Swedish component of the 'backwoodsmen' (Jordan and Kaups 1989).

It has been conventionally held, as self-evident, that these English-speaking immigrants, uneducated and of low birth, brought with them regional dialects – from England primarily, then (numerically, not necessarily chronologically) from Scotland, and finally (where needed to complete the historical picture) from Ireland. With development, complication and sophistication, this basic viewpoint has been upheld until the present time by linguists as different as Mufwene and Gilman (1988) and Viereck. The last puts it most explicitly (1980: 25):

'For to [sic] discuss such matters as the interrelationship of regional British and American English with some assurance, the dialectal structure of British English has to be established in some detail first.' A developing viewpoint, however, holds (Carver 1987: 76) that factors other than settlement patterns are of great importance. (see also Görlach 1987).

None of the English-speaking immigrant groups came into a linguistic or cultural vacuum. New Netherlands had representatives of a dozen European nationalities, with French-speaking Walloons at Fort Orange (now Albany); Norwegians, Danes, Germans, Scots and Irish along with the Dutch at Rensselaerswyck; and English coming from Connecticut in 1642. In 1644 it was said that eighteen different languages were spoken in Manhattan. After the English takeover in 1664, the polyglot complexity of New York tended to increase rather than to be simplified (Ellis *et al.* 1957/69: 105). In spite of the reduction of 'native' population in the immediate vicinity because of the plague of 1616–17 and wars, the two Massachusetts Puritan groups of 1621 and 1630 had important American Indian groups to deal with as well as Dutch and other European groups nearby. The earliest Virginia settlers found three linguistically different groups of American Indians. The Delaware Valley group found not only American Indians but also a colony called Nya Sverige (New Sweden), sent there by the then-powerful Swedish empire beginning in 1638. The Scandinavians there consisted of faster-proliferating Swedish and Finnish families (Jordan and Kaups 1989: 65). The Midland frontier group, which came through the Appalachians in the century after 1725, with the famous concentration of Scotch-Irish, perhaps comes closest to fitting the conventional picture (Jordan and Kaups 1989: 236).

> Persons of highland British ancestry, including Scotch–Irish, Welsh, Scots, and English settlers derived from hill areas such as Cornwall and the Pennines, probably formed a majority of the population on the Midland American frontier, though some claims of their numbers and proportions seem excessively high.

Where the Massachusetts Pilgrims are concerned, perhaps it should be remembered that they they were 'a small group of simple, inexperienced folk, unaccustomed to the rough and tumble of sea life' (Andrews 1934, I, 298). They may not – although the matter has hardly been examined – have fitted Malkiel's (1976: 588) description of immigrants arriving by ship:

'After two to three months at sea . . . the immigrants landed on the shores of the New World with their heads apparently replete and "buzzing" with the sailors' semi-technical jargon . . .' Had they been 'a company of undisciplined adventurers, such as had accompanied earlier [colonizing] efforts from Maine to the Amazon', they might well have found Samoset's English rather familiar. In spite of their experience with Dutch in Leyden, the Pilgrims were linguistically simple and inexperienced compared with sailors operating in a multinational activity where no one language had attained anything like the ascendancy their English has in the twentieth century.

One of the special factors of the history of American English – as in the history of any other American variety of a European language like French or Spanish – is that it was not always the clearly dominant language in any of the areas in which it was used. In England there might be problems enough concerning the dominant dialect, but there is no room for doubt that English was dominant over the remaining Celtic languages – or that, in spite of temporarily questionable status, it had soon re-established its dominance over Norse and Norman French. Since the thirteenth century, with complications in some domains until the sixteenth, the English treated in the histories of the language had been the clearly dominant language of England. Learned use of Latin might persist up to and through Milton's time, but there was no question of Latin becoming the everyday language of England. Effective, ordinary business was transacted in English.

In America, in the beginning, English was not so privileged. When Governor Bradford received communications from the Dutch 'plantation' of Manhattan, the letters were written in French and Dutch but not in English. Bradford was expected to read them – and, from all we are told, to reply – in one of those languages.

The Dutch 'had traded in these southern parts divers years before [the pilgrims] came, but they began no plantation here till four or five years after their coming and here beginning' (Bradford 1647/1901: 215–16). The Dutch under Hendrik Hudson had, after all, settled the Hudson River area in 1610, earlier than the Pilgrims themselves. The Englishmen were the interlopers when they moved into New Netherland around 1640 and established Southold and Southampton on Long Island. They may well have been the ones who had to adapt linguistically.

When Sir Edmund Andros was appointed governor of the colony of New York in the late seventeenth century, Dutch clergy were pleased that he was fluent in the Dutch language and

well disposed towards the Dutch church (Balmer 1989: 30).
Anglican missionaries such as John Barlow, *C.* 1710, enjoyed
success because they were able to use Dutch (Balmer 1989: 80).
A text like Hamilton's *Itinerarium* of 1744 shows 'the omnipresence of Dutch speech' (Needler 1967: 214) on a trip up the
Hudson to Albany. In 1750 Swedish naturalist Peter Kahn found
that, although the dress in Albany was English, the town's
language and manners were Dutch. The Dutch, in New Jersey as
well as New York, remained an important linguistic force until
the American Revolution. According to Higham (1968: 93),
'Dutch was still spoken fairly extensively in churches and homes
in New York and New Jersey . . .' As late as 1837, Captain
Frederick Marryat (1960: 89) considered Albany 'a Dutch city'.

Mixing of Dutch and English became pronounced, according to
popular reports, in the colonial period. Balmer (1989: 129)
asserts that, 'By the middle of the eighteenth century, the Dutch
spoken by ministers educated in the Netherlands could no longer
be understood by the Dutch of the Middle Colonies, whose
speech had become, in the words of one observer of 1744, a
"medley of Dutch and English that would have tired a horse".'
The late eighteenth century saw general, if not complete, English
dominance. By 1794 in New York City, according to one
statement, there was observed no language but English, 'even
among children of Dutch or German descent' (Balmer 1989:
153). Vanderbilt (1881) and van Loon (1938) indicate a
somewhat greater and longer persistence of Dutch.

As some of the dates of first attestation below tend to indicate,
Dutch borrowings into American English tend to *begin* rather
than to end at this period of 'bad' Dutch or of the greatly reduced
use of the language. The picture, however, is a commonplace one
in language history. One need only remember the preponderance
of loanwords from Norman French into English in the fourteenth
century, after the dominance of English had been re-established.
Reduced use of the Dutch (French) language in the country was
accompanied, not unnaturally, by the increased use of Dutch
(French) words in the emergingly dominant English language.

Perhaps from the 'colored people' whom Vanderbilt (1881)
identified among the users of 'bad' Dutch came one of the very
early borrowings. It may also have been in a general Creole
(Atlantic, according to Holm and Shilling 1982) that *boss* from
Dutch *baas* ('master') developed. The term *boss*, now widespread
in the Black English Vernacular and in the Creole of Surinam in
the meaning 'excellent, superior', developed somewhere around
the time when the English traded their mastery of Surinam for

the Dutch possession of New Amsterdam. Some time later, apparently, the term spread to South African *boss-boy* and to Australian *boss-cocky* ('person in authority'). The early attestations in the *Oxford English Dictionary* (hereinafter *OED*) are maritime. The first is from Purchase's *Pilgrims* (I, ii, 117): 'our Baase, for so a Dutch Captain is called'. The second is from G. Foster's translation of *Sparrman's Voyage* of 1785. In 1649, however, J. Winthrop recorded *work base*, which *OED* identifies as equal to Dutch *werk-baas*, and a 1653 attestation recorded the phrase 'at the Bosses house in the Manhatoes'. The *Dictionary of American Regional English* (hereinafter *DARE*), which is extremely conservative in these matters, finds the use of *boss* ('excellent') to occur 'especially among Black speakers', as are the compounds *bossman* and *boss lady*. The *Dictionary of Bahamian English* cites *boss missus* on Andros Island. It is probably not without significance that, at the time this maritime transmission was taking place, Pidgin English was creolizing not only in Surinam but in the continental United States.

Words derived from Dutch and rather clearly borrowed on the American continent include *bowery*, from the word originally (1650) meaning 'farm' that designated the country lane; the Bowery later (1787) became Manhattan's version of skid row. (*DARE* I found application of the term *bowery* to districts as far from New York as Pennsylvania and Amarillo, Texas, by 1967; the farm associations were undoubtedly long dead – or never alive – in those areas.) There are also *cookie* from Dutch *koekje* ('little cake'; first attested in American English in 1703) and *cruller* (Dutch *krulle*, 'a crooked piece of pastry', first attested in 1820). *Stoop* from Dutch *stoep* (1679; 'a small porch with seats or benches') was originally a raised, uncovered platform before the entrance of a house but is now used in various parts of the United States for 'porch' or 'veranda'. In such cases of specialization, doublets may well have been in existence in the early contact situation. *Scow* (1669), *sleigh* (1696), *span* (of horses, 1769), *snoop* (1832) were American borrowings from Dutch that have since spread to British English. Dutch *wafel* became American English *waffle* (1847, but 1744 in the compound *waffle frolic*), 'a batter cake baked on a waffle iron'; the word is distantly related to *wafer*, in use in English from medieval times and retained in American English in a meaning quite different. Dutch *pit* (1848) is used for the hard stone of the cherry, peach or plum that contains the seed. *Poppycock* ('soft dung') is treated today as a euphemism virtually equivalent to 'Nonsense!', but it could hardly have been so in colonial New York; interestingly, the first attestation (1865) is an allusion to the speeches of congressmen. *Logy*, of uncertain derivation, but possibly from Dutch, does not appear until Bartlett's *Americanisms* of 1859.

A number of compounds that have been closely translated came into English from Dutch in the Hudson Valley and East Jersey area, some of them remaining regional until the present. An example is *hay barrack*, for the more general *haystack*, first attested in 1767; the source is Dutch *hoi-berg* ('hay mountain'). *Storm Door*, first attested in 1878, may have been modelled on Dutch *storm deur*; *pot cheese* (1812), a localism for cottage cheese, is an obvious adaptation from Dutch *pot keese* – as in many cases, about half borrowing and half translation. *Hotcake* (Dutch *heetekoek*), first attested in 1683 but early used for 'freshly baked corncake' rather than as an alternative to *pancake*, is so little regionalized that it is a kind of stylistic alternative for Americans. (*Hotcake* is more colloquial; *selling like pancakes* would be as pretentious in an English conversation as switching into Spanish *como pan caliente*.) *Cole slaw* has certainly been deregionalized; folk etymology has made it *cold slaw* since 1794 (*DARE* I). There is the (apocryphal) story of kitchen personnel keeping it in the refrigerator 'because it's supposed to be cold'.

The way in which the British *Father Christmas* is represented in America by *Santa Claus* is an outstanding example of the multilingual context in which Dutch loanwords became a part of American English. Along with its more formal synonym, it came from Dutch *Sinter Klaas* around 1773. As a patron of sailors, among others, the saint himself was as appropriate to the coastally and nautically oriented colonies and new nation as to Holland. By the time of Clement Clarke Moore's 1823 poem 'A Visit from St Nicholas', many of the different features that Americans associate with Santa Claus had already developed. This St Nicholas, whose devotees originally gave each other gifts on 6 December had been absorbed into Christmas celebrations during the Middle Ages and his day changed to 25 December. In America the Germans brought in not only the Christmas tree but their name for the new-born Saviour, *Christkindlein* or *Christkind'l*, from which Americans made *Kriss Kringle*. The popular American designation 'Ol' Santa' – where probably not even the relationship to *sanctus* is recognized – removes virtually the last trace of etymological origin.

More than simple Dutch contact was involved in colonial New York and New Jersey. Palatine Germans began arriving in the Hudson Valley in 1709 as whole families, making up the largest non-English group of immigrants to New York in the colonial period (Carver 1987: 39). There were Frisians, Germans, Irish, English, French and Blacks – as well as the obvious Indians – along with the Hollanders. Together with German immigrants elsewhere, these Germans complicated the Dutch/English contact picture. The Americanism *dumb* ('ignorant or stupid' rather than 'mute'; 1823) may be either German or Dutch; most likely it combined the influence of both. *Sawbuck* (1842), now virtually obsolete slang for 'ten dollars', is first attested from 1869 and could come from either German *Saegebock* or Dutch *Zaagbock*; both refer to frames used in sawing wood, with an X-shape which visually recalls the Roman numeral for ten. (Whether or not the dictionaries recorded it, the comic strips of the 1930s and 1940s frequently used *double sawbuck* for twenty dollars.) *Speck* ('bacon') could also come from either language; its attestations in the *Dictionary of Americanisms* (*DA*) extend from 1691 to 1936, the last perhaps significantly in *Pennsylvania Dutch Cook Book*. Regional differences in origin, correlating with preponderance of German or of Dutch population, could be postulated but have no apparent supporting data.

The picture of modern borrowings (survivals) in American English from Dutch gives an artificaly diminished picture of Dutch influence in New York and New Jersey in the colonial and early national period. As late as 1910, J. Dyneley Prince found evidence of a contact variety of Dutch among Blacks in New Jersey. Vanderbilt (1881) has pointed out that this 'small colony of old Negroes' still had 'their own dialect of Jersey Dutch' but that they were 'shy' and difficult to approach. Prince, who apparently overcame this shyness, found forms thoroughly consistent with the thesis that the 'Negro' dialect of Jersey Dutch was a variety of Dutch Creole. (For further discussion, see Dillard 1985: 100–2.)

More mainstream Dutch forms have become completely nativized in American English; words like *stoop* appear quaint to some Americans because of their regional associations, not because of Dutch origin. These, like *olicook* ('fat cake'; first recorded as *olykoek* in 1809 in English, but obviously present in New York in Dutch for a long time before that) have become obscure even regionally; a wag would say that it is used more in dialectology classes than it is otherwise. According to Carver (1987: 39), the word had become obsolescent by the 1930s and it was 'unknown to *DARE* informants' in interviews conducted in the 1960s. *Blickey* (Dutch *blikje*, the diminutive of *blik*, 'pail'), 'a small bucket', is listed by *DARE* I as characteristic of 'chiefly southeast New York, New York City, and New Jersey' with its earliest attestation in 1859 from Bartlett's *Americanisms*. It would be a brave person who, relying upon the authority of *DARE*, would go into a hardware store in New York City and ask to buy a blickey. *DARE's* last actual citation is from its own field notes, in 1967 from north-west New Jersey. DARE I does not commit itself as to whether *blickey* ('a short coat or jacket') is from Dutch, although the term is also used in the New Jersey area.

Other words from Dutch seem now to be completely obsolete, even in the Hudson Valley and New Jersey. Among these are *overslaugh* ('a sand bar'; first recorded in *DA* in 1753 and last in 1901), *fetticus* ('a salad'; 1848–91), *pinkster* ('Whitsuntide'; 1797–1946, but the last is in a historical, reminiscing kind of context), *rolliche* ('a sort of sausage'; 1830–1949, but said to be disappearing fast by an informant in Kurath 1949), *boonder* ('a brush used in scrubbing'; 1791–1933), *blummie* ('a flower'; 1848–1936). A few words, such as *blickie* and *clove*, are not attested until seemingly rather late (1777). *Fly* ('a swamp'; 1645) drew the comment 'The word is old' in 1735; but *Fly Market* survived from 1775 to 1944, although the last attestation is in an archaic and reminiscing context.

In contrast, *cookie* is so Americanized that most Americans would probably be surprised to learn of its Dutch origin. Children and teenagers who gave a brief vogue to *That's the way the cookie crumbles* in the late 1950s (*OED* 1957–64) obviously thought of themselves as using a completely native word. For whatever reason, *cookie* exemplifies virtually the opposite tendency from *olicook*. Of the Dutch loanwords to American English, perhaps only *boom* (Dillard 1985: 100, 185) has been more thoroughly nativized. In fact, an American speaker is much less likely to associate *boom* with the meaning 'tree' than he is to associate *cookie* with 'cooking'. Again, whatever the state of the other Dutch loanwords, it is virtually certain that *boom* comes from maritime use.

Place names provide other evidence of the influence of Dutch upon colonial American English. The word *kill* ('creek'), for example, provided Catskill [Kaatskill], the country seat of Greene County, New York; Catskill Creek, NY; and the Catskill Mountains, along with Wynantskill, Sparkill, Peekskill, Fishkill, Wallkill, Plattekill, Poestenkill, Cobleskill and others. Schuykill ('hidden stream') gives its name not only to the Schuylkill River but to Schuylkill, Schuylkill County and Schuylkill Haven in Pennsylvania. In 1648, according to 'The Relation of Mr Garret van Sweeringen of the City of St Maries concerning his

Knowledge of the seateing of Delaware Bay', Englishmen, naming places for the characteristic activities there, called one place 'Whore-Kill, that is in England the Whores Creek' and another 'Murderers-Kill, that is Murders [sic] Creeke'.

*Clove* ('ravine, valley, or mountain pass') provides place names like Smith's Clove in south-east New York state and others farther north in the Catskill Mountains. An 1827 text has the compound *clove-road*. Schele de Vere (1872) mistook *clove* for *cove*, perhaps with some company among more recent speakers. Beverwyck ('beaver town') became Albany in a simple replacement; likewise Wiltwyck became Kingston, although the original was retained or recovered in the name of a boys' 'school'. New Netherland becoming New York is, of course, the most famous of the replacements. For Brede Wegh to become Broadway requires what might be called cognate translation, as it does for Roode Hoeck to become Red Hook; in *Hook* and Helle Gaat becoming Hell's Gate, false cognates got into the picture. The change from Vlissingen to Flushing is both phonological and orthographic, with a touch of folk etymology involved. Kinderhook (Dutch for 'children's corner') came only with a change of orthography – but with a loss, one might think, of meaning for most residents of New York State. When Martin van Buren adopted his political nickname Old Kinderhook for the 1845 campaign, complete anglicization (or, at least, de-dutchification) of the name had been completed. It all went a bit further when one of the many folk etymologies of *OK* was based on van Buren's nickname.

Had they been a little less other-worldly, these Pilgrims might well have had some contact with the Basque-tinged maritime variety. They might also have come into contact, as less sheltered Englishmen quite likely did, with a group of Walloons, or French-speaking Belgians, who became the first settlers of New Netherland by going to the Hudson in 1624. The Swedes who came to the Delaware River in 1638 – perhaps accompanied by some Finns – may have been a little bit out of their reach, but they were not far from several European language varieties before they became merged into Massachusetts in 1691. But no one in the general area could avoid Dutch completely. A text like Hamilton's *Itinerarium* of 1744 shows the 'omnipresence of Dutch speech' (Needler 1967: 214) on a trip up the Hudson to Albany. According to van Ginneken 1913 (cited in Holm 1989, II, 336), Dutch remained the official school language in New York until 1773, and disciplinary action was sometimes taken to force children to speak English when it became official there.

Although the Pilgrims came in 1621, major colonies were founded along the Atlantic Coast and on the lower Connecticut River between 1630 and 1645. For the first half-century or so, they had little contact with each other. Kurath (1972: 42–3) theorizes – although with no supporting data – that 'some regional differences' must have developed within about the first fifty years. If so, there is no record of them. Kurath's thesis of early-developing regional distribution is supported not with linguistic data but with a picture of the transportation system, radiating out from the old centres to the peripheral settlements. The availability of transportation, according to Kurath, served to consolidate these colonies economically, socially and culturally.

Feasible as this picture, conventional in dialect geography, is – centres of prestige with influence radiating out to more isolated areas which may easily become 'relic areas' when change takes place in the centres (cf. Wolfram and Christian 1976: 13) – there never seem to have been any linguistic data offered to substantiate such a development in the early colonies, or in the colonial period at all. The writings preserved from the period of around 1621–90 do not contradict such a supposition outright, but they do not support it either. In spite of Kurath's (1972) expressed hope, nothing in *DARE* I seems to bear it out either.

If it was true that the English-speaking immigrants became astonishingly unified in their use of English (see next chapter), levelling the dialects they brought from England, the seeds of a new diversity would have been sown by interaction with the Indians and the other groups which made up the extremely polyglot environment of the colonies, the new nation and especially the frontier.

This new kind of diversity thus characterized American English even in the colonial period. Some striking new types of uniformity also developed, however. Pidgin English, which continues to be attested throughout the westward movement of American English during the nineteenth century, may be looked upon from one viewpoint as a result of the language levelling in the multilingual communities of the North American colonies. Lacking some of the unusual features of ordinary English, it far better met communication needs – especially with speakers of American Indian languages. As such, its development paralleled the dialect levelling (see pp. 44–5) which took place somewhat later. The diversity of the American Indian languages, and the inability of the general European population to cope with them, made the pidgin now known as American Indian Pidgin English a significant factor in the colonial period and later. In the larger picture – whatever the genesis of AIPE or of pidgin in general – it was a major factor in the accommodation processes which ultimately made it possible to identify an 'American' English.

## Notes

1 An essentially transmissionist viewpoint is adopted in this work. For a different viewpoint, the 'bioprogram', see Bickerton 1982 and the considerable literature it generated. For a relatively neutral attitude, see Holm 1989, II, 628–30.
2 For the association of maritime usage, the language of the railroads and that of hobos – insofar as it is not self-evident – see Dillard 1985: 181–93.
3 On compounds with *big*, see numerous quotations herein and Dillard 1985: 46–7. There are reports that Indians of the West referred to the Virgin Mary as *big woman*. One story about the naming of Ohio as the 'Buckeye State' has it that, in 1788, a Colonel Sproat was called 'Big Buckeye' by a group of Indians. The term may have been a translation by Whites of the Indians' *Hetuck*, but it still seems relevant that the use of *big* in compounds to render Indian terms was well established and spread into the Ohio area (Winslow 1968: 132).

# Chapter 2

# Early diversity, levelling and rediversification

It is established that the earliest British migrants to the colonies carried a great diversity of dialects with them. It has not been possible, however, to identify the colonial dialects with any of the varieties of England – or those of Ireland or Scotland. Attempted reconstruction of the English of the American colonies has yielded virtually no insight into the English of the seventeenth and eighteenth centuries, the literature on which has concerned itself primarily with the last stages of the Great Vowel Shift and with developing purism. Perhaps this is why the traditional history of the language treated 'American English' after discussing Samuel Johnson's dictionary, as a special case of the usage problem. The colonists came 'promiscuously' (to use the term of an early observer) from many parts of England, although it might be objected that there was somewhat greater *social* than geographic selectivity among the colonizing population. Early North American groups are more readily identified as Puritans, Quakers, religious Dissenters of other types, or 'raw adventurers' than as natives of Sussex, Wessex or East Anglia. Even aboard ship on the voyage over, as Cressy (1987: 149–51) suggests, 'a new, if temporary, community' arose, 'a bonding among Atlantic travellers of the kind that is found among veterans of other intensive group experiences' which preceded even what social reorganization took place after arrival. Attempts to find origins in British regions for American regionalisms have led nowhere.

Noah Webster (1789: 384–5) was perhaps the first to suggest 'colonial lag', especially in New England. He reported that:

> . . . the New England common people . . . have been

sequestered in some measure from the world, and their language has not suffered material changes from their first settlement to the present time. Hence most of the phrases used by Shakespear, Congreve, and other writers who have described English manners and recorded the language of all classes of people, are still heard in the common discourse of the New England yeomanry.

According to Webster, these included the verb *be* 'in the present tense'; 'the word *dern* . . . [but not in] the sense it had formerly . . . now used as an adverb to qualify an adjective'; *this here* and *that there* (compared to French usage), *ax* for *ask*; *ferret* ('drive animals from their hiding places . . . but used in some parts of New England . . . applied figuratively to many transactions in life'); *without* ('in the sense of unless'); *peek* ('corruptedly' for *peep*); *chirk* for *chirp* ('wholly lost, except in New England'); *gin* or *gyn* for *given* ('as Bishop Wilkins remarks . . . in the North of England'); *shet* for *shut*; *an* for *if* (*DARE* I lists contracted *and* 'if' no earlier than 1909); *becase* for *because* (*DARE* I lists *becaise* from 1815 and 1837); and *sich* for *such*, traced back to '*swich* or *swiche*'. Notably, The 'Glossary of Provincialisms' in Humphreys' *Yankey in England* confirms Webster's *ax*, although using the spelling *aks* and *chirk*, and Pickering's *Vocabulary* of 1816 also confirms the latter. The following attestations of each are far from New England – Tennessee in both cases. Strikingly, Webster's New England 'archaisms' are a total mismatch for the New Englandisms of Samuel Kirkham (1829). Either there was rapid change or the composite offered by the two reporters is not reliable for developments in New England between 1789 and 1829.

New England was apparently the target of much of the early disapproval expressed about the speech of Americans. Other observers do not, however, refer to archaic usages. Read (1933) quotes Creswell (1777) as referring to a 'whining cadence' and Campbell (1792) as accusing New Englanders of being recognizable by a 'twang', even in western New York. Pilch (1980: 68) concludes that Webster eliminated graphic representation of /o/ from his spelling books after 1789, 'due to the fact that he recognized it as a New England peculiarity'.

Apparently, 'some parts of America' – but not necessarily New England – are the loci of *mought*, the survival of a verb used by some of 'our Saxon ancestors'. Read also quotes Boucher (1775) as identifying Virginia as its locale. Webster (1789: 382) also asserts that 'The dialect in America is peculiar to the descendants of the Scotch Irish', but the assertion comes in a context of prosody rather than of lexical, grammatical or other phonological matters. The question of the degree of cultural and personal connection with England remains a vexed one even among professional historians. Cressy (1987: 292) sees New England as a place where, 'During the first few generations of settlement the colonists looked homeward [towards England] rather than towards an American future and some went back to England.' Green (1989: 40) perhaps represents the consensus among historians more conventionally when he writes: 'Nevertheless, some historians will continue to believe that the intense religiosity and social communalism of New England . . . produced a greater contrast with the parent society than [Cressy] suggests.'

Perhaps it is well to emphasize here that coming to America was only a part of the total British emigration picture. Cressy (1987: 69) says that even at the peak of migration to New England, that destination accounted for 'just 30 percent of the migrants, with most of the rest going to the Chesapeake and the Caribbean'. The 'little bit of England' interpretation for the North American colonies overlooks the obvious fact that there were many other places to which the British emigrants went, all with their different eventual results. Among roughly contemporary observers, Captain Basil Hall, visiting (rather late for these purposes) in 1827 and 1828, found Canadians 'acting and looking like Englishmen, without any discernible differences' but in the United States 'the language, the thoughts, and even the tone of voice' were 'too obviously foreign and peculiar to the country, to escape notice' (Hall 1829: 265).

Diversity – in language dialect, and other respects – was a kind of keynote to the colonies through the first two decades of the eighteenth century. Because there was dialect diversity in England, it has been tempting to assume that the American diversity reflected that of the mother country. The point has never been proved, however.

The study of diversity in syntax, with no possibility of experimental manipulation, has been and probably must remain much more rudimentary than could be wished. Written records like those available from a writing system such as had evolved in English by the seventeenth century are notoriously difficult to evaluate in tracing phonological diversity, but some conclusions seem possible. Vocabulary variation, the easiest domain for study, has traditionally been regarded by linguists as the least reflective of the nature of language. Nevertheless, what has been concluded about early – and recent – dialects of American English has generally been based on word geography more than on any other factor.

Some syntactic studies have been made. In his study of Governor William Bradford's (and others') use of periphrastic *do*, Risannen (1985: 172) accounts for 'the higher frequency of [periphrastic] *do* in Winthrop's text', in comparison with Bradford's, by the interpretation that the former's '*Journal . . .* often smacks of officialese'. Bradford's *History*, on the other hand, 'consists of fairly simple narration', and 'the periphrastic *do* is very sparely used' (Rissanen 1985: 170). Rissanen refers also to 'the sensitivity of Winthrop's style to the level of formality of the text'. In Winthrop's official correspondence, periphrastic *do* occurs in 5.8 per cent of the cases; in his private correspondence, the percentage is as low as 1.7. It is clear that the colonists utilized a full range of language styles. Rissanen postulates 'a high frequency of *do*-periphrasis in spoken discourse', while admitting that he 'cannot hope to reconstruct spoken language as such'.

In late sixteenth-century England, Traugott (1972: 139) would have the situation somewhat different; there '[periphrastic *do*] is rarely used in the everyday speech of the bourgeoisie'. On the other hand, since there is no truly reliable reconstruction of that level of precision, it may well be that *do*-periphrasis in the Massachusetts colony, perhaps like a large number of other language features, was about the same as that of Shakespeare's plays, where 'archaic language' and 'fixed formal phrases' are the primary loci of the periphrastic structure. It is unfortunate for the historian of English, but hardly deniable, that the colonial documents do not represent anything like the variety of speech styles, dialects and usages that can be found even in the drama of the Elizabetho-Jacobean stage.

Where literary style is concerned, one relatively trivial feature of approximately Elizabethan English does seem to have made the trip to North America, but not to have been established with any permanence: the much- (and over-) discussed feature of 'inkhorn terms', the temporary fad of Latinate and Greekified polysyllables that Shakespeare satirized so marvellously in the pedant Holofernes of *Love's Labour's Lost*. Some of this type of quickly obsolescent words can be found in Nathaniel Ward's *The Simple Cobler of Aggawam in America* of 1647. Terms used include *Colluvies, Alchymized Coines, irritaments, tolerations*. Phrases like *the due latitudes of Love, the fair Compartments of*

*Christian fraternity*, *the frontiers of error*, *the redoubts of Schisme* and *the peerillous irritaments of carnal and spiritual enmity* almost suggest an ecclesiastical Euphues. But, in spite of Marckwardt's (1958:101) attempt to suggest a connection to frontier tall talk (another perhaps over-discussed matter), the literary fashion seems to have died on the Atlantic coast of America not long after it expired in England.

Ward lagged behind the literary fashion of England in his Euphuistic prose, and the anglocentric approach generally held that American vocabulary consisted either of such laggings or of 'barbarous' innovation, the latter often called 'wigwam words'. It is a commonplace of eighteenth century language history that certain condemned Americanisms were really obsolete Anglicisms (for a list, see Dillard 1975: 66). It is striking, however, that very few of these are chronologically colonial. *Calculate*, in the 'American' sense 'suppose', is attested in 1810; *budge* has its first American attestation in 1824; *bamboozle* in 1842. A few, like *clever* in the special sense 'affable, good-natured', appear in the late colonial period – 1758 in this case. The evidence, insofar as vocabulary evidence is concerned, does not point strongly to American retention of what was lost or being lost in England.

The written documents of the seventeenth century indicate some not entirely unambiguous forms correlatable with nine-teenth century British dialects in phonology (see below). Tjossem (1956: 18) cites Michael Wigglesworth's repeated rhyming of *devil* and *evil'*, which could represent a northern pronunciation of the latter, although he actually rejects that explanation in favour of 'pious' rhyming associations. He finds the Warwickshire vocabulary items *bing'd* and *crickling* in the poems of Edward Taylor but accepts from some (unstated) authoritative source that Taylor's 'other forms . . . occur in the various Midland and Northern counties'. Taylor's rhyme *unjust/Christ* probably reflects Warwickshire /jIst/ (Tjossem 1956: 100), and he 'shows most clearly the Midland characteristics one might expect from his Warwickshire origin' (1956: 25). The rhyme *who/woe* in Michael Wigglesworth is considered to be possibly a survival of northern [oː] in *who* (the Salem witch trial transcript has at least one occurrence of *whow*), and the rhyme *enough/cough* 'would have been a good one in 19th-century Yorkshire' (1956: 25). The rhyme *high/we* in the 1648 revision of the *Bay Psalm Book* may reflect a Lancashire pronunciation [eː], Henry Dunstable, one of the revisers, having been a native of Lancashire.

In the English of the early New England colonies, the medial cluster of *daughter* could be /-ft-/; Benes and Benes (1985: 6) cite eighteenth-century form *dafter* as 'an occasional variant in early New England manuscripts'. Alexander (1928: 395) points out that 'there are frequent spellings . . . *dafter* and *daughter* in the Salem witch trials of 1692', and Woodward's (1864) transcript, taken at face value, would indicate extreme variability among the Salem community in this and other respects. Graphic *-ft-* occurs frequently, quite notably in what is presented as a letter from Mary Towne of 7 September 1692. She writes *sarved* for *served* (see below) and both *dafter* and *dafters*, along with numerous spellings that would indicate marginal literacy. *Dater* also occurs in Woodward's transcript (1864, I, 234, for example), although not nearly so frequently as *dafter* or *daughter*.

In general, official documents like the indictments prefer *daughter* whereas *dafter* (and, to a lesser degree, *dater*) is recorded frequently in the testimonies. While it would be easy to make too much of this evidence (a Mrs Hoar or Hoare suffers frequently from having *w-* prefixed to her name, a certain man is located *at whom*, and *about* is frequently *abought* or *aboughte*), the occurrences of the spellings *dafter* and even of *daufter* (Woodward 1864, II, 55) seem to indicate that some members of the community used /-f-/ for [-x-] or 0. Webster (1789) writes of the 'imperative of the Saxon *thofian*, now pronounced *thof*. But it is generally pronounced as it is written *tho*.' Dobson (1968) presents some evidence that retention of [-x-] for written *-gh-* may have been a northern characteristic, but he tends to regard it more as a marker of 'typical educated St[andard] E[nglish]'. In a slightly different context he remarks (1968:671): '. . . in the early seventeenth century there was very real confusion in actual speech among those who attempted to preserve [an articulation where the *gh* spelling is now standard]'. In short, intrapersonal variation may have been almost as common in England as it seems to have been in the North American colonies.

For the Salem witch trial (and other seventeenth-century New England evidence) it seems best to be even more cautious than Dobson was about the pronunciations of England. Since individual scribes and even individual speakers are represented by different spellings of words like *daughter*, and since no other evidence appears to be even as clear as this, almost the only conclusion that can be reached is that there was some variation among the speakers and/or the transcribers at the hearings. Elsewhere in the colonies, according to Tjossem (1956: 44), there was some, if not conclusive, evidence of a not yet simplified /-ft-/ cluster, or at least something quite different from the modern English pronunciation, in Anne Bradstreet's rhyme *laughter/*

*slaughter*. Bradstreet's 'rhyme of *caught* with *bait* implies a late [!] survival of the old form *keight*, while *breadth* rhyming with *length* is evidence both for the pronunciation *lenth* and for the analogical *brenth*, a form still current in England and the United States' (Society for Pure English (SPE) Tract 27.201, 1927, quoted in *DARE* I)

Even when such questionable evidence as that from rhymes (where various literary traditions may intervene between the written and the phonological evidence) is accepted, there is no consistent picture of regional dialects from England in the North American colonies. Schele de Vere's statement (1872: 258) that *k-you* for *cow* 'in New England states, is the inheritance of early settlers from Essex, Norfolk, and Sussex' may be true, but the evidence is not overwhelming for this or any other such statement.

In the Salem witch trials and probably elsewhere, the use of graphic *a* before *r* in forms like *darst* (I, 177), *parsons* (I, 228; II, 85; II, 122, but compare *person* [II, 79]), *sarch* (II, 24), *sarved* (II, 39; II, 83; II, 118), *sartifie* (II, 40), *absarvations* (II, 40), *hard* (for *heard*), (II, 43) varies with graphic *-e-*. Dobson's study of the orthoepists, in England but at almost precisely the period in question, indicates that those who were based in the more northerly parts of England gave especially full evidence of the lowering of Middle English [er] to [ar] in words like *convert, serve, conserve*, but that [ʌr] from [er] occurs possibly as a variant in many of them, while others of the same type have [ər] (Dobson 1968: 435). Thus, with *sarve* and *dafter*, Mary Towne may have written a northern British dialect in 1692, although the evidence is far from conclusive.

Alexander (1928) finds evidence for the reduction of unstressed final syllables in some of the spellings of the Salem transcript. There are, for example, *danile* for *Daniel* and *Juner* for *Junior*; but there is also an occurrence of *John best Jwnear* [sic] (II, 21). *Seener* occurs, but there is also *senior* (II, 21). *Forten* for *fortune*, *lector* for *lecture*, *ventor* for *venture* and *tortor* for *torture* occur, but there are also a number of occurrences of *torture*. In general, it appears that *torture* is unusual in the indictments and other official documents, whereas *tortor* is recorded in the testimonies. On the other hand, one testimony (Elizabeth Hubbard) has *tortoree*, which is hard to reconcile with any dialect pronunciation or spelling convention. It seems difficult, or even impossible, to draw any conclusions from such evidence except that there was a great deal of variability in the written usage of the time and that some of the graphic variants tend to point to dialect usage by the speakers. It is obviously impossible, however, to identify the Salem community – or any other that has been studied – with a geographic dialect of England.

Scattered forms occur elsewhere in the colonial period. A letter written in New Hampshire in 1706 contains the spelling *chimlys*, possibly representing a Scots and northern England form current since the sixteenth century (*DARE* I). A puristic objection to *chimbly* in 1818 provides as good evidence as is generally available for the persistence of such a pronunciation. In this case, however, the British origin itself may well be called in question. Phonological developments ('excrescent' /b/ after /m/ and dissimilation of /n/ to /l/) must be invoked in order to explain the British dialect forms. There is no real reason why such developments could not have taken place independently in the colonies – and later in the United States, where the non-standard pronunciation is rather common.

Other indicators of what may reflect original dialect diversity abound in the Salem transcript, for example in the oblique form of the feminine singular personal pronoun: *her, har, hor* (all Woodward, II, 21)and *hur* in addition to these – all rather common (*passim*). Such evidence may, however, point rather to development towards [ə] and uncertainty as to how to represent it graphically than to diversity of pronunciation; for /-Vr/, see *gurl*, *gorle*, *garl* (II, 85) for *girl*.

Like many other texts of that time and the immediately ensuing period, the Salem transcript points as strongly in the direction of other kinds of variability as in that of the survival of British dialects. Even before 1700 the statement holds true. One is led to the conclusion of Şen (1973: 121) as to the 'amount of dialect variation which existed in the early American colonies with little regional distribution or social stratification.' Although there are social factors besides stratification, the context leads one to the conclusion that the variation was essentially intrapersonal rather than interpersonal. That is, individuals among the early American colonists varied their pronunciations, perhaps even more than the average speaker of a language, in order to adjust to their multidialectal environment.

If material is lacking on the geographic dialect provenience of any major group of colonial speakers, there is no lack of information on variation. Şen writes of 'early regional occurrence' of [I] for [ɛ] in *engine, yesterday* and *yet*, but also finds that it 'had a universal distribution among the colonies'. *Kiver* for *cover*, although not exactly the same phonological process, is apparently associated. In the nineteenth century, Humphreys' *A*

*Yankey in England* (1815) indicated the pronunciation, Eliason (1956) found an 1856 attestation in North Carolina, and Schele de Vere (1872: 497) found it 'common in New England and southward as far as Pennsylvania'. Şen considers the substitution acceptable 'among all ranges of the social scale' during the colonial period but 'only in rustic folk dialects and occasionally in the dialect of rural middle class persons in the twentieth [century] and now showing "regional patterning"'. American phonological similarities to British standard and regional forms are observable, but none traces clearly to the colonial period. Kurath and McDavid (1961: 111) find:

> The [au ~au] type of the American North and North Midland agrees with Standard British usage. American [æu~ɛu] and [eu~au] have their counterparts in British folk speech, the former type prevailing in the eastern counties (with the exception of Norfolk and eastern Suffolk and Essex), the latter in the west and in part of East Anglia. Marked positional variants are not current in English folk speech, except perhaps in the northern counties and in Scotland; hence Virginian usage is presumably an innovation.

No colonial American evidence seems to have been adduced, however, for transmission of these British 'counterparts' to early North America.

Others have not hesitated so much to find innovation. Pilch (1980: 63) concludes that American /æ/ in words like *half, staff, class, last, grasp, path, rather* is neither 'archaic' nor 'Elizabethan'. On the contrary, the neutralization of the former opposition constitutes an innovation over against the continued distinction of distributionally the same phoneme as æ≠a in southern British. Confirmation is found in Görlach (1987: 46).

Vocabulary turns out to be as disappointing a domain as phonology and syntax for those who would find British dialects among the colonists. Forms assumed to be British regionalisms transmitted to American dialects beginning in the colonial period turn out to have no attestations at all in that period. Kurath (1972: 44) made a case primarily on the very slight list *cosset* ('pet'), *cade (lamb)* ('pet lamb'), *hap* ('quilt'), and *nicker/whicker* ('noise made by a horse'), *tempest* ('storm'), along with some phonological data, but with no indication in the dictionaries of specifically American usage and thus no dating). It is suggested 'in passing' that 'such regional expressions as *cade, hap*, and *nicker* can, with proper caution, function as "tracers" of population movements or migration routes' and it is suggested that the (then) forthcoming *DARE* 'will vastly increase our resources' insofar as providing such 'tracers' is concerned.[1]

*DARE* I provides very few colonial examples of such 'tracers'. Aside from Cotton Mather's (1702) use of *been't* as negator of 'invariant' *be* (see especially the discussion in Chapter 3) and a couple of apparent dialect pronunciations, there are *brockle-faced* – 'used of a cow, having a mottled, pied, or blotchy face' (1665 in New York and moving by 1899 to South Dakota, but now 'chiefly West') – one of the very few western cattle terms showing such apparent transmission; *black man* – 'an evil spirit, devil' (1692 but not attested again until 1915); *bad* – 'seriously ill or injured' (1716 and 1737, 1840 – which may indicate greater permanence); *check* – 'a light dinner' (1775, attributed to Irish in the first attestation but traced to Scots by *DARE* I), *crab lantern* 'a fruit pie' (*c. 1770); chibbole* – 'a scallion' ('as of 1740s'), and *chop* – 'cracked or coarsely ground grain' (1733).

These terms arrived in the Americas, insofar as *DARE* I's attestations are concerned, earlier than the 'lamb words'. The first citation of *cade lamb* or *cade* alone is from Farmer's *Americanisms* of 1889. There is a north-easterly distribution and a likelihood that the noun and the compound were brought over well before the end of the nineteenth century, but no hard evidence of the latter assumption. A somewhat stronger case for early – but by no means colonial – transmission can be made for *cosset*. According to *DARE* I, it occurs as early as 1806 (Webster, *Compendious Dictionary*) as applied to a lamb and as early as 1816 (Pickering, *Vocabulary*) in the sense of 'a spoiled child or pet; a favorite'. A 'northern British' form *aboon* ('above, higher than') is cited as a 'rare' North Carolina regionalism, but the earliest attestation is 1891. *Angledog*, a Devonshire form according to English Dialect Dictionary (EDD), has a 'N[ew] Eng[land], esp[ecially] C[onnecticu]T and s[outh]w[est] MA[ine]' distribution according to *DARE* I, but its earliest North American occurrence is recorded in 1867. There are apparently no seventeenth- or eighteenth-century occurrences.

Following the strict chronology of the attestations, one would also conclude that many of these vocabulary items found their way into New England as a result of this kind of re-anglicization. They include the forms upon which Kurath (1972) based his thesis that British regional dialects were a, if not the, major formative influence upon American dialects.

With the lack of any substantial syntactic data, messy phonological data, and the chronological problems complicated rather than clarified by Kurath's (1972) list of 'tracers', the transfer of British regional dialects to America in any recognizable form seems less rather than more likely as further information becomes available. The appealing concept of colonial lag, with all its genealogical promise, does not seem to meet the test of chronology.

Aside from the problem of archaic British regionalisms, one would say that vocabulary change in the eighteenth century – during the period in which the colonies changed into the nation – was about that of 'normal' change in a standardized language; that is, it attracted the curiosity if not the condemnation of relative purists such as Benjamin Franklin. In his letter to Noah Webster of 26 December 1789, Franklin comments upon how the verb (apparently only the participial form) *improved* had changed in meaning. Franklin remarks that when he left Boston in 1757 the word had only the meaning 'ameliorated' or 'made better', but that when he returned to that city in 1785 he found the usages

> . . . A Country-House to be sold, which had been for more than thirty years *improved* as a tavern . . .

and

> . . . in the Character of a deceased Country Gentleman that he had been for more than 30 years *improved* as a Justice-of-the-Peace.

Franklin remarks that the use in question was 'peculiar to New England and . . . not to be met with among any other speakers of English, either on this or the other Side of the water'. Dickens, in *American Notes* (1842: 159), still found occasion to put the American use of the term in quotation marks.

When seekers after change can find only matters like the above to point out, the amount of diversity is probably not very great. There were quibbles about the American English of the period – hardly to be absent from the eighteenth century of Swift's agitation for an academy and of the first preface to Johnson's dictionary. Certain words were condemned as American innovations, and twentieth-century researchers such as Mencken (1945: 118) found that supposed Americanisms like *(city) square* had earlier attestations in England (1687). So did *expect* in the sense 'think, suppose' (1592), *fall* – 'season of the year' (1546), and others. Contrary to what Mencken thought, *OED* II now cites *belittle* (for which Jefferson was issued a famous rebuke) as occurring first in the United States, in 1782. Less well known, *boatable* (1683) appears now to be an 'Americanism' in the narrow sense of the branch dictionaries. Such nit-picking seems to illustrate, by its very pettiness, the close similarity between the standard variety of English and the usage of non-frontier White Americans of some education and socio-economic standing.

Franklin's long stay abroad was quite possibly the only reason he observed the particular change in *improved*. Between the time he left Boston and the time he wrote to Webster, a special development had been taking place in the colonies which were becoming the United States. It was not, however, the kind of development for which Franklin's background would have prepared him. It was, rather, a special kind of unification.

In religion, Franklin's trip abroad frames what has been called the Great Awakening. By the 1750s, the religion of the at least nominally Christian colonists was 'vigorous' but 'diversified, with habits of independence that were the continuing despair of emissaries sent by the Archbishop of Canterbury to assess the state of his church in America' (Ketcham 1974: 35). According to Jordan and Kaups (1989: 74), '"Low" Scotch–Irish influence probably prevailed in the religious sphere of the American backwoods frontier, but the Indian and Savo-Karelian Finn may also have contributed to frontier heathenism.'

Out of that diversity came the Great Awakening. It was part of a broad phenomenon also embracing German Pietism and English Methodism. Although George Whitefield's evangelistic tours 'were importantly stimulated by Europeans' (Ketcham 1974: 35), there seems to have been a different impact in America.

The frontier mixture referred to by Jordan and Kaups (1989) seems to have played an important part in the development. Prominent in the services was emotionalism, with highly passionate manifestations of conversion. Organizationally, without much regard for the cultural climate in which that specific development was possible, the beginnings are found in Jonathan Edwards' sermons in the Connecticut Valley in the 1730s (Ketcham 1974: 36) and in Whitefield's preachings from Georgia to New England along with the Tennents' evangelizing the middle colonies, and Samuel Davies and others breaking in upon what was considered complacent Anglicanism in the South. Possibly no single one of these – nor that combination – would have produced the same effect in a more homogeneous society than the frontier of the mid eighteenth century. At any rate, the 'colonies experienced their first mass unifying movement' (Ketcham 1974: 36). According to Balmer (1989: viii), Dutch resistance to the Great Awakening was an important feature in their continued struggle for autonomy in New York, but by the mid-eighteenth century that too was succumbing to the dominant English culture – and language.

As in dialect or any other area, 'unification' remains a highly relative term. Historians dealing with the Great Awakening would never assert that no 'complacent Anglicans', recalcitrant Catholics or plain sceptics were to be found. Yet there was a highly reportable development of unity as the many denominations, including even some dissident Anglicans, joined in evangelical fervour.

In dialect, also, the same set of metaphors or generalizations has the same kind of validity. In politics, to borrow the words of Ketcham (1974: 37), 'in the unfinished landscape and free air of the colonies the ferment produced by . . . radical doctrine had abundant opportunity to work'.

Language having a notably high threshold of awareness, out-of-awareness development would be more characteristic than in religion or politics. Yet this unifying pattern – highly reportable, although of course never absolute – is discernible in any overall viewpoint of the colonies in the mid-to-late eighteenth century – in other words, at just about the time when the Great Awakening had taken effect and when the political theories behind the independence movement had gained acceptance by such Americans as thought in those terms.

According to Kurath (1972: 67), 'at the time of settlement usage varied in each of the colonies . . . and relative uniformity developed several generations after the settlement'. It now appears that it may be possible to date the development of that uniformity with something approaching precision.

Like most theories about American history, it is controversial that 'the regions were becoming increasingly alike during the generations immediately preceding the American Revolution' (Greene 1989: 170, quoted in Egnal 1990: 296). Nevertheless, there was unification compared with the 'individualistic, disordered societies' which were the Chesapeake area, the middle colonies, the Lower South, and much of the West Indies (Greene 1988). The linguistic evidence appears to support the general hypothesis about American history.

During the Revolutionary period itself, a rather striking – and perhaps not to be repeated – unity was in evidence among the English-speaking colonists. Attempts of untrained observers to describe that uniformity (Read 1933) took the rather inept form of phrases like *perfect uniformity* and *great classical purity*, although an occasional observer saw fit to exclude 'the poor slaves' and probably none of them meant to include the Indians.

However imprecise, the phrases of eighteenth century visitors indicate that something different from the observers' own language situation was going on – something, in fact, strange and radically different. The London editor of [David] *Ramsay's History of the American Revolution* (1782) wrote: 'Before the late American Revolution, the English language had acquired a standard, (as far as any living language can acquire a standard) and the British colonists had attained a remarkable perfection in it.' Schele de Vere (1872: 429) quotes Waterton, *Wanderings in So[uth] A[merica]* (1824): 'He [the American] has certainly hit upon the way (but I couldn't find out by what means) of speaking a much purer English than that which is commonly spoken on the parent soil.'

The 'unity' period, insofar as it can be judged by such reports, was a quite narrow segment on a wide band of diversity. Again, social and political considerations (like those that led to the Whiskey Rebellion) seem to have begun even before the war of the American Revolution was officially over and the independence of the former colonies, by whatever method, secured. The period of 'striking uniformity' among the white settlers who had come to the thirteen colonies from England and who were located east of the mountains seems to have had an inception around 1740–50 and to have become as relatively complete as such things ever are by the early 1770s. It does not appear, by the latter time at least, to have been compartmentalized regionally, although such observers as thought about them (such as the London editor of *Ramsay's History of the American Revolution*, who specified 'the white inhabitants') excluded the slaves, who were at the time as prominent in the northern as in the southern colonies.

It would be naive to call even the political outlook completely unified at any time, but there was an observable and reportable trend in that direction. By analogy, the United States during World War II was certainly not without its dissenters from the 'war effort' (nor without its exclusion of Black labour from certain occupations even at a time when a labour shortage was a national problem); but, compared with the atmosphere of dissent in the 1960s, the attitude of consensus was striking. In the Revolutionary period itself, there were Tories, but most of them went away, many to Canada – where Captain Hall later could not find the foreignness that he observed in the new United States.

At the time of the American Revolution, there was in Canada 'an English speaking population of about 25,000 whose composition can be analyzed with reasonable accuracy' (Orkin 1971: 50).

Canada had had a long history of the use of English, perhaps beginning with Cabot in 1497, well before any permanent English-speaking settlement in the United States. Nevertheless, upon such a small population the linguistic consequences of Loyalist flight seem to have been great. Pringle (1983) credits the settlement from the United States as the first important factor in the development of Canadian English. Morton W. Bloomfield (1948) considered that 'The Loyalists . . . molded Canada, created its ruling caste and set its social standards among which was its language.'

Obviously, factors other than the Loyalist immigration have to be considered in accounting for the differences between Canadian and American English, even during the eighteenth century. Contact with England was one of them. The same Captain Hall wrote:

> . . . the intercourse carried on between those Colonies [i.e. Canadian, for the United States were no longer 'colonies'] and Great Britain employed, in the year 1828, no fewer than eighteen thousand seven hundred and fourteen seamen . . .
>
> In the same year, 1828, the total amount of British tonnage employed in trading with the United States was but little more than eighty thousand (strictly, 80,158) and the number of seamen employed was three thousand six hundred and forty-six (3646). So that our trade with the North American colonies alone, occupied five times as much tonnage, and more than five times as many British seamen, as the whole of the intercourse which we enjoyed with the United States.

Pringle (1983) points out that, by 1848, the 10,000 or so Loyalists who had settled in upper Canada were absorbed into almost 1,000,000 native speakers of English.

The ten thousand who fled the rebellious colonies eliminated, at any rate, a disunifying factor from the future United States. There were other destinations for those who did not share the revolutionary ideals. Troxler (1989: 563) points out how the British government considered pairing East Florida with Nova Scotia as a place of settlement for departing Loyalists. By 1783 East Florida had come to symbolize 'both British protection and the availability of land' (p. 565), and by the last quarter of 1775 St. Augustine 'became a nest of schemers against the revolutionaries' (p. 567).

With the Tories at least partly gone, the Indians subdued and the slaves generally counted out of the picture, the possibilities of unity were great in the eastern colonies. The reports of the observers of the time are thus probably indicative of real processes of change which can be dated and localized. Any identities between American and British dialects were blurred, apparently for ever, by this period.

There were, as stated above, always elements of disunity. But the real disunity, when it came, was nothing obscure. When either British visitors or American eastern travellers began to comment on the language of the frontier, terms like *unity* and *purity* were far from their minds. A really strong separation between the settled areas of the East Coast and the frontier seems to have developed, 'especially in the years after 1785' (Slaughter 1986: 47). (Comparative) Westerners in the states of Pennsylvania and even Massachusetts felt grievances against the Easterners and resented the affluence of the latter, which they attributed in part at least to 'internal' taxes like that on whiskey. Westerners saw the acquisition of right to navigate the Mississippi as a paramount issue; Easterners sought rather to avoid complicating relationships with Spain.

The most overt manifestation of Western discontent with what Easterners were doing – a distortion, from their point of view – with the American Revolution culminated, in the 1790s, in the Whiskey Rebellion. Even if the 'watermelon army' made rather short work of the 'whiskey boys', establishing among other things a precedent concerning the federal government's ability to tax local economic activities (Slaughter 1986), the occurrence itself of the events emphasizes the split between the prosperous, relatively effete East Coast and the frontier.

In this disunity – even though final political separation may not have been a really grave threat – the social differences of the two sections are emphasized. Significantly, Slaughter (1986: 270) refuses to focus upon some ethnic group, such as the Scotch–Irish, which so many revert to in explanations of American history.

The explanation here emphasizes the ideological, political, inter-regional, international, economic, and class dimensions over ethnic ones because the revolt certainly transcended ethnic and other cultural tensions, and because ethnic explanations tend to beg the wider questions that put native Americans on both sides of the controversy.

Jordan and Kaups (1989) trace an ethnic pattern more complicated than mere attribution to the Scotch–Irish. They stress the importance of early Scandinavian, especially Finnish, backwoodsmen in setting the cultural patterns.

The whole matter of Celtic influence, especially in the South

(McWhiney 1988), is strongly controversial among historians. The Celtic influence in the South is, strictly speaking, a different matter from that of a Scotch–Irish pattern on the backwoods frontier; the significant point here is that professional historians are strongly divided on these issues. Where the cultural and even demographic ascendancy of the individual geographic groups of English emigrants cannot be established, it seems best not to be dogmatic about transmission, particularly where contemporary reports point to an interactional rather than a transmission model.

Note especially Slaughter's use of *inter-regional*, even in the context of accounting for a conflict between Westerners and Easterners. The distinction seems a relatively obvious one. *Regional* would entail isolating little pockets, as conventionally done in dialect geography, separated by mountain ranges, rivers, etc., along with major commercial dividing factors. It is a different matter that regionally distinct groups of Westerners made common cause in this critical period of the development of diversity in American English. Linguistically, also, the development of diversity cannot be explained in terms of persistence of those original 'pockets' of settlers from England – linguistic 'islands' in the conventional terminology.

Whatever change was taking place in the period of around 1770–80 definitely carried American English further away from its British roots, even if it did not promote diversity in American English itself. Little that can be found during the period points to regional distribution of the results of these patterns of change. By the 'early 1800s' (Labov 1972b: 290), however, at least a segment of the population underwent a different kind of change. According to Leith (1983: 192), 'when "r-pronouncing" ceased to be prestigious in south-east England, cities like Boston, New York, Jamestown, and Charleston followed suit.' This statement about cities like Boston and New York is a familiar one. Labov makes essentially the same statement and adds that the phonological development 'reached a radius of approximately 150 miles from Charleston, but was confined to the immediate vicinity of New York City' (1972b: 290). Kroch (1976: 360) adopts Labov's presentation and the idea that the original adoption by upper-class Eastern Americans spread to the other classes, who imitated the dominant social group.

Thus, our theory predicts that /r/-less pronunciation in nineteenth-century America should be different from other prestige forms . . . it should appear in all of the speech styles of the lower and working classes and not be restricted to the formal styles. Also, it should not reflect social stratification due to preferential usage by the dominant class. All historical data . . . on New York City confirm these predictions.

(On Charleston, however, see below.) This statement has frequently been made, but the mechanisms have apparently not been examined.

The 'high' cultural connections between New England and 'old' England (centring upon London, which is geographically in the south-east) are well known. The communications and interactions of literary men like Hawthorne and Emerson, although so late that they must have been a product rather than a cause of the anglophilia, are well known to students of American literature and of American culture. In the New England they inhabited, at least, reintroduction of British patterns would not be unlikely.

Judging by the historical dictionaries, importation of British regionalisms was as strong or stronger in the early nineteenth century than in the colonial period. *DARE* I shows *banter* – 'haggle' (1793); *close* – adj. adv. (1815); *cowhanded* – 'awkward, clumsy' (1834); *brickle* – 'brittle, crisp' (1837); *chitterlings* – 'food made from intestines' (1841); *cause why* – 'for the reason that' (1854); *barm* – 'yeast' (1859). The ninety years or so between the Revolution and the Civil War were, to judge by the dictionaries, as conducive to British regionalisms in the United States as the 155 years between the landing of the Pilgrims and the Declaration of Independence. Numerous others, like *ash-cat* 'dirty or disheveled person' (1869), are not attested until after the war between the states. It is always possible that many of them were around for a long time before they were recorded; but, as has often been said of other possibilities in the history of American English (see Goddard 1978), possibility is not fact. Even allowing for such possibilities, however, there is no overwhelming evidence that Americans either in the colonial period or in the nineteenth century spoke anything closely resembling British regional dialects.

In more mundane terms, however, there remain many problems. Most Americans on the East Coast – and even more so those to the west – were busy with concerns of their own rather than with connections to England. Knights (1969) stresses the 'incredible' mobility of the Boston population between 1830 and 1860, roughly the period in which the change should have been taking hold. He asserts (1969: 164–5) that: 'It would seem, then, that overall population mobility in ante-bellum Boston was at

least as great as the oft-quoted modern figure for the United
States.' Whether such mobility would contribute to a stable,
invariant shift of /Vr/ to /V0/ appears to be something less than a
matter of socio-linguistic certainty. According to Griffen (1969:
57), in Newburyport between 1850 and 1880 the foreign-born
were overwhelmingly Irish, tending to polarize the community.
In nearby Poughkeepsie, however, a more receptive attitude
toward the foreign born accompanied a greater diversity of ethnic
groups, and those of Dutch descent aided in making German
immigrants more welcome. The picture of a stable community,
with the top group accepting a British innovation and the lower
classes placidly following suit, does not seem to follow.

With this kind of uncertainty in the supposedly clear-cut case
of British influence in the North, it seems doubly questionable
whether Charleston, very much in the centre of Black-influenced
speech by this time, can trace its /r/lessness' to England. The
linking of 'non-rhotic' Southern and American Black developments by Gilbert (1984) seems considerably more convincing.

It is well known that New England '/r/dropping' (in non-
prevocalic position) is accompanied by 'intrusive /r/' – not only
'Hahvahd' but also 'idear of it' – and that the latter especially is
subject to variable rules which make it more complicated in
performance than in reports by observers. The intrusive /r/ is not
so characteristic of the Charleston area so that, systemically, the
/r/lessness would not appear to be the same thing. Like the
transmission of *cade* and *cosset,* '/r/lessness' in New England
seems to have been part of the 're-anglicization' taking place
there but not in other parts of the United States in the early
nineteenth century.

It was primarily in the context of developing opposition
between Easterner and frontiersman – in other words, of the
abandonment or destruction of the short-lived unity – that
expansion to the West began, not in that of anglicization or re-
anglicization. Around 1787 large numbers of pioneers went down
to Ohio. Statistics can be cited, but sometimes a better
impression can be gained from a non-numerical approach like
that of Fearon (1818: 234).

On the road, every emigrant tells you he is going to Ohio;
when you arrive in Ohio, its inhabitants are 'moving' to
Missouri and Alabama; thus it is that the point for final
settlement is forever receding as you advance, and thus it will
thereafter proceed and only be terminated by that effectual
barrier – the Pacific Ocean.

About the same time, George W. Ogden (1823: 95), writing from Kentucky, reported that: 'Many of the inhabitants of this state emigrated from every part of the United States, and from most of the countries of Europe.' The settled peasantry of the type that produced European regional dialects does not seem to exist in this type of situation. Mobility was, and clearly remained for a long time, the pattern among English-speaking Americans.

Language forms seem to have had something of the same mobility. *DARE* I's designation of *clever* in the sense 'pleasant, good-natured, affable' as 'formerly N[ew] Eng[land]' (in the eighteenth century according to the attestations) but 'now chiefly S[ou]th, S[outh] Midl[and]' (nineteenth and twentieth centuries according to the citations) indicates a kind of regional shift which is by no means unique. What was developing in the early United States was a group of speech communities, roughly assignable to areas but still highly mobile. Other considerations, such as occupation, were at least as important as place of residence in determining membership in those communities. The composition of the extreme parts of the original states was different enough by 1795 that extreme differences in pronunciation between New England and the South could be recognized (Heath 1980: 24).

Henry C. Knight (pseudonym Arthur Singleton) distinguished (1824: 34) between regional communities primarily on the grounds of economic activity, citing among others 'the intelligent yeomen and dauntless mariners of the East' and 'the pioneering colonists of the West'. Captain Frederick Marryat, writing in 1837, found sectional differences on the basis of imputed character; Easterners pronounced those in the southern states to be 'choleric, restless, regardless of law, and indifferent as to religion' (1960: 39). The Southerners in turn considered the Easterners 'over-reaching pedlars, selling clocks and wooden nutmegs' (1960: 39).

Elsewhere, Knight offers comments like: 'What flat lands are in New-England called *intervales*, the Western planters call *bottoms* or *prairies*; and the Southern, *natural meadows* or *savannahs*'. *DARE* I calls *bottom* 'alluvial land, especially low-lying land near a stream', now 'chiefly S[ou]th, W[est] Midl[and]'. Knight also cites 'Virginia *phraseology*', which 'sounds a little peculiar to a northern ear at times', citing *grow* [a crop] for *raise* . . ., *be raised* for *be educated*, *gear* for *harness*, *lines* for *reins*, along with the much-discussed *reckon/guess*, *shuck* for New England *husk*, the latter word doing service for 'what we call cob' and for 'the external envelope of the kernel, which cannot be reduced to meal, and which makes the bran'. The use of *clever* ('intelligent'), he attributes to Virginians; however, 'we [Northerners] use it [*clever*] for a kind of negative character of weak intellect, but good disposition.' Having corroborated colonial observations about the New England usage (see above, p. 33), Knight concedes (1824: 82) that 'the correct meaning is rather with them [Southerners], than with us, as shrewd, cunning, dexterous'. *DARE* I's materials agree roughly with Knight's statement, calling the first meaning of *clever* 'formerly New England'. Actually, Knight's 'we [Northerners]' would be more inclusive, and the 1781 citation is from Philadelphia. According to *DARE* I, this particular usage has migrated in the interim and is now 'chiefly S[ou]th, S[outh] Midland'. Knight also points out (1824: 82) that 'What they call chamber, is the room where the madam sleeps, and is usually *below* stairs . . .' *DARE* I reports this word, in the sense 'an upper room or floor of a house, freq[uently] used as a bedroom', as 'chiefly N[ew] Eng[land]' with attestations in 1639, 1694, 1746, and 1800, and as 'a room on the main floor of a house, usu[ally] used as a setting room and a bedroom', with an attestation from Virginia in 1863. Knight's attestation of a relatively Southern, lower-floor *chamber* would appear, then, to be considerably earlier than *DARE* I's first. More importantly for chronological considerations, however, his evidence tends to place the developing regional differentiation around the 1820s, the period at which much of the other evidence of the same type is concentrated.

According to Knight also, 'what we [Northerners] call afternoon, they [Virginians] call evening, making no quarter divisions of the day.' By 1898, J. Fox in *Kentuckians* (p. 68) could report a misunderstanding as to the time of day, in a conversation between a Kentucky mountaineer and a presumptive Northerner; Fox was led to report 'The mountaineer's day has no afternoon.' The *Dictionary of Bahamian English* (hereinafter *DBE*) points out that the same usage is prevalent throughout the Caribbean and cites Portuguese *tarde*, while also pointing out that there is British dialectal usage of the same type. In the 1960s in the Cameroon, I observed frequent use of French *soir*, among Africans, in this sense.

Knight also reported that the Virginians, like the Kentuckians, 'tuck[ed] a *t* at the end of such words as onct, twict, skifft'. The Kentuckians themselves were observed to have, in 1824, their 'novel' phraseology. Knight cites *plunder* ('trunk or valise'); *nigh fainting under the pleasing punishment that women bear* ('a promised mother'); *human* as a noun (presumably for *human being*); *great* ('little', cited in the context of praising a lady's foot); *run* ('river'); *lot* ('section of land'); *stall* [a horse] ('overload . . .'); *cupping* ('milking'); *timothy* ('a kind of foxtail grass'); *fever and ague* ('"our" black-and-yellow caterpillar'); *collard* ('probably colewart'); and *cashaws*. Without giving equivalents from his own dialect, Knight cites *crablanterns* and *cobble*, which 'children wait for [at the oven]'. *DARE* I cites *crab lantern* ('A fruit pie shaped like a half-moon and fried') with a somewhat indecisive '?Midl[land] *old-fash*[*ioned*] from 1770 (Maryland), 1801,1818 in 1824 Knight', but cites nothing appropriate in this context for *cobble*.

According to Knight, some words were used 'even by genteel people, from their imperfect education, in a new sense' (1824: 106–7). 'The lower classes in [Kentuckian] society' had 'uncouth' usages, including:

> best book I ever read after . . .

According to *DARE* I, the last is the first citation for *after* 'Added, often without evident function, to certain verbs'. Knight also cites forms like *bresh* for *brush*. The latter is cited first from 1837 (Sherwood), called 'chiefly S[ou]th, S[outh] Midl[and]' by *DARE*, and is familiar to readers of comics, in Snuffy Smith's 'If that don't take the rag off'n the bresh' – regarded as a mountain or hillbilly usage.

The transmission of few if any of these forms can be traced to earlier occurrence in England or even to points further east in America, although it has frequently been assumed that occurrence of equivalent forms means that (unattested) transmission did take place. Some of the forms, especially the past tenses of verbs ( *I brung*) and past participles cited here and in other early reports of the 'bad' English of the frontier states and territories, are quite likely analogical developments although some may parallel forms in (nineteenth-century) *EDD*. Knight cites *I seen* from Kentucky, as much the victim of stereotyping during that period as Brooklyn was later to become; Kirkham (1929) cites *I seen, have saw* and *seed* from Pennsylvania, just about exhausting the 'incorrect' possibilities. Mencken could hardly have done better in his composite American Vernacular, and Kirkham throws in *I done* and *have did*. Something of the same might be said about Knight's *drap* and *fotch*. Just as an illustration of the possibilities, the tendency of Pidgin English to use the base form of the verb (or sometimes a base like *lef* rather than *leave*, *loss* rather than *lose*[2] or *took* rather than *take*) would provide an obvious difference from the standard past-tense forms. Uneducated frontiersmen could easily form a past tense *brung* by analogy with verbs like *sunk* or *sung*. *See, saw, (have) seen* simplifies to *see, seen (have) seen* or *see, saw, (have) saw* in a pattern long familiar in English strong verbs – and still without reducing the number of forms as much as is regularly done in Pidgin.

Fanny Kemble, an actress and 'professionally trained to listen to the spoken word' (McCrum, Cran and MacNeil 1986: 43), observed that 'The southern, western and eastern states of America have each their strong peculiarities of enunciation, which render them easy of recognition.' McCrum, Cran and MacNeil use that observation to come to a conclusion which is identical to the assumption of more academic writers on the same topic – that 'pockets' of British dialect were the dominant pattern in the formation of American English. Kemble's observations were made in the late 1830s, however, a time at which regionalization was well under way (see Chapter 7.) She offers no specifics of these 'enunciation' patterns, but her place in the chronology of observations accords well with those of Knight and Kirkham.

Kirkham's *English Grammar in Familiar Lectures*, which had an eleventh edition in 1829, introduced 'Provincialisms' which had not appeared in his *Compendium* of 1823, although the earlier work (or version of the same work) did have his 'Exercises . . . in False Syntax, &c', the popularity of which seems to indicate self-consciousness about usage by many Americans of the 1820s. The book, which had already been popular as a prescriptive grammar, was even more successful with the cautionary material on 'Provincialisms' added. It is likely, in terms of the general dialect history of the United States, that some of the 'provincialisms' had changed by the latest editions, which ran until 1857 (Laird 1970: 299–300). Users apparently did not, however, lose confidence in the work because of glaring inaccuracies. One would guess that Kirkham's notion of regional distribution accorded fairly well with theirs, with no glaringly obvious discrepancies.

Kirkham seems to indicate, and Knight not to disagree, that in the early 1820s there were noteworthy non-standard forms characteristic of four groups: one social – the Irish; the others regional – New England or New York; Pennsylvania; Maryland, Virginia, Kentucky or Mississippi. The first of these regional groups (New England or New York) included *O, the pesky criter*! [*sic*, but obviously *critter*], 'corrected' to *O, the paltry fellow* . The historical dictionaries list *critter* from 1815, by Humphreys, *A Yankey in England*, where even metaphorical application to human beings is not certain: 'Cooking for the crew, and taking care of the dumb critters.'[3]

Notably, Kirkham did not differentiate New England and New York. Later writers seemed more confident of the difference. Featherstonhaugh (1844: 134), steaming on the Mississippi from Little Rock to New Orleans, had a fellow passenger who 'from his language was evidently from New England'. Featherstonhaugh, however, apparently based his conclusion as to origin in New England, 'where the young men are generally well brought up', on a pleasing manner and the young man's being 'decently dressed'.

For Pennsylvania Kirkham recorded numerous expressions, including:

> Leave me be, for Ime afear'd.

Neutralization of *leave* and *let*, both expressed in German by *lassen*, is perhaps the best known feature of the Pennsylvania Dutch dialect (Springer 1980). Germans who moved into the Pennsylvania area in the seventeenth and eighteenth centuries may well have made their influence felt by 1829. It was a Frenchman, on the other hand (Michaut 1804: 27), who cited '*Le route*, turn-pike-road' from Philadelphia.

For his Irish category, Kirkham cites:

> Not here the day; he went till Pittsburgh.
> Let us be after pairsing a wee bit.
> Where did you loss it?

Note that he does not include

> be V-ing

among Irish usages, although he does include the familiar Irish idiom *be after* as a kind of indicator of futurity or intention.

Noteworthy among Kirkham's New England or New York examples are the 'invariant' *be* forms, including the oft-cited

> I be goin

With at least the possibility of early occurrence in Newfoundland, the early occurrence in New England almost unavoidably suggests spread southwards and into Black English. On possible origins for 'invariant' *be*, see, however, Dillard (1985: 116–19). More importantly, Kirkham's New England or New York *be* is negated *bain't*; *been't*, as a 'chiefly N[ew] Eng[land], *old fash[ioned]*' form, is attested by *DARE* I as early as Cotton Mather's *Magnalia* in 1702. Frederick Law Olmsted (1972: 266) reported *bean't* from Tennessee Whites in the 1850s. This is notably unlike the Black English Vernacular negative pattern *don't be*, emphasizing what Stewart (all references) Loflin (all references) and others have often said: that what is distinctive about the BEV is not the (surface) occurrence of certain words or phrases but their place in the entire grammatical structure. Although less has been done on the New England and New York dialect of the early nineteenth century, something of the same principle may well apply.

The BEV version of *be V-ing*, as is well known, may also include a final *-s*: *be's*. The dialect of Newfoundland, for an extent of time which has not yet been studied, has had a special 'invariant' (with the same exception noted), although there has been no evidence adduced except for the twentieth century (Paddock 1966: 20–1). Newfoundland was probably part of the maritime contact language area and probably took the 'invariant' *be* from that source. Whether it actually agrees with the BEV form – or with that cited for New York and New England by Kirkham – remains to be studied. Paddock calls the Newfoundland form 'non-past' because, while time is not specified, as notably in the BEV, it is not definitely present. It may also have a suffix /-s/, not dependent upon agreement in person. Paddock reports contrasts between this 'non-past' and 'present'

| | |
|---|---|
| I bees sick | I'm sick |
| He bees sick | He's sick |
| They bees sick | They're sick |

Also like the Black English Vernacular, the Newfoundland folk dialect has /-s/ with other verbs independent of the third person singular agreement pattern of ordinary English: *I expects, you haves, you does, I hates* – with a reported *he do*.

Story, Kirwin and Widdowson (1982) list 'principal grammatical features of Newfoundland and Labrador English' which include non-redundant pluralization (a noun does not need an *-s* plural in the proper environment), *-0* rather than *-s* with third person singular, present-tense verbs; and a distribution of *am*, *is*, *are* for present-moment 'events', as opposed to the 'continuous or repeated' use of *be* as in the examples above from Paddock (1966).

It has been conventional to trace the dialect diversity beginning to emerge during this period to the areas from which the migrants came, but there seems to have been no migration pattern which included 'New England or New York' and Newfoundland. Undoubtedly Kirkham's distribution is too narrow. Just as likely, the general patterns of language contact and special contact varieties – perhaps the same that 'produced' the Black English Vernacular *be(s)* – were operative along the East Coast at least up to Kirkham's time. Survivals in Newfoundland (and Labrador) folk speech thus provide a general parallel to BEV insofar as this and perhaps some other features are concerned.

Other non-standard developments were taking place further west, although perhaps at a slightly later period than that reported on by Knight and Kirkham. The reports of the period stress the diversity ('bad grammar', 'frontier defects' and the like) of Westerners. Featherstonhaugh's 1844 *Excursions . . .* reports how, at St Louis, 'the bar-room was filled with vagabond idle-looking fellows, drinking, smoking, and swearing in *American* '. The emphasis is in the original; 'American' was considered somehow related to what these 'idle-looking fellows' were doing. That is, it was so considered in 1834 and would have been by Dickens during his travels in America in the early 1840s. It would not have been so considered, on the East Coast and from White speakers, between 1770 and 1780, and hardly between 1750 and 1820. But Featherstonhaugh (1844: 105) also found in Little Rock a 'gentleman' who offended the writer by the manner in which he drawled out his ungrammatical absurdities.

According to Caruso (1962: 323), 'correct speech' joined 'gentlemanly bearing' and 'neat clothing' as sufficient motivations to make a frontier 'bully' want to fight the bearer of those attributes. Another way of putting the same thing would be to say that the 'bully' or frontiersman recognized cultural, including linguistic, patterns different from his own and reacted to them with hostility.

Apparently, no one ever called the frontiersman's dialect 'classically pure' or even 'uniform'. The koiné-like dialect of the East Coast around the Revolutionary period apparently never developed beyond the mountains. On the other hand, factors leading to diversification were more abundant there than on the coast. Hesitations between forms like *brung* and *brought*, *burst* and *busted*, *dragged* or *drug* (as past of transitive *drag*), *drank* or *drunk* (as preterite or past participle of *drink*) – linguistic uncertainties which were common at the time of Atwood (1953) – may well have been as commonplace as 'variation among the noncultured types' on the early frontier.

Uninterrupted diversity was apparent in other domains of activity as well. In religion, the tendency of Scotch–Irish to be

Presbyterians and of Germans to be Lutherans was only part of a complex pattern. With this kind of diversity, the phrasal collocations characteristic of the unifying Great Awakening should not have dominated the religious usage of frontiersmen. The Great Awakening has been perceived as a time when, with a tolerance for racial and other differences rare for its time, there was achieved a unity of values (Mullin 1989). If Hirshberg (1982) is correct, the religious vocabulary which spread to the South, to the plantations and to the slaves, 'derives directly from the revivalist movements of the late eighteenth and nineteenth centuries' (1982: 56) rather than from the Great Awakening.[4] Given the incomplete nature of the documentation, however, it might be thought that some of it may go back to the Great Awakening. In any case, Hirshberg deals only with *amen corner* (1860), *breaking exercise* (1948; treated not of itself but by analogy to *falling exercise, jerking* and especially '*singing exercise* . . . attested in white as well as black sources'). At least some of the vocabulary treated under 'Religion' in Dillard (1977) may have spread to – or from! – the slaves in that temporary (and restricted) democratizing period. Some of it is even preserved today in the vocabulary of the Black church. For example, *seeking* ('pertaining to a religious search', *DBE*) is characteristic of Bahamian Black usage as well as of the Black church in the United States. Coalescence of religious terminology did not in most views result even in complete and final religious unification nor in anything like cultural uniformity.

It is clear that complete Black identity with White religious practices did not remain, if it ever came about, after the Great Awakening or the revivalist movements. Later statements, both from Blacks and from Whites, indicate a great deal of difference. James L. Smith (1881), a freed slave recording his experiences on a Virginia plantation at the time of Nat Turner's rebellion, states:

> The way in which we [the slaves] worshiped is almost indescribable. The singing was accompanied by a certain ecstacy of motion, clapping of hands, which would continue without cessation for about half an hour; one would lead off in a kind of recitative style, others joining in the chorus.

In southern Virginia, according to 'The Camp Meeting at Gray's Hill', (*The Southern Bivouac*, Vol. II, No. 1 [June 1886], pp. 232–4):

> After a short exhortation, the shouting begins, for a negro would scorn a Christian who did not shout. The ceremony of

shouting is terrifying to a spectator. A sort of fury seems to seize the negroes, especially the women, who scream at the top of their voices, throw their arms wildly about, jump up and down for hours and seem entirely out of their minds.   (p. 233, column B)

This shouting in the Black church does not refer to 'calling out in a loud voice'; W. F. Allen in 1865 (Jackson 1967: 80) correctly identified the shout as a 'kind of shuffling dance'.

There undoubtedly was sharing between between Black and White groups – as between either of the two and the Indians – in the colonial period and in the nineteenth century. Separateness, including cultural and linguistic separateness, remained insofar as the great majority of those identified with the groups were concerned. The unifying tendencies of the Revolutionary period, with relatively few exceptions, excluded 'the poor slaves'. It was this socially identified group from which developed the greatest of all the diversities that emerged in American English.

## Notes

1 Kurath also issued numerous cautions (e.g. 1972: 67) against the suggestion of 'clear and simple' relationships between British and American. In general, however, it does not seem a distortion to characterize as a Linguistic Atlas approach the historical thesis advanced in the works of such writers as McDavid (1967). While acknowledging the great importance of Kurath's contributions, there seems to be no way to avoid the admission that the thesis of this book is almost directly contrary to that approach.

2 The attributions of base forms like *loss* to pidgin and to British dialects ('Irish' here) are not mutually exclusive. Hancock (1985 ) attributes many of the verb forms of Pidgin English to British regional provenience. A certain number of such forms, regional in England at the time of the *EDD* and perhaps even earlier, may have come to American English through pidgin transmission. Strictly speaking, neither transmission is established beyond doubt.

3 Kirkham's list of expressions for New York and New England is quite long – much longer, for example, than that of Webster (1793). There will be considerable discussion of forms cited by Kirkham in later chapters.

4 Note again, however, that, as with so many such researchers, a time lapse of up to a century is accorded little importance.

# Chapter 3

# The development of Black English

The first clearly discernible and reportable dialect of American English appears, almost paradoxically, to be the last recognized by the academic world – Black English, often referred to as the Black English Vernacular (BEV). Many early literary records are available, going back to the early decades of the eighteenth century, with some hints of the existence of the variety as early as the late seventeenth, and the early examples are consistent with the thesis that a West African form of Pidgin English was in use in the slave community in the colonies and the early United States quite as much as it was in the West Indies. The question of West African 'substratum' influence remains controversial, in terms of data as well as of theory, but the history of the variety does not depend upon the resolution of that problem.

Records of recognizable West African languages could hardly be kept by the Whites, who were the only recorders and were not, with the very fewest exceptions, able even to recognize specific West African languages. We are not fully able to account for what made British traveller J. F. D. Smyth (1784) 'not understand . . . one syllable of his [a slave's] language', making it necessary for Smyth to sell that first slave, whom he had bought in Petersburg, Virginia, and to buy another from a plantation in North Carolina. That the first slave spoke a West African language seems entirely likely; on the other hand, that he was *monolingual* in that language, or lacked some language of wider communication, would seem almost impossible at that date, over 150 years after the introduction of slaves into the general area. Smyth's second slave, Richmond, spoke pidgin- or creole-like English according to Smyth's transcription.

Mixing of tribal and language groups of Africans is one of the commonplaces of the history of slavery. From Richard Simson's *Voyage to the Straits of Magellan & S. Seas* in the year 1689, we read (Rediker 1987: 48; Sloane MS. 86, BL, f. 87):

> The means used by those who trade to Guinea, to
> keep the Negroes quiet, is to choose them from severall parts
> of ye Country, of different Languages; so that they find they
> cannot act joyntly, when they are not in a Capacity of
> Consulting one an other, and this they can not doe, in soe farr
> as they understand not one an other.

Exceptions to this practice have also been reported, but by far the greater number conform to the general pattern. Atkins (1735: 172) asserts that 'Caution where a cargo is of one language is so much more the requisite,' and Hancock (n.d.: 15) observes from a general study of slave ship reports off the coast of Africa that, 'while it was not always possible, efforts were made to keep slaves speaking the same language separate from each other'.

For those slave ship captains who were not so careful, there could be 'bloody . . . mutinies' like those of the *Eagle Galley* (1704), the *Henry*, the *Elizabeth* (1721) and the *Ferrar Galley* on which 300 slaves 'of one Town Language' mutinied three times before being brought to Jamaica (Rediker 1987: 49). Yet Smith and Atkins, among others, report how the ship captains had learnt their lessons and avoided just such situations.

Selective purchasing practices by owners in the Americas, which would have tended in some cases to reunite Africans from the same tribe and language even if the separation practised by the slavers had been fully effective, have also been reported. Individual west African languages, in restricted circumstances, may well have survived longer than has generally been assumed. On the whole, however, it seems highly unlikely that slaves who had not been forced to learn a new language (often two or three according to the advertisements for escaped slaves) were anything like commonplace. A pidginized form of English was certainly one – and probably the earliest and most frequent – of those languages. Krapp (1925) cites, apparently unknowingly, examples of Pidgin English used by slaves in the early period; Stewart (1967, 1968) is more explicit about the significance of such attestations.

Littlefield (1981: 157) provides statistics concerning reports of those slaves' language abilities which were commented upon by their masters. Of these, 30 per cent were said to speak 'no English at all'; 45 per cent were judged as speaking 'good to excellent' English; the remaining 25 per cent spoke 'some

English'. As Littlefield and many others have noted, artisans and house servants were far more likely than any others to come in the group judged 'good to excellent'. Whether 'no English at all' is to be taken literally is a moot point. The meaning of 'some English' or of 'a little English', as often reported in the African records, perhaps remains to be judged rather by what records we have than by the testing qualifications of the masters who rated them. Littlefield's sources classify slaves as 'inferior [in] language ability' when what is meant is clearly that those slaves had learnt less English than the others; ability in other languages, such as west African languages, would not have been subject to the judgement of the owners.

Pidgin English would have been available to Africans by the period in question. Hancock (ms. 15) dates the origins of 'Guinea Coast Creole English . . . at least back to the early 1600s'. As noted in Chapter 1, there is documentary evidence that Pidgin English was spoken in the Massachusetts area by American Indians as well as by Black slaves. There may well have been some kind of interchange between the two non-white groups, African slaves having been brought to the New England area at about the same time the earliest Pidgin English records there occur. Numerous examples of Pidgin or pidgin-like English are attested from slaves within what is now the United States between about 1690 and 1790. A 'Jin, native of Guinea' in Deerfield, Massachusetts, is quoted in 1732 (Sheldon 1895–6):

. . . and we nebber see our mudders any more.

Between 1743 and 1783 in Abingdon, Massachusetts, a Cuff (probably based on Cuffee, the day name for Friday among the Ashanti, with other meanings in other West African languages) is quoted, (Hobart 1866):

By-and-by you die, and go to the bad place, and after a while Cuff die and go and knock at the good gate.

As indicated below, slaves speaking Pidgin English were imported from Africa until about 1830, but the Pidgin English of those who arrived after about 1820 seemed anomalous on the plantations and was even ridiculed by other slaves. Such factors of change do not, of course, prove 'creolization', but that remains perhaps the most obvious possibility. Not even the question of creolization, however. is absolutely critical to the history of the Black English Vernacular and of its influence upon American English.

Unless all the records are false, the auxiliary languages the slaves learned did not include what is today called Southern dialect. The first West Africans – except for those brought by the Spanish – were brought to Virginia in 1619. Before there was any large population of slaves in the Deep South there was an appreciable number in New England and New York. It was in New York City in 1741 that Daniel P. Horsmanden recorded a form of *buckra* ('white man'), now a regionalism and distributed with a typical – for American regionalisms at any rate – disjunctive range in 'coastal S[outh] C[arolina] and G[eorgia]' according to *DARE* I and in the 'Seminole' Gullah-speaking community in Bracketville, Texas (Hancock 1980). Horsmanden's citation is:

. . . and then they would be rich like the backarara.
[Horsmanden's note] Negro language, signifies white people.[1]

The word (sometimes in the slightly variant form *bakra*) is widespread in the West Indies, although little historical evidence has been gathered. The *Dictionary of Jamaican English* (hereinafter DJE) cites an example from 1688. Benjamin Franklin gave the form *Boccarorra* in 1787; there is no reason not to believe that the clearly pidgin speech in which the term is included was meant to represent Black speech in Philadelphia. The third occurrence listed in *DARE* I (1800) is from Maryland, but Samuel Lowe's *The Politician Outwitted*, written in 1788 but published in 1789 (Walser 1955: 172), contains what is obviously the same word in the spelling *buckaraw*. Thomas Dibbin's *The Irishman in London* of about 1800 has the form *bochro*, in context an obvious antonym to *poor black*. The variant spellings, as Mason (1960) suggested, indicate some problems the recorders had with the phonology of the word. Longstreet's 1835 story 'The Character of a Native Georgian', set in Savannah, contains the form *buckera-man*. Considering the transmission by the Florida Seminoles, it is believable that the word was distributed well to the south of South Carolina before Seminole removal. It is only in 1838 that a South Carolina attestation is recorded.

More material about the speech of slaves in New York City around the middle of the eighteenth century can be gleaned from Horsmanden's materials. The associate justice also quotes the sentence:

His master live in tall house Broadway. Ben ride the fat horse.

The 'loss' of final -s for the third person singular present tense, with its multiple possibilities for origin, is the most commonplace feature of Black English – and of a number of other dialects. Omission of the preposition before *Broadway*, while not unknown in British dialects, is paralleled in the twentieth-century Caribbean. *Fat* raises something of a problem also. Since horses are more regularly – and perhaps 'naturally' – distinguished by colour than by weight, it is likely that Jack (the speaker of this sentence) meant a 'white' horse rather than an 'obese' one. Initial *f-* in Black English for ordinary English *wh-* is fairly commonplace in the nineteenth-century plantation literature and occurs in Breckenridge's *Modern Chivalry* of 1792 (*fat* for *what* in the speech by Cuff). Monophthongization of stressed vowels, as /a/ or /a:/ from /ay/, by Black speakers emerges even from twentieth-century Linguistic Atlas work on Black informants, with nuclei different from those of White speakers in the same region (Dorrill 1986).[2]

Horsmanden also records (p. 244) that *the house* 'in the negroes dialect signifies houses, i.e., the town'. The usual pidgin and creole pattern is that noun plurals occur non-redundantly and are absent from phrases with modifiers indicating plurality.

The province of New York contained 'more than two thousand Negroes, a little over thirteen percent of the total population' at the beginning of the eighteenth century (Ottley and Weatherby 1967: 19). The Dutch had brought in African slaves until the time of the English conquest in 1664, and the English resumed the trade when they established themselves as masters, buying some from pirates (Ottley and Weatherby 1967: 18). According to Ellis, Frost, Syrett and Carman (1957/69), Blacks fluctuated from 12 to 24 per cent ot the total population during the period, being found in every county of the colony, although most of them resided in or around New York City. Most of them had been brought from the West Indies – as early as 1626 from Curaçao by the Dutch, although some had come from Africa. In 1741, at about the time of the incident Horsmanden described, New York clearly had a large enough population of slaves for the Whites to be virtually obsessed by the danger of revolt.

More important than the demographic representation of Blacks in the colony and early state of New York was their relative autonomy in cultural terms. Ellis, *et al.* (1957/69) put it succinctly: 'The Negroes created a subterranean society of their own . . .' In fact, Jack, the user of the 'Negro and unintelligible' English according to Horsmanden, was the suspected leader of the perhaps imaginary Negro Plot. It was this social relationship, not mere numbers or propinquity, which made possible the existence of Black English in New York long before the notice of the nation came to the 'ghettoes' of the inner cities after World War II.

Horsmanden indicates the linguistic complexity of the group of slaves on Manhattan Island around 1740. A witness at the trial named Mary Burton testified that Comfort's Jack (also referred to as 'Captain Jack') spoke 'a little English and some other language that she did not understand'. Another, Sara Hughson, says of John Ury that, when baptizing some slaves, he 'talked in a language which she did not understand'. It may, of course, have been Dutch, which was still in widespread use in New York at this time. In Horsmanden's transcript, a letter in 'female Dutch' from Elezabet [sic] Romme to her husband Johannis Romme is introduced into the testimony. Some French is also introduced in connection with the practices of Jesuits supposed to be involved in the 'plot'. Latin and questions about the use of Latin are introduced into the testimony

Terms like *Negroes' language* are used about the Blacks, who have names like Quaco/Quack/Jack, Quash, Kuamino, Pompey, Cato, Caesar, Mars, 'Juan alias Wan' (p. 167), 'Pablo alias Powlus' (p. 167), Othello, Prince, London, Indian London, Ticklepitcher, Fortune and Braveboy. Some were called 'Spanish negroes' and one was known as 'Curacao [sic] Dick' and was thought to be able to 'talk Spanish'. Jack, the most extreme of them all, uttered the sentence quoted above and is reported to have had 'a dialect so perfectly negro and unintelligible, it was thought that it would be impossible to make anything of him without the help of an interpreter', although his language is represented as a variety of English. There were, in fact, not one but two interpreters available. 'Two young men, sons-in-law of Jack's master', had been around Jack, had learnt his variety of English, and in court 'made a shift to understand his language' and to interpret for him.

Slaves coming to virtually any part of the East Coast in the eighteenth century are very likely to have known some version of Pidgin English. From the evidence we have, what was spoken in West Africa and at sea was rather similar to what was being used in the American colonies, and not just in the South. Hancock (1986, ms. 15) quotes Bolingbroke (1799–1806: 71), who quotes an African sailor from the Gambia but located in Demarara for two years:

Kie, massa, you sabby talk me country

and

> Massa, me been see that white man in me country, in de town where me live, he been come dere one night for sleep, one blacksmith countreyman for me been with him, me been give him rice for he supper, and soon, soon in the morning he been go towards the Moor's country.

Aside from the questionable *towards*, the *-'s* on *Moor's*, and perhaps *that* where *se* or *say* would be expected, Bolingbroke's quotation has strikingly pidgin/creole features such as anterior marker *been + Verb*, complementizer *for*, invariant pronouns in subject form *me* and possessive *he*, possibly *one* for the 'article' *a*, and /d/ for /ð/. The expression *soon in the morning* is still widely used in the American Black community; *EDD* records similar (though not identical) phrases from 1850 – later than the maritime/African attestation.[3]

West African Pidgin English was obviously more maritime than terrestrial at this period. Fayer (ms., n.d.: 2), reporting on a study of the Pidgin English of a diary kept in Old Calabar from 1785 to 1786, asserts that 'One way to learn [Pidgin] was to serve on a British ship. Other [Africans] were placed on British ships when the ships were in the river at Old Calabar.'

In Philadelphia, a somewhat newer port than Boston or New York, trade in the 1740s and later in the eighteenth century was conducted 'with Lisbon, the Madeira Islands, France and its colonies, and, increasingly, Africa' (Rediker 1987: 69). Benjamin Franklin's 'Advice . . .', the 1787 text which contains a probable attestation of *buckra* closely matching Horsmanden's in New York, has other pidgin characteristics in the speech attributed to a Black.

> Boccarorra (meaning white man) make de black man workee, make de horse workee, make de ox workee, make ebery ting workee . . . .

Phonological characteristics like /b/ for /v/, /t/ for /θ/, and the enclitic vowel fulfilling the pidgin tendency towards a canonical CVCV syllable pattern (/r/, as a semi-vowel, would not count; or very likely the speech would have been 'r-less', with the *r* added only by orthographic convention) join the 'loss' of inflectional *-s* as pidgin characteristics. Many of the same characteristics are observable in attestations of the same time, a little earlier, and later. Horsmanden, an associate judge of the Supreme Court of the colony of New York, and Franklin are unlikely to have faked their representations, even though their skill in presentation is not that of a professional linguist. The probability that they would have invented independently a form of *buckra/bakra* seems very slight indeed.

Horsmanden's account of the 'Negro Plot' makes it clear that residents of New York City were strongly aware of, even frightened of, the slave population of that city in the early decades of the eighteenth century. Until 1754–85 there were 'field negroes' in poor living accommodation remote from the master's house, known as the 'Negro quarters' (Ottley and Weatherby 1967: 31–2). The somewhat limited observations by Horsmanden are also enough to reveal that there was a recognizable 'Negro' dialect – although not spoken equally by all Blacks in the city – with recognizable phonological, morphological and lexical characteristics.

The documentary evidence suggests that, prior to the 1741–87 dates represented by Horsmanden and Franklin, a special variety of English, at the very least strongly resembling Pidgin and Creole English in most particulars, was spoken by at least some of the African-derived residents of New York and Philadelphia as well as in West Africa and on ships at sea between Africa and America. Literary evidence suggests, although somewhat more weakly, that the same may have been true of Massachusetts, Connecticut and some of the other more northerly colonies. A dating of 1690 (the date of Tituba's testimony at the Salem witch trials) to *c.* 1790 for the use of Pidgin/Creole English by Black slaves in the northern colonies and states is by no means extreme. There seems to be no reason to assume any earlier date for the southern colonies and states. South Carolina's 'Negro Plot' of 1740 was only one year earlier – and only slightly more productive of unmotivated hangings – than that of New York City, and no records of Black speech from the more southerly state at that period seem to have been reported. If a Black variety of speech did exist in South Carolina before 1800, there is no reason to believe that it was very much different to that reported from New York City and from Philadelphia.

Georgia, founded in 1733, did not officially permit slavery until 2 January 1751, after the Trustee's prohibition against slavery was repealed, although surreptitious use of enslaved Blacks had taken place as early as 1734, the slaves coming from South Carolina (B. Wood 1984: 61). Imports from west Africa began in the mid-1760s, although the trade with South Carolina continued. The population of the colony itself grew from 3000 Whites and 600 Blacks in 1750 to 18,000 Whites and 15,000 Blacks in 1773 (B. Wood 1984: 89) The spread of English-speaking slave owners and slaves into Alabama, Mississippi and Louisiana was later still. Clark (1969: 295) writes of 'the phenomenal increase in Alabama from 21,780 slaves in 1820 to 127,360 in 1840'. The 'Southernization' of Black English, with the increasing concentration of reports of the variety from the South, traces only from this period.

Abolition in the North was preceded by a change in attitudes and treatment: 'Slavery [in New York] had become a domestic institution . . . . [After 1754] slaves lived under the same roof and ate the same food as the rest of the family'. Many were 'scrupulously' baptized and received religious instruction along with the children of the family (Ottley and Weatherby 1967: 31–2). Under these circumstances, more rapid change towards the mainstream dialect(s) of English would certainly be favoured. But earlier conditions had favoured the existence of a separate Black dialect.

In the polyglot environments of, especially, Philadelphia (Rediker 1987: 70) and New York, there would have seemed nothing strange about a special language variety for a group highly 'visible' in terms of colour and rather different in culture. Those who wrote about those port cities rather casually gave examples of the speech of those African-derived workers and slaves. In the eighteenth century, as has been evident at least since Greene (1942), the location of slaves was not exclusively or even dominantly southern. Thompson (1907) asserts that Maryland around 1690–1700 had 30,000 inhabitants, of whom about 3000 were 'negroes'. The greater part of these 'negroes' came from Africa; some had been born in Maryland; some came from Barbados, and a few from Virginia. In a letter of 20 August 1698, Governor Nicholson of Maryland wrote of '396 ['negroes' imported] in one ship directly from Guiny', along with fifty from 'Virginy' ( Thompson 1907), twenty from Pennsylvania and ultimately from Barbados, and 'a few others from other places'. Nicholson reported that *the major part* of the negros speak English, (emphasis added).' Since he does not distinguish the 'English' of Guinea Blacks from that of the ones from Pennsylvania, and since the 'Guinea' version of English spoken by slaves is attested elsewhere as highly non-standard, Nicholson must mean that a part of the slaves, even in Maryland, did not speak English at all. Since any non-African language for the non-English-speaking slaves would be extremely difficult to explain, it seems likely that some of them did speak African languages. On the other hand, modern English Creole varieties like Saramaccan (in some accounts) and Ndjuka might be likely to sound 'non-English' to an observer like Nicholson.

The early attestations of Pidgin English-like speech, far from being confined to, or even centred in, the South, are rather northerly in geographic distribution in the seventeenth and eighteenth centuries. South Carolinian attestations, as indicated, are rather late. Georgia's relatively late acceptance of slavery drew comments in 1754 that the slaves there were 'ignorant of ye English Language' and elsewhere that a missionary needed to learn the 'dialect peculiar to those Negroes who had been born in our colonies, or have long been there' in order to convert them (B. Wood 1984: 160). Transmission to those colonies did not lag long behind the existence of Pidgin English among the slaves of the more northern colonies, but there is no evidence whatsoever that the variety in the South preceded that in the North. There is also no certainty that it was identical, although it did have at least some of the same characteristics.

According to Walser (1955: 271), the 'dialect of the Southern Negro' on the stage at any rate, first appeared in Leacock's *The Fall of British Tyranny* in 1776. Cudjo, the escaped slave quoted, identifies himself and his companions as being from Virginia. Cudjo's contribution to the dialogue, however, has the characteristics of Pidgin English rather than of specifically 'Virginian' dialect:

> No, massa, me no crissen.
> 'No, master, I have not been christened.'

> Eas, massa, you terra me, me shoot him down dead.
> 'Yes, master, [if] you tell me, I [will] shoot him down dead.'

Walser (1955: 272) also cites the 'Negro dialect' attributed to a Boston house servant in an anonymous play, *Occurrence of the Times* (1789):

> . . . Twixt you and I massa he no courage . . . shentlemen you no de law.

Whether because of the more northerly locale, the slightly later date or his different status, the Boston house servant is represented as speaking something less like Pidgin English than Cudjo; the former not only does not have the invariant pronoun form *me* in subject function but even has an apparent hypercorrection, *I* for *me* as part of the compound object of a preposition. Both, however, have the negation pattern NP *no* Pred.

It will probably be noticed that any discussion of Gullah is so far missing from this account. There appear to be no attestations of that well-known (since Turner 1949) variety of the Georgia–South Carolina low country ('sea islands') from this period, and no reason to assume that it was an early development. In the past it has been assumed that the most extreme variety must be the earliest; and Gullah has been given general treatment as the earliest of Black American dialects for that reason. Recent work by Singler (forthcoming a), however, indicates that creolization, even the transmission of 'Africanisms', may occur relatively late in such a process.

Demographic dominance, if it is the only factor to be invoked, could easily mean that all residents of every future state except South Carolina 'spoke white'. Even by the 1730s, according to Meinig (1986: 124), 'The population of South Carolina was estimated to be . . . about 30,000, of whom 20,000 were Blacks.' Note, however, that demographic accounts often leave out the American Indians, many of whom spoke Pidgin English and many of whom interacted more easily with the African-derived slaves than they did with the immigrants from Europe. Wood (1974: 116) cites a contemporary account that, while Blacks outnumbered Whites in the colony of South Carolina in 1710, the Indians were still a plurality of the population. Towards the end of the eighteenth century, slave runaways to the Indian tribes became an important factor in the total demographic and cultural picture.

A purely demographic picture can give the wrong impression. In the colony of New York at about the same time, the Dutch had become a minority, yet the evidence from loanwords (Chapter 1) is that Dutch influence on English in the area was stronger than ever during that period. Like the reports of Dutch in New York and New Jersey, reports of a Black variety of English throughout most of the colonies counteract deductions based upon demography. The materials to be found in sources like the journal of a trip by Baltimore physician Alexander Hamilton through New England and the Middle Atlantic colonies in 1744 (Needler 1967) attest both Dutch and a 'Black' variety of English – and communication problems on the part of both. Hamilton records of the Dutch (Needler 1967: 215): 'now their language and customs begin pretty much to wear out and would very soon die were it not for a parcel of Dominies here, who . . . endevor [sic] to preserve the Dutch customs as much as possible'. At Albany, 'the devil a word but Dutch was bandied about between the sailors and him [a Dutch gentleman, Volckert

Douw], and in general there was such a medley of Dutch and English as would have tired a horse' (p. 214).

Of the Blacks, Hamilton records from his slave, Dromo, sentences like:

Dis de way to York?

You a damn black bitch

. . . trow away his stones, de horse be better ballast.

Based upon demographic considerations alone, it has been held (D'Eloia 1973) that creolization could happen only on large plantations, but these, except perhaps in South Carolina, were definitely in the minority even in the South. Elsewhere, large groups of slaves living together were quite rare. Myers (1965) shows that, in New York City in 1705, of 733 slaves, almost equally male and female, only two groups of thirteen and fourteen belonged to individual owners (Derick Ten Eyck twelve male and one female, Peter Pieret eleven male, one female, one male child and one female child); the others were distributed so that each owner had one to five slaves, often including a child or two. This is hardly the demography of plantations. On the other hand, a less than threefold increase in numbers – with no indication of any greater congregation in the ownership of one master – accompanied the kind of language situation indicated by Horsmanden (see above) less than forty years later.

A different picture is possible if factors other than numbers and density of communication – cultural, not just demographic – are taken into account.[4] Horsmanden's report shows rather clearly that inter-racial interaction patterns were limited; only two young white men, who had worked beside Jack, were well enough acquainted with him to be able to interpret for him. Yet Jack was at least a suspected leader among the slaves. The language repertory of the two groups was by no means identical. Communication networks and symbolic identification patterns, of the sort that linked the slaves in New York City in the early 1740s, continued to link especially field hands on farms – agricultural enterprises far too small to be called plantations at least in the modern sense – to others of their social status.

Knight (1824: 74) was one of the earliest of many to point out that 'The field slaves are the plebeians; the house slaves the patricians.' Harris (1990: 11) writes of Georgia slaves in the mid-nineteenth century: 'The Miller farm was by no means the boundary of the slaves' social world. They attended church on

Sunday . . ., they occasionally visited Sandersville, the nearest town; they had five days off at Christmas . . . and they worked frequently with other slaves in the neighborhood'. Shared features of many types indicate that a more widespread creolized variety than present-day Gullah was spoken quite early and continued well past Emancipation.

The most easily diagnostic feature of the creole stage of the Black English Vernacular has always been *been* + Verb (in a non-passive context), although it does not illustrate the more basic grammatical pattern of dominance of aspect over tense so well as the more intensively studied and bitterly debated *be* + Verb-ing. Poe's Jupiter in 'The Gold Bug', set on South Carolina's Sullivan's Island, says

Somebody bin lef' him head up de tree . . .

in a passage where a more recent action (i.e., necessarily *after* the head had been left) is also represented:

de crows done gobble ebery bit of det meat . . . .

This attestation (1839) may well be the first for Gullah. It was not, however, the first among African-derived speakers. See, for example, the Bolingbroke quotation above from possibly before 1800. Holm and Shilling (1982) describe it as 'found on both sides of the Atlantic Ocean, specifically in the English-based creoles of both the Caribbean and the West African coast'.

Although this preverbal anterior marker *been* can be traced to British English *been and V*, the syntactic function is strikingly similar to that of Haitian Creole *te* (probably from *était*) and Iberian Creole *taba* (from *estaba*), although there are some limitations to the distribution of the latter in present-day Iberian-based creoles. In Caribbean and West African creoles, including Cameroonian Pidgin/Creole, this anterior marker combines with the durative or continuative (*de, da, a, le*) to form a past continuous *bina*. Again comparisons are obvious to French Creole *tap* from *te* + *ap* and Iberian Creole *tabata* from *taba* + *ta*.

There have been those recently who have wished to say that this *been* + V is severely limited, with a view to confining it to Gullah and geographic distribution in the Georgia–South Carolina Low Country. Schneider (1983: 58) has referred to this structure as the result of 'neo-Creolization' and asserts that it 'was most likely restricted to a few big plantations in the antebellum South', an explanation for its 'limited spreading'.

Modern distributional evidence, as well as historical documentation, is strongly against that point of view. A seventy-two-year-
old Black lady in Natchitoches, Louisiana, said to me in one
short conversation on 20 December 1986:

He oughta been put some money into it . . .

She shoulda been told them people to go away.

This lady has no history of residence in or near South Carolina,
she and her parents having spent their lifetimes in north-west
Louisiana. She does not know where her grandparents, who were
in 'slavery time', were born, but she does know that they lived in
the same parish at least after she was born. And a Black athlete
at Northwestern State University, Natchitoches, notably Black in
culture and maladjusted to the (White) university cultural
pattern, in desperation trying to fulfil an assignment on 'How I
Study for my English Final', wrote that he relied upon

. . . what I been know about English.

The septuagenarian lady referred to above frequently uses *I been
know* or *you been know* in an emphatic context.

  The clause quoted above was the only occurrence of this
structure in thousands of essays written by Black students at the
same school. On the other hand, in at least twice as many total
essays written by all students at the same college, the word *ain't*
did not occur even once. I am quite sure, however, that *ain't* is
part of the language of many of the students. Language historians
who rely upon the WPA (Work Progress Administration) ex-
slave narratives for their information, including geographic
distribution and chronology, on Black English are simply falling
victim to the fact that *been* + Verb is very seldom used with
White outsiders – almost never unless the Black speaker has a
high degree of confidence in his interlocutor.[5]

'Decreolization' – change in the direction of more mainstream
English, varieties more easily identifiable as being spoken by
Whites – began well before Emancipation. It took place at
different rates among different populations, and complete
creolization may never have taken place in some areas where
identifiable Black usages can still be traced historically. At least
there is evidence of the development of non-creole grammatical
forms more nearly resembling on the surface the usage of
mainstream Whites but not identical with that usage. A favourite
example, developed in principle by Stewart (1967, 1968), is:

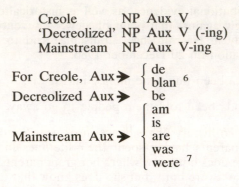

Creole          NP  Aux  V
'Decreolized'   NP  Aux  V (-ing)
Mainstream      NP  Aux  V-ing

For Creole, Aux ➤  { de
                    { blan  6

Decreolized Aux ➤  be

Mainstream Aux ➤   { am
                   { is
                   { are
                   { was
                   { were  7

Except for Gullah, the *de* form, one of the salient characteristics of the African-influenced Atlantic English creoles, either disappeared very early in the North American colonies or was never widely used.

The reason for the disappearance alternative does not seem especially esoteric nor obscure. The form *de* is highly 'visible' as not belonging to ordinary English and would be quite 'naturally' eliminated by a speaker of a creole-like variety moving towards more nearly standard usage. The possibility remains that the form was very widespread in early Black English (that is, until about 1820) and then disappeared except for Gullah (including that form of Gullah which was soon transmitted to Bracketville, Texas). On the other hand, lack of early attestation – even in Sea Island Gullah – argues against any dogmatic assertion that such was the case.

Pre-verbal auxiliaries like *de* and *be* can never be treated completely in isolation. The Atlantic (African and Afro-American) varieties which have either generally have a 'zero copula', so that there is a contrast between

NP 0  Complement

and

NP be Complement.

(Complement, for these purposes, is usually either a verb or an adjective. In special circumstances, a noun complement may occur.) Both sequences appear in the colonies in the eighteenth century. The quotes from Hamilton's *Itinerarium* of 1744 (above) illustrate the point.

At this stage, it is intended only to remind the reader of the existence of both. The precise function of *be*, much less its origin, is not yet under examination. The two forms continue to be attested through the eighteenth century into the nineteenth, as in J.W. Page's *Uncle Robin* of 1853:

Juner [Juno] be me conger . . .

and into the twentieth (Stewart 1967, 1968).

The relationship between these forms and *de* is not immediately self-evident. David Brainerd's materials (1745) apparently have both *be* and zero copula, but there seems to be no attestation of *de* either among the Indians Brainerd quoted or among the slaves outside the Low Country. In fact, Gullah attestations of the form come rather late. Eighteenth-century drama contains approximations of the form in speech attributed to West Indians (Walser 1955), and the indications are that the American audiences understood the speeches in general, but of course there is no proof that they had heard all the forms used in their own country. The presence and fairly widespread awareness of West Indians, among whom there is little argument about the existence of *de* + Verb forms, in the early East Coast states is well documented, as is the importance of contacts between those states and the West Indies. Among other things, perhaps the first complete oratorio presented in the United States, in New York in 1788, was *Jonah* by Jamaican resident Samuel Felsted.

Fearon (1818: 153) presents a testimony by a Jamaican in a Philadelphia court:

Not guilty, gentimman. I was going long street groggy, man groggy too . . . me go long so bad groggy, lay down, put saw by side, man steal saw from me, me not steal saw from no man.

The Jamaican is styled a 'man of colour' and referred to as 'yellow boy'. His reported speech shows the West Indian, including Jamaican, usage (the first occurrence only) of *man* as a generalized form of address, some apparent code-switching or different stylistic levels (*me*/*I* as subject), and something apparently like mesolectal status of his English. Fearon also attests (1818: 168) racial segregation in the churches in Philadelphia and prejudice against 'a man, whose body is (in American estimation) *cursed* with even a twentieth portion of the blood of his African ancestry'. Yet Fearon's Jamaican does not use *de*.

Given Singler's (forthcoming a) concept of the possible lateness of African substratal influence, it seems quite possible that *de* was established rather late. If we go by documentary evidence alone, there appears to be no reason to believe that it was present even in Gullah before 1856, when William Gilmore Simms recorded it in *Eutaw* (cited in Brasch 1981: 40):

I day look for young maussa.

Perhaps the first recording of the form by an academic was that of William Francis Allen, who under the pseudonym Marcel published in the December 1865 issue of *The Nation*: 'Present time is made definite by the auxiliary *do* or *da*, as in the refrains "Bell da ring," "Jericho da worry me" ' (Jackson 1967: 77). The same article also reports (p. 80):

'Jesus da comin'.

Although earlier direct attestation is lacking, strong circumstantial evidence exists in the Bracketville, Texas, Gullah-like dialect (Hancock 1980), carried there in Seminole removal in 1837. Although considered Seminoles by Andrew Jackson and his agents in 'Indian removal', these were largely Black escaped slaves and their descendants. Many of the strikingly creole Gullah features, like anterior marker *been* –

. . . a boy that been left

and aspect marker *de*

You de mean the old Caesar

(Hancock 1980: 316) – existed in Bracketville 'Seminole' when Hancock did his fieldwork there in the 1970s. It would be difficult to explain how these (and numerous other) features were transmitted to Texas in the 1830s if they came to the South Carolina–Georgia–Florida variety which was their source only in the 1850s. Recognizably BEV grammatical and phonological features characterize the speech of these 'Seminoles' with casual outsiders.

Nevertheless, there is no reason to think that Gullah existed in the colonial period. The particular process that produced Gullah, of the Sea Islands or of Bracketville, remains historically unclear. Statements (e.g. Mufwene and Gilman 1989: 122) about the presence of 'various rural dialects' in the formative background are subject to ambiguous interpretation. If they mean 'rural British dialects', there is good chronological reason to doubt their accuracy, although the statement referred to here is presented as a truism.

There are other implications. Sentimentally, it is appealing to think of the Africans as being the innovators in the language situation. Simplistically, it is attractive to think of Gullah as having been more widespread than the Low Country. On the other hand, a number of the forms involved are attested just as early or earlier for other populations – such as the American Indians. This might mean that the maritime pidgin transmitted to Indians on the East Coast, and becoming more widespread among them as tribal life was disrupted and communication with previously distant groups (including the Europeans) became an important factor, was actually transmitted from the Indians to the slaves. It is well known that slaves (sometimes technically 'indentured servants') imported from Africa and American Indians formed closer contacts, especially in the seventeenth and eighteenth centuries, than either did with the European immigrants (Greene 1942).[8] For the second point, while it is still likely that Gullah once had wider distribution than the Low Country, that specific variety may well not have spread far beyond the Georgia–South Carolina plantations. This would mean that two rather distinct Black varieties, the relatively more widespread (than today) Gullah and a second lacking *de* or *blan*, existed at least as early as the 1880s, and probably long before. Some of the features of Gullah, including the *de V* structure, need not have been produced until relatively late in the history of the Black variety.

Statements strongly motivated by a desire for Black unity, as in Pharr (1969), look to a pre-Civil War unity and a later difference based only upon the independence of the Gullah ('they were never reconstructed' – 1969: 199). At the very least, the postulated two varieties would have been strikingly similar, sharing many features including some vocabulary (see material on *buckra/bakra* above). The verbal system, involving especially dominance of aspect over tense, and considerations of a wider systemic nature are the strongest arguments against separating the two geographic varieties in any basic sense. The verbal aspect system proves perhaps the major obstacle to such a tempting hypothesis.[9] At any rate, one such variety, sharing many characteristics with AIPE and known even on southern farms only to those whites closely associated with the Black community, would have been widely used in the Black community even in the northern colonies before the end of the eighteenth century.

The term *creole* seems to provide an unnecessary obstacle here. If Gullah as known recently in the Low Country is a creole, and different varieties known early even in the New England area and later in the Mississippi Basin are different, then perhaps a term like *creoloid* should be applied to them. At any rate, the terminology is the least important part of the history. Only social conditions involved in the use of the variety/varieties (first language use by children of an early generation, virtual disappearance of African languages) preclude the description as a pidgin, or an 'extended pidgin'.

Grammatically, it should be noted carefully that creole/creoloid and 'decreolized' forms like *be* V(-ing) and *de* V translate mainstream English forms in the past as well as in the present ('progressive') tense. Terminology such as 'tenseless' is, thus, often used. This particular function of *be* V, but without -*ing*, is apparently the stage represented in the speech of Cuff in Hugh Henry Breckenridge's *Modern Chivalry* (1792):

> I be cash [catch] crabs . . .

a sentence which sets the background for a past action which Cuff is reporting. In this sentence, *be* must be [+continuative] or [−completive] and [+past] or at least [−present]. It designates an ongoing action in the context of which a past action occurred. According to Holm (1989, II, 490), Bahamian use of *be* with 'the simple form of the verb'

> People be row right up

alternates with *be V-ing* forms like

> They just be playing

'to indicate habitual action, even in the past'.

Because of the focus of most serious studies on 'deep' or 'radical' creoles, information about such sequences in many of the creole-related varieties of the New World often has to come from less trustworthy popular sources. But there are indications that *be* preceding 'the simple form of the verb' is characteristic, today, of the mesolect of some Creole English varieties. The Kingston (Jamaica) *Daily Gleaner* of the 1960–2 period ran cartoons with captions in a kind of urban, mesolectal Jamaican Creole; one in my collection reads:

> 'So dem arrest a ship.'
> 'What big hand-cuffs dem mus' be use!'

And on the BBC series *The Story of English*, a Barbadian truck driver says

> I be see the level of the truck coming . . .

even though McCrum, Cran and MacNeil (1986) did not choose to write down the text in the accompanying book. The Nigerian

Pidgin English that Chinua Achebe writes in *A Man of the People* (1966: 62) has:

I be think say . . . .

Even in the literary evidence, forms like *be V* as distinct from *be V-ing* are rare, even though the first represents a close parallel to *de V* and often Blacks in, for example, Charleston, South Carolina, tend to replace *de V* with *be V-ing*, as in the comment by two small boys who observed the filming of *The Story of English* with camera equipment on a balcony:

Dey be filmin' – *Romeo an' Juliet.*

For various reasons, *be V-ing* seems to have replaced *be V* within a fairly short period of time, possibly between 1792 and 1830.[10]

The paucity of evidence makes it necessary to treat the auxiliaries of this type preposed to adjectives in the same manner as if they preceded verbs. There are some problems in paralleling such structures to any currently extant 'deep' creole, but in principle the practice is not too far-fetched. Stewart (1980: 231) cites, from Kemble's *Journal of Residence on a Georgia Plantation in 1838–9* (Kemble 1862: 52), the *be + Adj* form:

Missus only give we, we be so clean forever.

Since material cited by Stewart from the same source (p. 118) also includes zero copula with adjective complement –

She just sick a little while

– a contrast which is part of the twentieth-century Black English Vernacular system seems to be attested among the very earliest materials which indicate a special Black variety in the Low Country, either Gullah or a predecessor in some sense of Gullah. Tabitha Tenney's 1829 sentence (cited from *DARE* I) –

Soon he want to know how old you be first

– is from Philadelphia; earlier than the Kemble attestations, it also tends better to fit the geographic pattern (origin or adoption into Black English to the north of South Carolina). The systemic function of the word, which must remain the most important consideration, is not as clear as the form cited by Stewart.

Within such a context, the Kemble citation is later than Kirkham's (1829)

I be goin'.

Kirkham's ethnically non-identified materials do not, however, provide for the contrast with zero copula; and, as has constantly been pointed out, it is the system involved, not just the 'innovation' of one sequence, which provides the evidence for a separate variety which can be called Black English (Vernacular). Kirkham's (1829: 207)

You bain't from the Jerseys, be you?

is as unlike an equivalent syntactic sequence from Black English, at any stage of its development, as it would be possible to contrive without simply randomizing the order.

The similar occurrence in Irish English is often cited in this connection. It is noteworthy, however, that Kirkham does not place *I be goin'* among the Irish dialect features he cites. Although there appears to be little or no evidence as to the chronological development of the structure, Irish English tends to favour strongly *NP do/does be V-ing* which is rare in Black English. Negation, in the regular Black English basilect pattern –

They don't be jokin'

– is the Black English pattern which today most closely represents the Irish usage and the surface result of the ordinary English *do*-support rule. The use of 'invariant' *be* (which, as in Black English, 'varies' with *be's*) is also characteristic of Newfoundland folk speech (Paddock 1966 and discussion, Chapter 2), and there are many other possible sources for non-infinitival, non-subjunctive *be* in auxiliary function (see discussion in Dillard 1985: 117). Replacement of *de* may have been going on, as indicated by the *Modern Chivalry* occurrence, around 1792. Another possibility is that an underlying aspect-dominant system, lacking the unattested *de*, was realized by an 'invariant' *be* which was taken over from some source like the New England usage cited by Kirkham. Note, however, that sources in the forms cited by Kirkham or Paddock seem to require a non-Southern development of the *be-ing* pattern. Kirkham, however (1829: 107), cites not only the negative *bain't* but the question form *Be you . . .?* which would have had to change to *Do you be . . .?* by some as yet unexplained process in order to produce the syntax of the Black English basilect.

Some evidence is provided in the forms of Liberian Settler English. Singler (1989) concludes that the creole-like features of that variety were brought with them from the United States rather than developing or being acquired in Liberia. Singler also asserts (forthcoming b: 33) that American ex-slave emigrants to

Liberia, 'arriving from more northerly states (Virginia and above) tended to dominate Settler society'. Liberian Settler English today contains forms like

(2) NP be V-ing

but apparently not like

(1) NP be V

Singler (1989: 49) reports

When my pa be preaching . . .

and specifies that 'pa' in question has been dead for years. (For Black American English Vernacular *be* in non-present context, see *DARE be* B3f; Loflin, Sobin and Dillard 1969.) The presence in Liberian Settler English of (2) but not (1) would seem to indicate that by about 1820, an effective date for the transmission of American Black English through 'recolonization' (see Singler 1989), the *-ing* affix had become obligatory in the American form. The period of development from *be V* to *be V-ing* can thus be fairly well located in the period 1792–1820, largely in the Black English of the Eastern Seaboard, excluding at least the Mississippi Basin.

One of the earliest first-hand observers who could not be accused of racism or of pro-slavery sentiments would be Frederick Douglass, who gives an interesting report on the 'imperfect' state of English on Colonel Lloyd's plantation in Maryland in the 1820s (Douglass 1855: 76–7). Douglass called the dialect 'a mixture of Guinea [then used in the general meaning 'African'] and everything else you please'. At the time, there were slaves from the coast of Africa who 'never used the 's' in indication of the possessive case . . . *Oo you dem long to* means, "Whom do you belong to?" *Oo dem got any peachy?* means, "Have you got any peaches?"' Even though born on the plantation, Douglass asserts he 'could scarcely understand them . . . so broken was their speech'.

For the 'imperfect' English of other slaves, Douglass presented little except the verb *tote* (1855: 46) – describing the way his grandmother brought him, a child of about seven, to the master's house – the clause *better day comin'* (1855: 76), and the speech of Sandy, the root man (1855: 284–5):

. . . and furder, honey, watch de Friday night dream; dare is sumpon in it, shose [sic] you born; dare is, indeed, honey.

Reference to the 'jargon' of the 'rude, and apparently incoherent songs' (pp. 98–9) of the slaves may refer to disguise vocabulary, although of course other interpretations are possible.

The account of Douglass indicates that specifically Black features, although most concentrated among the Africans, were part of the 'imperfect' speech of the plantation. His *you dem* and *oo dem* seem to attest the common Atlantic use of the third person plural pronoun as noun pluralizer, not the frequently used Africanism *una* or *wuna*. The *-y* on *peachy* may represent the enclitic vowel of the pidgin canonical syllable, also reported (imperfectly) by Benjamin Franklin. Above all, Douglass's report indicates diversity (in currently fashionable terms 'variability') on Colonel Lloyd's plantation – and quite possibly on many others. An incident of Douglass's bondage depends upon his lack of understanding of the terms *in ox* and *off ox*; after becoming free, he met with some scepticism because he did not talk like a slave.

Although some pidgin-like features and some African vocabulary and phonology are reported in the northern colonies earlier than in the southern, a creole or an extended pidgin either did not develop there or changed earlier in the direction of more ordinary English in states such as New York and Massachusetts. The elimination of such features was well advanced – though certainly not complete – in the early nineteenth century. The New York *Evening Post* for 1 September 1802 published a poem satirizing Thomas Jefferson and purported to be by 'Quashee' ('Sunday', as a day name) which used pidgin/creole negation patterns (*Quashee no hab de one no hab de oder*), the resumptive pronoun (*Our man Jefferson he*), lack of *-s* for third person singular (*he say*), and phonological features like *b* for /v/ and *d* /for /ð/. In 1845 Alexander Mackay in *The Western World* recorded a speech from a competitive driver:

> Cheap! Neber mind him, sa; he's only a nigga from Baltimore, just come to Philadelphy . . . I'se born here, sa
> . . .

The change proceeded with intermediate speed on the smaller farms of the Eastern Seaboard South, especially slowly among the field hands; and slowest of all on the large plantations in the Sea Islands/Low Country. Note, however, that length of retention does not necessarily correlate with priority in development. According to Stewart, Garaty and Mufwene (personal comunications), there were greatly decreolized but still recognizably Gullah forms in the Low Country in the late 1980s.

The Liberian evidence, and general lack of early attestation, argues for a somewhat different variety in the non-Eastern Seaboard South, still found primarily among field hands rather than house servants, still having pidgin morphosyntactic and African lexical features, and still known to but not used proficiently by some Whites. Singler (forthcoming b) cites Sinoe in Liberia, where a distinctive form of Settler English is traced to the 'Mississippi plantation' origins of the Sinoe group. Although Singler finds that Georgia and South Carolina emigrants became dominant in the 1865–72 period, he does not indicate that any significant portion of that group came from the Low Country.

Virginia (38 per cent), North Carolina (18 per cent), and Maryland (11 per cent) accounted, according to Singler's figures, for the dominant group of liberated slave emigrants to Liberia in the pre-Civil War period. These emigrants appear to have spoken a partly decreolized English. It is difficult, however, to reconcile such a conclusion with the notion that creolized English existed only in the Low Country – or in the Deep South, for that matter. Poplach and Sankoff (1987) have argued that, since the English now spoken by the Samaná community in the Dominican Republic shows no more creole features than American Black English (Black English Vernacular) in the United States in general, the Black community in the United States at the time of the migration to Hispaniola – again, with the exception of those in the Low Country – did not have creolized speech and that the close match between the English of the residents of Samaná and that of Philadelphia (and other inner city populations in the United States) indicates that little change (decreolization or other) has taken place in the English of Black America between 1820 and the 1980s. Poplach and Sankoff cite, however, reports that the emigrants to Samaná came primarily from Virginia and Maryland, which would be from a relatively decreolized (or, alternatively, never completely creolized) population. The dialect transmitted to Samaná, although subject to subsequent changes, appears to have been approximately what Frederick Douglass reported from Colonel Lloyd's plantation in Maryland – excluding, quite naturally, those from the 'Guinea coast'.

There appears, therefore, to be a less major conflict between the Liberian evidence and that from Samaná than would otherwise be concluded, even though dominant elements came to both at about the same time and from approximately the same area. The language contacts of the two groups have been strikingly different. In addition to the African languages in use in Liberia, the Settlers certainly came in contact with some form of the Pidgin English spoken along the west African coast since well before the repatriation period. Among the Samaná group there were very different contacts, including some from the continental United States and from England. Some members, according to self report (Hoetink 1974: 7), were more proficient at Spanish than English. The Methodist Church, an important influence in the cultural life of the 'Americans' in the Dominican Republic, procured a preacher in the person of the Reverend William Tindell from the Wesleyan Methodist Church of England in 1834. The church kept a school directed in the 1870s by George Lewis Judd, son of a White American father. Trade was carried on with the surrounding islands, including St Thomas (Hoetink 1974: 10).

Even in places like the Mississsippi Basin, pidgin/creole features continued to be available for export to Liberia. As indicated elsewhere, early attestations of the Black English Vernacular have dealt little with the Mississippi Basin area. However, slaves were brought there very early – before English-speaking settlers, as a matter of fact. The area became known for the extremity of its treatment of Blacks. Williams (1883, II, 3) asserts that 'Alabama and Mississippi became the most cruel slave states in the United States.' Ingraham (1835: 236) reports the anticipated terrors of a slave self-reported to be from 'Ol' Wirginy' upon coming to the lower Mississippi area. Williams also asserts that the slave population of the Mississippi Territory grew from 3489 in 1800 to 32,814 in 1820, to 65,659 in 1830 and to 195,211 in 1840. Many of the Mississippi slaves came from Virginia. Around 1835 Joseph Holt Ingraham, a writer born in Portland, Maine, in 1790 but moving to the South at the age of twenty-one, in *The Southwest by a Yankee*, reported that 'probably two-thirds of the first slaves came into this state [Mississippi] from Virginia'. Kentucky, he said, had provided 'a small number, which is probably increasing', and Missouri was to provide $200,000 worth of slaves (at contemporary prices, around 250 slaves) 'this season for the Natchez market' (Ingraham 1835, II, 237). He reported (p. 234) 'Thus Virginia has become the field for the purchaser and the phrase "he is gone to Virginia to buy negroes" . . . as often applied to a temporarily absent planter, as "he is gone to Boston to buy goods," to a New England country merchant.' He also (p. 195) quotes a slave named George as saying:

Yes, master, me full blood Wirginny

and

. . . you never be sorry you buy George.

This is represented as a Virginia-derived slave, with characteristics like the enclitic vowel (*wishy* as a verb) but no *be + V-ing*. While there is a kind of zero copula–*be* contrast, the use of *be* is subject to the oft-cited phonological contraction and deletion (*will*, '*ll* and zero in this case) and the match with the Black English Vernacular, where *be V-ing* can refer to past time as well as to present or (with 'deletion') to future, is not clear. At any rate, the existence of this most characteristic BEV contrast pattern is suggested but not conclusively demonstrated. Ingraham (1835, II, *passim*) reports abundant examples from Mississippi of Black dialect features like zero copula, *done bring*, negation with *no* (*what enter into de mouth no defile de man; niger no keep de debil down he throat*), invariant pronouns (*me* as subject, *he family*), and indication of phonological features like written *d* for /ð/.

Where *be V-ing* is concerned, *DARE* I's evidence includes nothing closer to the Mississippi Basin than Georgia, and that from Joel Chandler Harris in 1887:

> He holler dat out eve'day, en den, wile he be talkin', he'd stop en look roun'.

The form *be talkin'*, in sequential terms like that of Cuff's *be cash* except that the latter is paratactic whereas Harris's form has the subordinator *wile*, fits the pattern of durative but atemporal characteristics observed elsewhere (Loflin 1967, 1969). Harrison's (1884) worse than amateurish attempt at presentation of 'Negro English' contains no example of the structure, although he does claim to have used the writings of Harris as one of his sources. Arthur Huff Fauset's excellent Black folklore collection from Alabama, Louisiana and Mississippi, 'with a few from Tennessee' (Fauset 1925: 214), has only one unambiguous case:

> One be playin' the fiddle, one callin' the figures.

The WPA ex-slave narratives, collected in the 1930s from living ex-slaves who must have been extremely young at the time of Emancipation, show some use of the form. The circumstances of collection of these narratives were far from the standards of good fieldwork, and the results are part of – not a corrective to – the literary tradition of Black English.

Certain features are recorded as common to Black (field hand) speakers in the South. Schele de Vere (1872: 607) made no distinction of states or other features of locale when he reported that *gwine* instead of *going* was 'the uniform pronunciation of the negroes in the South'. The graphic *gw-* may well mark implosive articulation, characteristic of numerous West African languages although varying from one to another in precise phonological function.

Recent researchers, who base their conclusions almost entirely upon current fieldwork and draw historical conclusions only from differences in age groups (Bailey and Maynor 1985, 1987; NWAVE 1987), have found extensive evidence of 'invariant' *be* + *V-ing* in eastern Texas, Louisiana, Mississippi and Alabama. It is used much more frequently by Blacks than by Whites, but not exclusively by either group. Evidence from these groups seems to be lacking as to whether the 'atemporal' function is characteristic of either group. The form may not have been in these states early on. Other features now associated with the Black English Vernacular, on the other hand, almost certainly were. Unification of Black groups after Emancipation, but especially in the late nineteenth century, the World War I migration and the World War II migration to the inner cities of the North and elsewhere may actually have seen a spreading of the form beyond its mid-nineteenth-century limits.

Folk history seems to have some such chronology. A Black woman in Louisiana, completely untrained in linguistics but broad-minded about Black English and its differences from ordinary English, once explained it to me in these terms: The 'subjunctive' (her school-grammar-based term for the form) *be* had not been heard in her area (western Louisiana, eastern Texas, and perhaps southern Arkansas) before World War II. She acknowledged that it had 'spread rapidly' and then become relatively general by the time of the conversation (approximately 1976).

Folk dialect geography seems also to accord fairly well with this view. In Washington, DC in 1967, a group of young Black males trying to make a pick-up from an automobile met rejection with counter-rejection:

> We don't want no Bamas.

*DARE* I's evidence on *Bama*, although not directly confirming this statement, does not contradict it. The meaning 'rustic or countrified person, especially one from the South' fits fairly well, but the first attestation, from 1966, is *Bama chucker* ('A Southern white rustic'). The sense 'an "unhip" person' from South Dakota in 1970 better fits the inner-city pattern.

This is not to say that there is any special folk wisdom involved here. The young men referred to above did not have opportunity

– even if they were adequately skilled – to determine whether the girls who rejected their advances were from the Mississippi Basin, or even from the South. There may well, however, be some validity to the Black folk tradition of differences – among which speech differences would be part – in behaviour patterns ('hipness'). Compare the phrase *square from Delaware*, reportedly from the refrain 'I'm just a square from Delaware, / Come to town for to see the fair.'

Vocabulary differences seem to exist between the two major geographical divisions of the Black English Vernacular. *Calinda*, familiar in the French *danser Calinda*, has been in Louisiana English since 1763 (DA) but has hardly been known outside except to folklorists. Dickinson (1976: 2) reports: 'In Louisiana, Arkansas, and Mississippi, these charms ['hands'] also are known as gris-gris and juju, West African terms for fetiches.' Various conjure terms are certainly known in the South Carolina, including Gullah, community; *hand* seems to be universal. Although the popular imagination associates *mojo*, often used in compound with *hand* and occurring in many disguise forms like *Joe Moore*, with Louisiana and the immediately adjoining area, Turner (1949) found *moco* ('witchcraft, magic') in the Low Country and suggested an African language origin. Desire to characterize the 'South Carolina, Georgia Low Country', rather than to deal with widespread terms of African origin like *mojo/moco* and *goobers* ('peanuts'), apparently motivated McDavid's (1954/6: 524) list: *bloody-noun, cooter, pinders* ('peanuts'), *yard-ax, pinto* ('coffin') and *buckra*. The legends of Black music hold it that *jazz*, both the term and the music it designates, originated in New Orleans. Some of the originally Black collocations (Dillard 1977: 60–83) may have spread in the same direction, at the same time, and by the same process. Such a possibility does not necessarily contradict the belief of many musicologists and folklorists that the blues which underlies the musical style itself was used wherever there were field hand slaves.

The famous migration up the Mississippi to Chicago of, especially, New Orleanian jazz musicians (King Oliver, Louis Armstrong, Jelly Roll Morton and many others) might be said to have been responsible also for the spread of terms like *jelly roll* and the other food-for-sex terminology (Dillard 1977: 25–8) famous in blues and jazz lyrics but so unknown in the 1920s that Black singers were able to escape a censorship then very narrow on sexual matters. Singers on 'race records', such as Bessie Smith's 'Empty Bed Blues', were able to indulge in a sexual explicitness not again found in American popular music until perhaps the 1970s.

The picture of the Virginia–North Carolina slave presented by writers like Thomas Nelson Page, especially through his character Edinburg of *In Ole Virginia* (1887), is the subservient, not unintelligent but perhaps rather artless person. This is the Uncle Tom stereotype that Harriet Beecher Stowe established or utilized in *Uncle Tom's Cabin*. Looking back at the earliest blues records, on the other hand, we see a striking picture of Black singers very *artfully* taking advantage of 'the man' – in this case the censor – with an elaborate, detailed and graphic sexual vocabulary which would not have been permitted on records of the time if the terminology had been understood. This is the *hipster* – a term Dalby (1972) convincingly linked to Wolof *hipicat* and to other west African languages, *cat* (based on the second element of the term quoted above or on something similar in West African languages) having achieved very wide currency in American English, especially among musicians. This artful person is scornful of the phony *hep* (as against the genuine *hip)* and of the *alligator* ('a person who pretends to jazz knowledge'). *DARE* I traces the last to 1937, but Louis Armstrong makes it clear that the term was common on the riverboats on which he played two decades earlier. It likened the pseudo-cognoscenti of jazz to the alligators which followed the ships to feed on the garbage; that is, it depicted a person who would 'swallow anything'.

*DARE* I refers to the 'non-regional catch phrase' *see you later, alligator* as deriving from this usage. It is also the probable source of *Greetings, gate* [i.e., 'gator] temporarily popular with radio comedians of the early 1940s. Many other popular 'slang' terms have had origin or transmission through the Black musical and entertainment community. So, almost certainly, did the *hippie* subculture, modelled upon the ghetto *hipster* and imitating the (superficial, some would say) features of Black culture. Much of Black terminology worked its way into the jargon of popular music and then into the terms by which teenagers (usually White) marked themselves as going through their peculiar rites of passage. Such vocabulary is, stereotypically, evanescent, but it lasts longer than popular commentators want to think. A Washington, DC newspaper once called to ask me whether *jonin'*, one of the names for the widespread Black verbal insult contest known elsewhere as *sounding* or *the dozens*, were actually based on the name of television talk show hostess Joan Rivers! *Rap*, fairly recent as such things go in musical terminology, has also been around a long time, although only recently has it been applied to music rather than to another aspect of Black verbal style (Kochman 1972).

It is very likely that the 'hip' Black existed, although more covertly, even on the plantation. Littlefield (1981: 134) writes of a 'Boston, of John's Island . . . born in Guinea but spoke excellent English, Spanish, and Portuguese . . . [and] was a cunning, artful fellow'. Among other evidence of his artfulness, he convinced two others, who could not even speak English, to join in his escape.

The division into 'artful' slave and 'Uncle Tom' may well be as basic and as important as the geographic division. Careful examination of the records will probably show that both personality types existed in both areas. The evidence for farm creole comes, unfortunately, from White observers from whom such traits were characteristically concealed. Modern Blacks, understandably, prefer to think of 'Black English' in terms of the 'hip' vocabulary rather than in terms of *be V-ing, been V, de* V, 0 for *-s* as a verb ending, possession by juxtaposition (*he book*), non-redundant or reduced-redundancy pluralization (*them three boy all got bicycles*) and non-redundant tense marking (*He was scared, and he holdin' his mother's hand*). The public school system, which has not achieved the level of linguistic sophistication needed to recognize the necessity of some redundancy in all language – its rhetoric textbooks inveighing against *audible to the ear* and *visible to the eye* – is far from being able to transmit to Black students the notion that 'non-redundancy' in their own language is not so different from that desired result. Certainly the further principle that redundancies in different varieties are ultimately equal is beyond any kind of widespread language policy, public or private, that we can call upon.

Ethnic awareness has little to do with one of the features of Black pronunciation often found in their speech in areas where Whites are different. This is the use of /ant/ for 'mother's sister', as well as /antiy/ (Pippin, Jones and Dillard forthcoming). The latter might ordinarily be thought of as the intimate form, but Black speakers can invest it with what seems like an especially high degree of respect. *DARE* I refers to the non-/ænt/ articulation as 'sometimes considered affected' by Americans, but it does not seem to be so among Black speakers in the South. Such speakers do not follow the pattern of using /a/ in *pass, path, dance*, etc. A much wider use of /a/ for American English /æ/ is observed in the West Indies and in West Africa, in both of which it is often rationalized as 'British', even in a context of heavily

African phonology. The Louisiana speakers with whom I am most familiar do not so rationalize it; they simply consider /ant/ to be 'correct'.[11] Holm (1989, I, 113) finds /a/ but not /æ/ in possibly substratum west African languages, but the lack of Black substitution of /a/ in other words makes such an origin a far-fetched guess. The same should be said, however, about any theory of anglicization.

By the apparent period of general regionalization of American English (see Chapter 7), Black English had been very nearly – although not without some exceptions, noted already – become limited to the South. In spite of the selling of slaves, with oft-lamented consequences such as the separating of families, the slaves were tied to the land, even those on farms which could not be called plantations. With the exception of the necessarily smaller group of land and slave owners, they constituted for a critical period the most geographically stable element in the South. In fact, with the possible exception of some Appalachian Whites, they constituted the nearest approximation to a settled peasantry which has developed in America. Even though they were numerous in that section, they played a larger part in the linguistic and cultural history of the area than their numbers considered alone would lead one to expect.

## Notes

1 *DARE* I and DBE cite as source Efik *mbakára* ('he who surrounds or governs'). Turner (1949) also lists Ibibo.
2 See also Schneider 1989: 312. The speakers whom Dorrill and Schneider consider are from Maryland, North Carolina and Virginia – roughly the same locale as that of Cuff in Breckenridge's *Modern Chivalry*.
3 On 'Tom Moore's Farm', Texas Folklore Society 77–LA–12–13a, Side Two, Band Four, both Sam 'Lightnin' Hopkins and an anonymous singer, who refuses to have his name published for fear of the 'big boss', sing

> Soon in the morning you'll get [variant *he'll give you*] ham and [variant *scrambled*] eggs . . . .

Black graduate students in English linguistics classes in north-western Louisiana cheerfully volunteered the information that they or some of their elderly relatives used the phrase. *EDD* lists s[outh] Lan[cashire] *soon on in th' morning* and n[orth] Y[or]ks[hire] . . . *seaner on than 6 o'clock*, both later than the Bolingbroke attestation.
4 Compare Alleyne (1989: 307): 'Dominance here is not merely a factor of numbers, but of cultural salience and ethnic aggressiveness . . .'

5 Another factor in the distribution of this preverbal *been* is that it virtually never occurs in blues lyrics – at least in those recorded and widely distributed. My own experience is that it is more likely to be used in a quarter-hour's conversation than in hundreds of hours of jazz and blues lyrics. On the other hand, preverbal *done* is quite ordinary in the latter context.

6 Stewart (personal communication) has insisted that *blan* is what is 'relexified' by BEV *be*. The sentence

> Buh Alligator blan come out de river . . .

– describing an habitual action, does indeed come close to the function of *be V-ing* and earlier *be V*. Early occurrences do not, however, appear to have been discovered. *DARE* I lists the word, considered there a form of *belong*, from a Gullah text of 1888. *Belong* has special use in many varieties of Pidgin English; however, this particular one seems to be peculiar to Gullah.

Another issue raised by Stewart (1969) is that *de/da* is most directly replaced by *-ing (in')* in a scheme of internal reconstruction; specifically *dem da fish* becomes *Dem (is) fishin'*, both meaning 'they are fishing'. Neither the hypothesis offered by Stewart nor its emendation by Fasold (1976) offers any *chronological* data, although Stewart's position is supported by abundant documentation. Stewart's reconstruction –

$$
\begin{array}{ll}
\text{de V} \longrightarrow \text{V-ing} \\
\text{*blan de V} \longrightarrow \text{be V-ing}
\end{array}
$$

is the neatest solution which seems possible. On the other hand, in addition to the apparent lack of attestation of *blan de V* there are the chronological limitations discussed above. Again, this particular reconstruction, with the chronology indicated by the attestations, would seem to favour the notion of Gullah and, *a fortiori*, its decreolization as relatively late developments. Note also that the 1865 attestations by W. Allen include both *da V* and *da V-ing*.

7 Problems of the past-tense functions of *was* and *were* are overlooked in presenting these columns. The Black English Vernacular has methods of marking past progressive, including its own use of *was V-ing* and *were V-ing*.

8 Space limitations preclude dwelling upon these and certain historically important distinctions which have no clear relation to the language.

9 Atwood (1953: 44 ) almost certainly perceived that the problem of the Black use of English was one of system rather than of 'usage' or of the forms in isolation as in Linguistic Atlas work. His statement that 'preterite' use of forms like *bring, throw, take, drink, dive, climb*, and *wake* is 'entirely, or almost entirely' restricted to Negro informants and is linked to syntactic 'peculiarities' like *I done bring* and *Is you drink?*, used by the same speakers, makes it clear that he saw the systemic nature of Black differences. His natural caution may

be what prevented him from going further with such an investigation. In spite of all the attention given (herein and elsewhere) to individual features like *be* and *be's*, statements about Black English, apart from such systemic considerations, are certain to be inconclusive.

10 For reasons discussed at some length above and in the references, it simply does not matter that Noah Webster, in 1789, cited 'the ancient manner, I *be*, you *be*'. For discussion, see Dillard 1985: 117.

11 Phonological factors, like monophthongal pronunciations and 'r-lessness', are dealt with elsewhere in this or another chapter. Others (assignment of stress in clauses and in sentences, simplification of final consonant clusters) are omitted largely because of the difficulty of obtaining historical information on them. In the (deservedly) prestigious work of Labov, many of the factors treated here, in Dillard (1972, 1985) and elsewhere are considered phonological deletions rather than grammatical differences. While not denying the importance of such factors as final cluster simplification, I simply cannot agree that features like zero copula are phonological deletions in origin.

**Chapter 4**

# The development of Southern

The nature of Southern has constituted one of the most controversial parts of American English dialectology. The controversies cannot be said to have been resolved, and certainly sweeping historical conclusions cannot be drawn from the dialect material generally made available. Special persistence of older English processes and strong Celtic (or Scotch–Irish) influences have been postulated from the anglophile point of view. The folk typology, on the other hand, has long held that Black influence on the language of Southern Whites was especially strong – a hypothesis rejected in its entirety by the Linguistic Atlas projects. Early observers such as Knight (1824: 34) focused upon 'the slave-hording nabobs of the South' as a characterization of that community, perceived as notably different from other American communities in the late eighteenth and early nineteeth centuries.

In apparent opposition to such a tradition, Carver (1987: 166–7) refers to a 'folksy' quality, tracing some of the Southern folksiness to 'the old-fashioned or relic nature' of words like *brickle* or *brickly* meaning 'brittle' or 'fragile'. *DARE* I shows *brickle* as 'chiefly S[ou]th, Midl[and]', but with no attestation before 1837 – in Georgia but hardly in the seventeenth or eighteenth century. (There is also an 1890 attestation from Louisiana, one in 1893 from Mississippi and one in 1899 from Virginia.) As in so many other cases, evidence like this does not rule out the influence of archaic survivals but hardly provides conclusive evidence for such a thesis.

So far as the Scotch–Irish influence is concerned, in a surprising number of cases forms are first attested around the 1830 period of regionalization (Chapter 7). Carver cites *fornent* ('opposite, near to against'), which he finds first in Davy Crockett's 1835 *Tour to*

*the North and Down East.* Carver (1987: 171) finds that Scottish
*scoot* (in the meaning 'to slide or to move') is first attested in
Pennsylvania in 1837 and in New England in 1838, but that the
'original' Scottish meaning, 'to eject or squirt' something
apparently never made it to the United States. (The first sense is
apparently intransitive, the second transitive.) Here the Linguistic Atlas and branch dictionary traditions have apparently missed
a bit of evidence in support of their basic positions. Friends of
mine from southern Florida and from Savannah, Georgia, White,
middle-aged, academic and (incidentally) female, use just this
form. It seems bizarre, however, to me – a north-east Texan,
slightly older than the others but with a family history of
migration from Mississippi on one side and from Kentucky on the
other.

The alternative to the 'folksy' interpretation of Southern will
depend upon the nature of Early Black English itself. If the latter
was only a matter of a slight skewing of features from British
rural dialects through slavery and segregation, as has been often
asserted, then there was obviously nothing in Black English itself,
however much black 'mammies' and their children may have
influenced 'li'l massa' on the plantation, to effect any major
changes. If, however, at some *very early* stage, the most extreme
variety in use among the field hands resembled – as a
communication variety *internal* to the slave community –
something like Sranan Tongo of Surinam or 'deep' Jamaican as
the oldest layer, contact influence could have produced much
more extensive changes.[1] (The survival of African languages long
enough to have a 'substratum' influence is a straw man which will
simply be ignored herein.) If Southern dialect was recognized
before the Great Migration of 1816–18 and especially that of the
1830s brought Celtic and regional British influences – which
seems to be the case – then influence from the Black variety
extensively attested throughout the eighteenth century would be
a more likely factor in producing something recognizably
Southern. It also is not necessarily true that 'Southern' as
recognized in the late eighteenth and early nineteenth centuries
was identical to what was spoken in the same area after the
'folksy' terms came in with the migrations of 1816–18 and the
1830s. The nature of Black English (farm or 'plantation' creole)
has been dealt with in the last chapter and in many other places.
The questions of its influence, the mechanisms of whatever
influence there may have been, and the chronology remain to be
addressed.

It might be well to start outside North America, in Surinam, where the existence of 'radical' creoles is not in doubt and where there are Pidgin English-like attestations in Dutch texts going back to the early eighteenth century (Herlein 1718) and a likelihood that the general slave Pidgin English was in use before the English left in 1664. R. Sanford's *Surinam Justice* (1662) is prefaced by an address 'To the Reader', with an apology for possible non-English 'idioms', for which 'it is more than an excuse to say, I was transplanted in my very childhood into the West Indies . . . . Near twenty years have I been absent from my native Europe, the greater and better part of which I lost in places unrefined from their aboriginal Barbarisme.' In the historical context, it is no great feat to translate *Barbarisme* as 'Pidgin English' or ' English Creole'.

Within the North American continental colonies, it was not long before equivalent statements were forthcoming. Read (1933) quotes G. L. Campbell, *The London Magazine*, in 1746: 'One Thing they are very faulty in, with regard to their Children, which is, that when young, they suffer them to prowl amongst the young Negros, which insensibly causes them to imbibe their Manners and broken Speech.' Read also cites C. J. Janson, *The Stranger in America* (1807, p. 383), who quoted the geographer Morse to the same effect. Read reports that John Davis, in the South in 1799, wrote: 'Each child has its *Momma*, whose gestures and accent it will necessarily copy, for children we all know are imitative beings.' Campbell here appears, less affected by the stereotype than does Davis, since 'momma' (or *mammy* in the usual report) had offspring who served as play children for 'Massa's' children and more naturally transmitted the dialect to them. See Dillard (1972: Ch. 5) for further examples.

From a strictly chronological point of view, these observations precede the transmission of any substantial number of 'folksy' British dialect forms. If *tote* (see below) is indeed an Africanism, it would have had to be transmitted quite early. *OED* II points out, in apparent rebuttal, that the term is attested in Virginia in 1676–7 and that the citation 'does not refer to Negroes'.[2] On the other hand, West Africans had been brought to Virginia more than four decades earlier than the citation, and it seems an unrealistic constraint to demand that an African-derived word refer to Africans ('Negroes'). In the history of Middle English, for example, it is not required that a word refer to Frenchmen in its first attestation in order to be credited to Norman French influence.

As indicated above, while eighteenth-century assertions of Black influence on (especially) Southern speech exist, early

nineteenth-century reports of the process abound. An early
observer of the influence of Blacks on the speech of white
Southerners is Henry C. Knight (pseudonym Arthur Singleton)
who reports: 'Children learn from the slaves some odd phrases
. . .' (1824: 82). Frederick Douglass (1845: 59), reporting about
Maryland at about the same time as Knight but from the
viewpoint of an escaped slave, is another who reported, obliquely
as usual in such cases, Black English influence on Southern White
speakers. Even 'Mas' Daniel', by his association

> with his father's slaves, had measurably adopted their dialect
> and their ideas . . . . The equality of nature is strongly asserted
> in childhood, and childhood requires children for associates.
> Color makes no difference with a child. Are you a child with
> wants, tastes and pursuits common to children not put on, but
> natural? Then, were you black as ebony you would be welcome
> to the child of alabaster white.

Douglass's report (more of which has been quoted in Chapter 3)
asserted that some of the newly imported slaves used *oo-dem* as a
plural of the second person pronoun. Although the direct
influence is obscure, it is clear that a second person plural
pronoun, contrasting apparently with the singular, was part of
those slaves' linguistic repertory. West African Pidgin English
would be expected to furnish the form *unu/una/wunu/wuna*
instead of *oo-dem*, but special developments in the pronoun of
the second person have been a major issue in the development
and identification of Southern dialect. Eventually there developed *you all*, cited by Knight (1824: 82) as one of the 'odd
phrases that southern white children learned from slaves'.
Edwards (1974: 14) asserts that: 'In the white plantation English
of Louisiana, the form *y'all* functioned precisely as did the *unu* of
the slaves. The use of *y'all* (semantically *unu*) was probably
learned by white children from black mammies and children in
familiar domestic situations.' Edwards finds the occasional use of
*unuaal* (*unu* + *all*). Holm (1980: 38–9) points out white
Bahamian *you-nay* ('you' plural) and /yin/ in Virgin Islands
Dutch Creole, citing African forms like Limba *yina*, Mbundu
*(y)enu*, Kongo *yeno*, and Wolof *yena*. South Carolina regionalisms
for the plural of *you* include *unner, yunnuh*, and *yinnah*.
Particularly since Holm establishes clear African influence on the
English of white Bahamians, there seems to be little reason to
hesitate to attribute at least some influence in the formation of
*you all* (*y'all*), the most frequently cited indicator of Southern
dialect, to Black influence.

Perhaps the most oft-mentioned phonological feature in Southern dialect – or in American English, or in English altogether – is non-prevocalic /r/. 'Dropping' of the /-r/ in northern areas like eastern New England and New York City (variably, as it turns out) is conventionally linked to the British influence of the early nineteenth century (see Chapter 2. p. 50). Although that dating itself appears to be based more nearly on authority than on chronological data, Southern offers additional complications. For one thing, it tends to differ in not having 'linking' and 'intrusive' /r/. According to McDavid and O'Cain (1980: 172, Map 157), the Upper South has nearly eliminated the 'linking' /r/ and the Lower South wavers in usage. . . Southern usage is clearly an American innovation, although the loss of /r/ in *your aunt* is sporadically attested in the English counties of Northampton, Suffolk, and Essex.'

A different kind of influence is suggested by studies like Gilbert (1984: 5–6), which attributes that phonological development to

the creole English of the Caribbean and the creole and pidgin English of West Africa. The 'extremely non-rhotic character' of southern English (Wells 1982: 543) is linked with the similar non-rhoticity of most types of Caribbean and West African English . . . in connection with features such as absence of linking *r* and the deletion of shwa offglide, which are rare in non-rhotic New York City and Eastern New England, as well as in Britain . . .

In the absence of any historical data concerning the transmission of British dialects from which selective retention could be made, it seems much more likely that – given both the structural pattern and the literary records – the major difference in non-prevocalic /r/ distribution relates to the greater persistence, wider distribution and stronger influence of Black English Vernacular in the South. Just as often, on the other hand, more than one influence may well have been operative.

Another – if even less precise – point of attack is the 'Southern drawl'. Except for Sledd (1966) and Brooks (1935, 1985), phonologists have done little with it. Sledd sees the drawl as a continuation of the historical English processes of breaking and umlaut, processes however which represent earlier stages of English historical phonology than those represented in colonization. Brooks, whose early work especially was highly influential, cites correspondences between Southern American and regional

British forms in an apparently reconstructive theoretical framework, asserting the apparent impossibility of such correpon-
dences developing except through transmission from England to
America. Nothing is suggested, however, about the chronology
of that transmission, and independent developments are simply
considered out of the question.

The drawl has always represented the very core of popular
observations about Southern speech. It was also noted, in 1801,
as a characteristic of certain White residents of the West Indies.
Lady Nugent's *Journal* (1966) of her stay in Jamaica from 1801 to
1805 reports of a certain Mrs C. that she 'says little, and drawls
out that little . . .' (p. 52) and generalizes about ladies 'who have
not been educated in England', who speak with 'an indolent
drawling out of their words . . .' (p. 98). Lengthening (diphthon-
gization and even triphthongization) of vowels is, obviously, the
most important feature. 'Slowness' of that speech has always
been a popular perception; phonologists' statements about
duration of a phoneme have often met with scepticism from low-
level students, who are generally 'sure' that Southern speech is
slower. During World War II, Northern servicemen developed
stereotypes of Southern speech on the order of 'If you ask a
Southern girl for a kiss, by the time she says no it's too late.'
What the popular view sees as slowness, a more objective view
sees as addition of phonemes, lengthening or the like. As a native
speaker of a modified Southern variety, I have always felt that
the slowing-down contributes, metalinguistically, to an interactional factor of politeness. Southerners notoriously consider the
'clipped' Northern speech as brusque, even discourteous.

Early Southern, whether or not influenced by Black English,
was distinguishable, according to reports, from, especially, 'the
New Jersey man'. Smyth (1784, I, 278–9) reported that
inhabitants of western North Carolina had rejected an inhabitant
of New Jersey who sought refuge in a fort during an Indian scare
because of his accent, and Davis (1809: 367) remarked that a
person from that area was 'distinguished by his provincial
dialect'. New Jersey was, it will be remembered, one of the areas
of greatest Dutch influence. Read (1933) cites Jonathan Boucher's
(1775) localizing the 'croaking, gutteral idioms of the Dutch' in
an area 'near New York', which should include New Jersey.
Prince (1909) shows that Dutch influence on the English of the
area, which should have been at its height between 1775 and 1809
(see Chapter 1), continued into the twentieth century. Smyth
remarked that 'after spending several years in the Southern
colonies' he had noticed a difference between that dialect and

that of New England, 'greatly to the disadvantage of' the latter (1784, II, 363). That a Dutch-influenced New Jersey dialect could be distinguished from a Black Creole-influenced Southern dialect – or from the more standard English of educated Southerners on their guard – would come as no surprise.

Kirkham's (1829) list of usages from Maryland, Virginia, Kentucky and Mississippi contain a number for which there seems to be no reason to refer to Black influence; for example, *Have you fotcht the water?* which he characteristically 'corrected' to *Have you fetched or brought the water?* Schele de Vere (1872: 470) asserted that by his time, *fetch* 'in the sense of bringing' was almost unknown in the South but still used for 'bringing up children'. The 'very old participle *fotch*', however, was 'still very general among the negroes of the South', and he also commented upon the 'negro' production of the 'hybrid *fotched*'. Harrison's (1884) list of '[Negro] Archaisms' contains *fetch*. Although the transmission of these forms is not documented, it seems quite likely that some of these are genuine cases of Black retention of relatively archaic features. Later observers have found mutual influence between Black English and White varieties.

It was predominantly after 1800 that many Northerners with their slaves moved into the interior South. At the same time there came to the area 'one-time pioneer hunter-farmers and their families, and Southern planters and their slaves' (Wood 1971: 4). On the not very radical theory that dialect resides in populations rather than in areas, it might be assumed that real changes came about in the South consequent upon the persons new to the area.

As we have seen above, some hint of Southern characteristics was to be found before 1800. The 'folksy' character of the dialect of the South may well, as the historical attestations tend to indicate, have begun fitting into the general timetable of regionalization in American English, for which an attempt at presentation will be made in Chapter 7.

Accepting this intermixing of Black-influenced and 'folksy' influences on Southern dialect makes possible a kind of progressive treatment of nineteenth century observations. One of Kirkham's (1828) usages localized only as Maryland, Virginia, Kentucky or Mississippi (that is, perhaps, from his point of view, generally southwards) is *whar you gwine?* – corrected, according to Kirkham's regular practice, to *where are you going?* As a rendering of slave usage of *going*, *gwine* is prominent in the plantation literature. The articulation possibly indicated thereby (implosive /g/) is among the possible Africanisms of Black

English which spread to Southern Whites. There is little reason
to draw the same conclusion about Kirkham's 'Southern' *in
cohoot with*, corrected to *partnership*, which is actually the first
attestation of the phrase, more usually *in cahoots with* and, in
twentieth century usage at any rate, having a pejorative
connotation. The first attestation in which the sense of 'plot'
rather than 'partnership' is clearly present is in Jones's *Negro
Myths*, of 1888 and from the Georgia coast, although there are
intermediate and indeterminate (semantically and geographically)
attestations. No reference at all to Black English influence would
be needed to account for Kirkham's *come of* [that habit]
corrected to *overcome* or *get rid of* . . . The term is not listed at
all in *DARE* I. If it is a mistake for or an early form of *come off*
('quit, stop!'), it far precedes the earliest citation (1892) and is a
striking exception to the early New York, New England
distribution.

*Plunder*, corrected to *baggage*, in Kirkham's Southern list, was
more likely to have merited the locale designation 'frontier' than
'Southern' in Kirkham's time. An 1822 citation in *OED* II calls it
a 'cant term used in the western country', where *cant* probably
has none of the technical meaning it can be assigned. Probable
derivation from Dutch, with an ultimate but not immediate
relationship to its verbal and nounal homophones, would indicate
a more northerly origin under 'normal' circumstances. Flexner
(1985) bravely – and, I think, accurately – defies *DA*'s denial, on
geographic grounds, of Dutch origin.[3] *OED* II concedes that the
specifically American nounal use 'may be immediately due' to
Dutch. In a highly mobile society like the American, it is not a
question of where Lewis of Lewis and Clark, who provides the
first (1806) attestation, came from or where he was when he
wrote down the word. The important factor is that the Lewis and
Clark expedition, like so much of what was going on in the
United States, was trans- and even ultra-regional. Samuel Taylor
Coleridge, who in spite of his Horne Tooke-inspired fancifulness
in linguistic theory was very observant of new words, regarded it
as used 'in America' in a letter of 1826 (quoted in Mencken,
McDavid and Maurer 1963: 30)

Except that Webster (1789: 384) also attributed *holp* ('help') to
Virginia – although it is in a context ambiguous as to whether
*holpe* or *holp* was used elsewhere – one would be inclined to
overlook Kirkham's statement about *Who hoped you to sell it?*
corrected to *Who helped you sell it?* Schele de Vere (1872: 489)
writes '*Holpen*, the old participle . . . is still often heard,
especially in Kentucky, while in Virginia and by negroes of the

South a mongrel form, holped, is made for the preterite of I help.' *Holp(ed)* is of course one of the most familiar of archaisms, a survival of the strong verb *helpan* in Old English which became weak relatively late in the process of such changes. The notion that *help* is confused with *hope* in the Ozarks or in some other rural area (including areas of Louisiana and Texas) is familiar to everyone who has ever taught a dialectology or American English course in a small university; the explanation that it is not really confusion usually comes at about the same time that the instructor explains that residents of Brooklyn do not say *Earl* for *oil* and *oil* for *Earl*.

If we conceive provisionally of a Black English-influenced 'early Southern', from approximately 1750–1830, the two points of view – Black influence and later 'folksiness' – can be partially reconciled. On the other hand, statements about Black English influence on Southern dialect (Dillard 1972: Ch. 5) have tacitly assumed that later – even twentieth-century – Southern dialects show that influence. Continuing and overlapping influences seem more likely than neat chronological compartmentalization.

The same Knight (1824) who characterized Southerners as primarily slave owners also observed that Virginians at least used *mad* for *angry*, 'as do the Irish'. The 'Celtic' hypothesis of influence on Southern culture has been most strongly advanced by McWhiney (1988), especially in collaboration with Forrest McDonald. The latter's Prologue states: 'the American colonies south and west of Pennsylvania were peopled during the seventeenth and eighteenth century by immigrants from the 'Celtic fringe' of the British archipelago.' McWhiney himself interprets Jordan's (1981) characteristics of 'Anglo' cattle culture in the South-east and South (see Chapters 5 and 6) as being Celtic in nature. The hypothesis has apparently never been tested in terms of any substantial linguistic evidence. McWhiney (1989: 208) cites *Spboi*, a 'Southern call or shout . . . used in managing swine' as 'reputedly' of Irish origin, and the phrase *Devil take the hindmost* as derived from the 'Welsh admonition':

> Home, home, let each try to be first, and may the tailless sow [symbol of the Devil] take the hindmost.

These are rather minor details, but the materials provided by, for example, Carver (1987) supplement them to some degree.

Celtic or not, *antebellum* white Southerners were not a settled lot. McWhiney (1989: 12–13) asserts:

> Migration was a constant in the lives of many of these

antebellum Southerners . . . The mobility of antebellum
Southerners can be illustrated by . . . Lowndes County,
Mississippi, [which] had somewhat over 1,600 heads of
families, of whom only 103 were born in the state. The vast
majority came from other Southern states; only 77 were from
the northern United States, and only 11 were foreign-born.

White Southerners in the *antebellum* period, except perhaps for
the very small group of plantation owners, were hardly tied to the
land. Their mobility itself argues against the direct transmission
of British regional dialects to the South in regionally formulated
patterns. The slaves, on the other hand, come closest to the kind
of settled, tied-to-the-land peasantry upon which dialect zones
have generally been based. Although being sold – including that
kind of selling which broke up families – and other factors
worked against stability for African-derived slaves, Frederick
Douglass (1845: 176) expressed the opinion, in the immediate
context of reporting the sale of slaves from Colonel Lloyd's
plantation and the consequent breaking-up of families, that not
only free Southerners but even 'people of the north' 'have less
attachment to the places where they are born and brought up,
than have the slaves'.

Continuing Black influence, even after 'folksiness' had begun
to enter the picture, is apparent. Certain relatively Southern
usages documented by Kirkham (1828), who lumped together
Maryland, Virginia, Kentucky and Mississippi, seem directly
relevant. For the group of states with which he dealt, Kirkham
pointed out these interesting usages:

> Carry the horse to water (corrected to 'Lead the horse to
> water')
> Tote the wood to the river (corrected to 'Carry the wood . . .').

Thomas Nelson Page's *In Ol' Virginy* (1887) has the speech of the
slave Edinburg showing:

> . . . de mens dee was totin' in de wood
> (pp. 67–8)
> [I] toted 'im back, jes' like I did dat day when he was a baby
> . . . .
> (p. 34)

Almost immediately in the second passage, referring to the same
event, Edinburg reports:

> . . . I kyar'd 'im 'way off.

*Carry* meaning 'lead' (as Kirkham pointed out, specifying a homey usage) is Southern, although *DARE* reports that *carry* as 'to escort, accompany' was 'formerly freq[uent] in N[ew] Eng[land]; now chiefly S[ou]th, S[outh] Midl[and]'. There is no citation earlier than – or even as early as – Kirkham, however, the *Familiar Lectures* attestation being inexplicably omitted and nothing for the meaning 'escort, accompany' being reported earlier than 1861. *DBE* reports it of 'Atlantic [English Creole]' distribution, labelling it *'arch[aic]*'; Brit[ish] dial[ectal], Northern Irel[and], U.S. South idem' with an 1832 citation – later than Kirkham but earlier than anything in *DARE*. Given Holm and Shilling's statement (1982: v) that 'American loyalists and their slaves had profound demographic and linguistic consequences' on the Bahamas, it seems entirely possible that the forms *tote* and *carry* as 'escort, accompany' would have been carried from the American mainland to the Bahamas at about the time of the American Revolution, in spite of the fact that no one has cited an attestation from so early.

The arguments about whether the words (and meanings) involved are 'Anglo-Saxon', African, Atlantic Creole or Southern seem all to partake of special pleading. Kirkham's indication of the distribution of *tote* and *carry* remained true in rural eastern Texas – and probably through most of the South – through the second quarter of the twentieth century. the usage of *carry* is 'frozen' in the lyric of the popular song 'Carry Me Back to Ole Virginy', and 'Tote Me Back to Ole Virginy' would incite snickers in the South quite as much as the actual title does in the North. The plantation literature, which generally treats these forms and meanings as of Black – if not necessarily African – transmission, records materials consistent with these facts.

The influence of Black English upon Southern dialect, although preceding the 'folksy' component, would have continued to the Civil War and beyond: In the South, as well as in the North in the earliest period. Black and White culture, like Black and White English, could differ greatly, although of course there were differential rates of assimilation among different social and occupational groups of Blacks.

The influence, like anything else in language, was not monolithic. Dickens, Kemble and others (cited in Dillard 1972: Ch. 5) who specified that girls and women tended to retain the Black influence most completely, young men being sent away for an education and either becoming bidialectal or repressing the farm/plantation dialect, are limited to the Atlantic coastal slave states in their observations, Kemble primarily to South Carolina and Dickens to the plantation he visited in Virginia. Their observations took place within approximately a twenty-year period. At other times, and in other places, the influence would have been different. For example, a contrasting situation may have obtained in the lower Mississippi Basin area. Ingraham (1835: 208), between the time of Kemble and that of Dickens, observed that the daughters of the Mississippi planters were given more education than the sons: 'Many [Mississippi] planters are opposed to giving their sons, whom they destine to succeed them as farmers, a classical education. A common practical education they consider sufficient for young gentlemen who are to bury themselves for life in the retirement of a plantation.'

Such factors could reverse the situation, in sex-grading at any rate, and might mean that the relationships between Black and White English were different in what may have been two major areas of slave language. In the preceding chapter it is suggested that one of those two areas included but extended far beyond the South Carolina–Georgia Low Country, and that the other included the lower Mississippi Basin states of Mississippi, Alabama, northern Louisiana, and eventually Texas. Westernmost parts of Georgia and Florida should probably be included with this group.

There are a number of implications of such a division. At that period, female speakers were in any case much more inclined to delicacy than were males and would have picked up different expressions from the slave population. Influencing the males of the Mississippi area, for example, slaves would have transmitted *cock* ('female genitalia'); the women of the Georgia–South Carolina area and its sphere of influence would have been unlikely to adopt the same form.

Edwards (1974: 21) suggests restriction of the word in that sense to Southern (White) males. See also the *DARE* I citations from 1944 and 1970. *DARE* also cites *cock* – 'sexual intercourse, *especially among Black speakers*'. In that meaning, of course, both the features [+masc] and [+fem] must be present. Dillard (1977: 25–44) cites numerous examples of 'unisex' ([+masc] [+fem]) features in the Black English lexicon. In a similar manner, the Black word game called 'the dozens', 'sounding', 'jonin', etc., must have spread to the Whites in the Mississippi area where the dominant influence was on the males (Jackson 1966).

More conventional evidence for such a geographic dichotomy may be found in the much-examined matter of 'invariant' *be* (with its variant *be's*). For Mississippi and Louisiana, Bailey and Bassett (1986: 11) have pointed out that 'Invariant *be*' is 'clearly not unique to black speech. In fact, the form has a similar pattern of distribution for both races, with education, age, and sex all influencing the pattern. However, among blacks the form is much more common and is used by a larger segment of the population.' Although the authors may intend this statement to rule against Black origin or transmission, the opposite seems to be its effect. *DARE* I lists no form of this type (its B2f) earlier than Joel Chandler Harris's *Free Joe* of 1887. Its next listing, 1935, is from Zora Neale Hurston's *Mules and Men*, a study of Black folklore primarily in Florida. Only in 1966, from *DARE*'s field records, do they list White usages – and then not clearly in anything more than the surface form. The forms cited are:

NP be PP
NP be ADJ (all right).

Bailey-Bassett's white usages are:

NP don't be Adj (sandy)
NP be Adj (together)
NP don't be Adj (spongy).

Although none of these has

NP be V-ing

the structure seems present in principle. No real conclusion can be drawn, however, in the absence of consideration of the 'atemporal' function discussed in Chapter 3.

Joy L. Miller (1972) attempts to dispose of the basically Black distribution of this structure by pointing out usage by White racists, including members of the Ku Klux Klan. Those who can remember the segregated South, however, can well recall that the most racist Whites (well represented by Lyle Britton in James Baldwin's *Blues for Mr Charlie*) were the most avid imitators and parodists of Black behavioural and speech patterns. It may be unpleasant to recall such matters at a time when some real progress has been made in race relations in the South, but histories cannot be written by using only those materials that are pleasant to contemplate. But, getting back to language history, it cannot be denied that the surface form *be + V-ing* has early attestation among White Americans.

The indication of mixing of Black English and other influences on Southern dialect continues into the latter half of the nineteenth century and beyond. Payne (1908–9), in the words of Brooks (1985: 11), 'naturally in his day, interpreted that fact [use of 'Black' pronunciations by white men] as a borrowing by whites from the blacks.' Actually, Payne seems to have represented rather well the folk traditions about mutual influence between Blacks and Whites, although he attempted to exclude 'pure Negroisms' from his picture of eastern Alabama White dialect.

More formally and more recently, projects such as the East Texas Dialect Project, conducted by linguists and folklorists at the University of Texas, Austin (Galvan and Troike 1969) have found linguistic and cultural differences – and, of course, many similarities – between White and Black east Texans who have lived in proximity for quite lengthy periods, with frequent and often close contact between the two groups (but, a native of the area would say, in restricted domains of interaction). Galvan and Troike feel that 'sociolinguistic isoglosses' could be drawn because of the differences, but that few linguistic features, if any, would be completely exclusive to one ethnic group.

By the time of the Civil War, the South was certainly set apart from the North in the popular imagination. (That same popular viewpoint conveniently forgot that widespread use of African slaves had been much more widespread in New England and New York than in what had come to be called, in the mid-nineteenth century, the 'slave states'.) 'Yankees' and 'Rebels' were mutually exclusive terms. Enlisted men in the armed forces into World War II, at least, maintained that distinction. Insofar as symbolic identification figures in dialect diversification, the war between the states must have contributed greatly to the polarization of the two major regions of the nation at that time. Whether or not the Southern use of /griyziy/ as against the Northern use of /griysiy/, one of the most perfect isogloss distinctions ever presented (Atwood 1950), had developed by this time remains unknown. There appears to be no chronological evidence.

Whatever its sources, the post-war Southern dialect was well recognized by the time of Schele de Vere (1972). He contrasted 'New England' *do tell* with 'southern' *You don't say* (1872: 436), identified *fair off* ('stop raining') as a Southern term (p. 468), pointed out that *evening* replaced *afternoon* in the South and West, and observed that 'axe' (apparently /æks/) survived in Southern speech with 'astonishing vitality' and was 'almost uniformly used by the negro population' (p. 433). The last two (*evening* for *afternoon* and *ax* for *ask*) are also used in the Bahamas and in other places in the Caribbean. Both have English dialect distribution, but there may be more to their history than simple diffusion of British dialects.

As *DBE* points out, *EDD* shows *evening* for *afternoon* as British dialect, from 'Mid, East'. An attestation is given from Shropshire in 1788, but there is no special reason to believe that

Shropshire lads dominated the diffusion of English in the period of maritime expansion, and even less that they formed the basis of the population of the American South. The same meaning is current in Australia and New Zealand (Turner 1966); early and widespread distribution – not just to North America – seems to be indicated. As *DBE* points out, the usage is general Caribbean and parallels in semantics the Portuguese *tarde*. Furthermore, even Cameroonian French *soir* tends to replace *après midi* (from my own experience in Yaoundé in 1963–4).

The stigmatized rural Southern form /æks/ for *ask* provides another case of possibly more than one influence. *DBE* classifies *aks* for *ask* as the 'Atlantic' form and also points out one of the very best known facts of English-language history, that Old English *axian* was the regular form, /-ks-/ having been metathesized to /-sk-/ or replaced by the Northern form *-sk* in the history of the word. Furthermore, '*ax* . . . survived down to nearly 1600 [as] the regular literary form'. *DARE* I points out that *ax, axe* in this meaning was 'formerly especially New England, now chiefly S[ou]th, Midl[and]', listing it from Webster's *Dissertations* of 1789 as 'still [NB!] frequent in New England', and from Humphreys' 1815 *Yankey in England*, 'Glossary of Provincialisms', as 'N[ew] Eng[land]'. *DARE* I also lists an 1836 attestation from west Tennessee and a statement from Mississippi in 1893 that the form was 'Negro for *ask*'.

This would appear to be the strongest evidence available for the familiar idea that Black English represents an extreme form of archaic retention, but there seems no reason to assume the direct transmission of a British regional dialect form on such evidence. Transmission rather to a contact variety just around 1600, when *ax* was still 'the regular literary form', seems much more likely. The English-based pidgins and creoles of both the Atlantic and the Pacific (Todd 1974: 12) have forms like Krio, Cameroonian and Jamaican *aks* (the last varying with *haks*), Sranan Tongo of Surinam adds apparently enclitic *-i*, and Neo-Melanesian has *haskim*, where the final syllable is apparently the transitivizer marker. Since *haski+ -im* would have yielded *haskim*, the enclitic vowel may well have developed in at least some of both the Atlantic and the Pacific varieties. Holm (1989, I, 76) discusses prosthetic /h/ in West African and Caribbean creoles, rejecting the hypothesis of African influence and calling the addition of /h-/ to a number of West Indian forms (e.g. *hear* for *ear*) 'yet another Caribbean mystery'. There appears no special reason to explain the Neo-Melanesian *haskim* as derived from any of the Atlantic forms.

Taking *DARE* I's attestations at face value, one would assume that the route of *ax* in America was from New England to western Tennessee and then to Mississippi. With a detour to a 'P[ennsylvani]a M[oun]t[ain]s' attestation of 1930 'as of' 1900, the form would go to Mississippi attestations in Faulkner's *Go Down Moses* (1940) by a country Black speaker who also uses *leff* as the base form instead of *leave* ('Leff her look at you,') and *hit* for the neuter pronoun in quite recognizable (literary) Black dialect. Schele de Vere's 1872 material would intervene, and so would numerous other occurrences which overwhelmingly designate the form as 'Negro'. The attestation from a Black speaker in Boston (Walser 1955: 272) is quite as early (1789) as the attestation from Webster which *DARE* I chooses to use, and the occurrence of the Surinam forms *hakisi* and *aksi* (Lichtveld 1951) suggests a multiple (or at least double) transmission for the Southern form rather than simple retention of an archaic form which was 'formerly N[ew] Eng[land]'.

By the 1870s a Southern dialect – apparently without need for further subdivisions – was recognizable by certain features about which there was virtually no room for doubt. New Englanders would recognize streams smaller than rivers 'only' by *brooks* (*DARE* I shows New England use of the term by 1668), although later use of the word tends to scatter out a little; educated people anywhere in the English-speaking world could hardly have found Shakespeare's *books in running brooks* bizarre. *Run* and *branch* were Southern, according to our observer. *DARE* I finds the latter in Virginia as early as 1624 (but in the writings of Captain John Smith), in Virginia for probably the first significant attestation in 1663, and in Georgia in 1746, 1844 and 1870. Schele de Vere found *breakdown* to be used in America, 'as in England', for 'a noisy dance' but to be especially applicable and 'universally applied to the violent performances of the negroes' (1972: 447). *DARE* I has an 1843 reference to 'nigger breakdowns'.

Schele de Vere is careful to specify that both 'negro and white' use pleonastic *at* in *Where is it at? Where have you been at?* and *Where does she lie at?* (1872: 436). He finds *tote* for *carry* 'constantly used in Virginia and the South'. Nevertheless, similarity is not identity and it remained possible to distinguish most Black (especially field hands and their descendants) from most White Southerners until at least the time of Lambert and Tucker (1969).

By the third quarter of the nineteenth century, outsiders are insistent upon recognizing something special about Southern

dialect. Samuel Clemens (Mark Twain), in *Life on the Mississippi*
(1883: 359), makes some comments about the 'pleasing' Southern
'intonations and elisions' – relatively trite observations, one
would think, even for Twain's own day. Like so many others,
he focuses upon non-prevocalic /r/, asserting 'The educated
Southerner has no use for it, except at the beginning of a word.'
He apparently perceived some difference from 'Northern' *r*-
dropping, for he asserts that 'it [the dropping] was not from the
North' and he also claims that it 'was not inherited from
England'. (It is rather striking how closely Twain agrees with
Gilbert 1984.) He also points out the palatalization ('putting a *y*
into') of /k-/, a factor not unreported elsewhere (see p. 100).
Typically, also, Twain observed 'some infelicities' including
commonplace 'mistakes' such as *like* for *as* (reporting that he had
heard 'an educated gentleman' say 'Like the flag-officer did') and
pleonastic *at*, both of which have very widespread use outside the
South. Twain had been in the West already (1861–4) and should
have known of the more widespread character of these usages by
the time he wrote *Old Times on the Mississippi* (1872–6) or issued
it in book form as *Life on the Mississippi* (1882).

Twain's emphasis, insofar as *like* is concerned, seems to be
social – where the distribution may well have been different in
the South. He also pointed out that this gentleman's 'cook or his
butler' would have said 'Like the flag-officer done'. He had heard
gentlemen say 'Where have you been at?' and a 'street Arab' say
'I was a-ask'n' Tom what you was a settin' at.' Twain also
reported that the 'unpolished' often used 'went' for 'gone', which
he found 'nearly as bad as the Northern "hadn't ought"'. For
Northerners, in his own area of residence at that time, he reports
'He hadn't ought to have went.' Clemens and Schele de Vere
agree on this particular of geographic distribution.

Some of Twain's comments clearly reflect the genteel tradition
in grammar rather than any special insight into language history,
as when he indulges in the biblical allusion that 'the very elect'
say ' "will" when they mean "shall" '. On the other hand, he
seems on solid ground when he reports: 'The Northern word
"guess" – imported from England where it used to be common,
and now regarded by satirical Englishmen as a Yankee original –
is but little used among Southerners. They say 'reckon' . . .' And
one must wonder about his statement that there is no *doesn't* in
their language: 'they all say "don't" instead'.

Twain was inspired to these observations at the end of a trip
down the Mississippi, a sentimental journey of sorts in memory
of his days as a river-boat pilot. The specific reminders of

Southern came in New Orleans, although he had also stopped at other Southern towns along the Mississippi. In the same section he points out *levee* and *lagniappe*, both associated in some way (for *lagniappe* see Chapter 5) with French influence. Twain's Southernisms appear as a kind of amalgam of 'folksiness', grammatical 'sloppiness' (more notable in the lower socio-economic classes) and something very close to stereotyping.

The forms which attracted the local colour writers who dealt with the South after the Civil War are often those which seem to have 'migrated' from other areas. Joel Chandler Harris, in *Free Joe* (1887), set in Georgia, uses *ary* ('any, either') which had been in a list of 'Provincialisms' in Vermont in 1818 It appeared in western Tennessee in 1836. *DARE* I now calls it 'throughout US, but esp[ecially] S[outh], Midl[and]'.

Harris and Twain, who had specified in *Huckleberry Finn* that he was representing the dialect of a Negro slave in Jim (a 'yard Negro', closer to a house servant than a field hand, by most accounts from the period of slavery), along with many others of the period, differentiated between Black and White speakers in the same area. In Daddy Jack, Harris (1883) distinguished between a Gullah speaker and other Blacks from the more inland South. The Black/White distinction remained a striking one throughout the South. Black novelist Charles Waddell Chesnutt, in *The Marrow of Tradition* (1901), made a critical part of his plot depend upon the failure of Southern Whites to recognize by his speech a Black man who had been educated in the North. They simply assumed – as, apparently, did Chesnutt – that a Southern Negro, the only kind they expected to encounter, would be distinguishable by his speech. Lambert and Tucker (1969) established, by a variant of their matched-guise test, that Blacks and Whites in Tougaloo, Mississippi, were distinguishable by tape-recorded evidence.

Although Twain's writings contain some indication that Louisiana is different from the remainder of the South, and although Schele de Vere separated different states with some consistency, there is a vast gulf between the picture they present of variations in Southern and the many sub-dialect areas found in even the relatively early works of the dialect geographers.

Black-influenced, 'folksy', 'Celtic' stereotypically or just as a result of imputed sloppiness, Southerners in general seem to constitute a recognizable population beginning in the early nineteenth century and continuing until the present. (On recent developments, however, see Chapter 7.) The exact boundaries of this Southern are not generally agreed upon, and even the

features which make for the general regional recognition have
not always been easy to specify.

In phonology, simplification of the /ay/ and /ɔy/ diphthongs
is widespread and have been generally recognized in dialectology, but there is little indication of the time of that simplification.
Neutralization of /ɛ/ and /ɪ/ before nasals is widespread; it was
one of the more convincing arguments, in the 1960s, that Black
English in the North's inner cities represented simply an
importation of Southernisms. The dialects which have that
neutralization tend *not* to neutralize /a/ and /ɔ/ (*cot* and *caught*)
except sometimes before /-rC/. Various reflexes of /əy/ in *third*,
*bird*, *shirt* occur fairly widely in the Gulf states but never seem to
have figured strongly in stereotypical recognition of Southern,
that particular feature being reserved for 'Brooklynese'.

In vocabulary, the popular stereotype prefers food terms
(*cornpone, ham hocks, butterbeans*) which would not satisfy any
dialectologist. Wood (1971: 28) gives a test vocabulary for
general Southern in *barn lot*, *corn shucks*, *light bread* and *pallet*,
with *snack* and *kerosene* suggested somewhat hesitantly because
of commercial associations. For the first of these, *DARE* I has a
New Hampshire attestation in 1724, an 1867 occurrence in
Virginia, a 1905 citation in north-west Arkansas, a 1949
attestation in Kentucky with a statement by Kurath (1949) that
the word occurs 'from the Rappahannock southward', and
slightly later examples from fieldwork showing occurrence in
South Midland. The compound is rated 'chiefly Midl[and],
S[ou]th'. *Corn chucks* is not represented in *DARE* I and is
therefore, apparently, judged non-regional. But *corn shucking* ('a
social gathering at which corn is picked or husked') is considered
'chiefly S[ou]th, S[outh] Midl[and]' and attested from south-
western Indiana in 1823, South Carolina in 1859, eastern
Tennessee in 1895, eastern Alabama and western Georgia in
1908, south-west Virginia in 1915 and other general Southern or
south Midland areas until 1965–70 and presumably the present.
*Light bread* is not attested before 1821. *Pallet* is not an
Americanism in any sense; maritime usage intervenes, chronologically at least, between its Middle English usage and anything
Southern. *Snack* has no special American attestations in the
historical dictionaries; its 1807 British citation refers to Irish
usage. *Kerosene* is first attested around the time of its invention,
1854–5, and is not indicated as particularly Southern at any early
time.

The picture that seems to emerge from the cited vocabulary,
except for the words and expressions quite probably Black in

origin, is of a relatively late movement towards the South, with no very clear line between 'General Southern' and South Midland even in this farming vocabulary. Carver (1987: 164), in partial agreement with C.-J.N. Bailey (1968), refers to 'upper Southern' rather than to South Midland: 'Nearly all the southern Appalachians, Kentucky, eastern Tennessee, northern Alabama, and northern Arkansas are the heart of this region, with peripheral areas in southern Indiana and Illinois, almost all of Missouri, Oklahoma, and much of northeastern Texas.' Carver (1987: 259) suggests the following distribution of twentieth-century Lower Southern dialects:

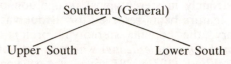

He makes little distinction between what he considers Upper Southern and what is also called South Midland. Aside from certain farming terms, he lists *bloody flux* (not included in *DARE* I) and *bad sick* (1928, South Carolina, from Peterkin's *Scarlet Sister Mary*; 1929, Mississippi, from Sale's *Tree Named John*; 1939, northern West Virginia; 1942, northern Kansas; 1965–70, from *DARE's* own fieldwork, 'scattered S[outh] Midl[and], but esp[ecially] Inland S[ou]th', with occurrences in 1966 in North Carolina, 1969 in Kentucky and 1979 in Missouri). The last expression, first attested in Black or strongly Black-influenced texts, seems to have moved recently into the 'Upper South'. Carver (1987: 165) reports that only two *DARE* informants, both in Kentucky, gave *brought on* as a response to the question 'What do you call a piece of clothing not made at home?' Other evidence, primarily written, establishes that the expression is uniquely Upper South. *DARE* I lists the term from 1895 in western North Carolina and eastern Tennessee, in 1905 from north-west Arkansas, in 1917 from western North Carolina, Iowa and Kentucky, in 1931 from eastern Kentucky, in 1937 from the 's[outh] Appalachians, and later from Tennessee and Kentucky'. Evidence of this sort would not indicate that the Upper South dialect developed at any early period. So far as the colonial period, as a *terminus a quo*, is concerned, there is no clear evidence even of a germ of this particular dialect or dialect complex. In fact, little indication of its origins by around 1830, a time of more realistic expectation, is to be found.

A kind of scheme of Carver's 'Lower South' would appear to be

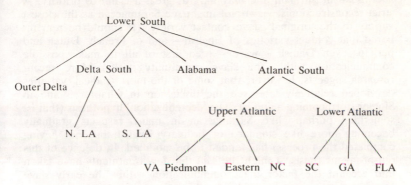

As a general scheme of dialect (especially word) geography, such a picture offers little to object to. Only the relationship between north and south Louisiana is puzzling, and any objection there might be on basically the historical ground that French was much more important in the former than in the latter. In that respect, north-west Louisiana at least is strikingly like eastern Texas and south-eastern Arkansas.

Such lines do not, however, map out anything like the history of the dialects; chronological factors, insofar as we have them recorded in the historical dictionaries and so far as any other evidence is immediately available, would seem to have only the roughest correlations with such a scheme. And the pattern so presented still does not answer Wood's (1970) disturbing (implied) synchronic question about Southern: how far west does it go? Even less does the scheme indicate when, how far and how that westward diffusion took place diachronically.

However great the value of the traditional scheme, elaborated by *DARE*, Carver and others, for synchronic dialectology, it seems to say little about historical diffusion. The next two chapters attempts to deal with at least some of the reasons why this may be true.

## Notes

1 Least affected by 'white' varieties of English are the creoles of Surinam. Saramaccan is the most 'radical' form of English Creole in the New World and in some ways more so than the frequently

described West African varieties like Krio. Other varieties like Sranan Tongo (sometimes referred to by the international term Taki Taki) are also found in Surinam and may have as great a claim to priority. A strict reconstructionist viewpoint might see Saramaccan as the closest variety to the 'original' slave contact variety. (It should be remembered that contact varieties of English – and of French, Dutch and perhaps even Danish – were – used first of all to make possible communication within the slave community itself.) More recent research suggests, however, that some of the more 'radical' varieties developed relatively late; see the discussion in Chapter 3 and in Singler (forthcoming a and b). The 'decreolization' hypothesis (that is, something perhaps like Saramaccan in many respects gradually becoming more like standard or ordinary English but not having completed the process) has tended to be modified. In defence of this out-of-favour thesis, it might be said that few treatments have taken into account the factor that communication within the early slave community was most likely different from – and in many ways more important to the slaves themselves than – communication with the master.

2 There was a reaction against Turner's (1949) etymology of *tote* as African, some rather extreme attempts being made to find a Middle English source. *DBE*, however, calls it 'Atlantic [English Creole]' and traces it to Kongo *tota* ('to pick up') and Mbundu *tutu* ('to carry'), citing also, after Hancock, Anglo-Saxon *tùtian*. The Old English verb, however, means 'to look' (Bosworth and Toller), posing a very difficult semantic problem; and the [o:] vowel regularly becomes [u:] or [u] (/_t) in modern English. There is a modern English dialectal *toot* meaning 'peek' (*EDD*) which fits the pattern of historical phonology much better and which poses fewer semantic problems than the development from 'look' to 'carry'. Whether or not the word is an 'Africanism', there is a striking uniformity among early sources in attributing the word to slaves. Clapin (1902) calls it 'Much used in the South' but also points out that *tote load* ('as much as one can carry'), *tote team* ('team used in hauling from one place to another') and *toting up* ('going from one place to another') were used by the lumbermen in much more northerly areas.

3 Atwood (1962: 45, 93) attributes *plunder* and *plunder room* in Texas to 'German influence' and not to the older Southern vocabulary he postulates for Texas.

# Chapter 5

# The early history of the Gulf Corridor

Chronologically, the treatment of the South-east and the Gulf Corridor would have to begin almost as early as that of New England. English came into the area late relative to Spanish and French; it is therefore not surprising that the south-eastern states, beginning with Florida and comprising what was in early times included in West Florida, have received very little attention. On the other hand, vestiges of the early language situation seem to survive even into the twentieth century, and the dialect history might possibly turn out to be significant for much of the history of other sections. Having been under five flags (only one less than Texas), and until being sold to the United States by Spain in 1819 subject to loss and reconquest by three nations, Florida has had as varied a history as even Texas and Louisiana since Juan Ponce de Leon and Alvar Nuñez Cabeza de Vaca explored it in the second decade of the sixteenth century. Hernán de Soto landed in Tampa Bay on his way across the Gulf Corridor in 1539, coming up from Peru; his army perhaps even brought a few lasting Quechuanisms (see below) with them as they crossed to Mexico by 1842, leaving de Soto buried in the Mississippi River. The Inca Garcilaso de la Vega, ironically, was the first and still almost ignored chronicler of Spanish exploration of the Gulf Corridor.

After failed expeditions by Fray Luis Cancer and Tristan de Luna, Menéndez founded St Augustine in 1564, along with fortification on the St Johns River (1565), a kind of buffer against the French Huguenot colonies founded in what is now South Carolina. Driven to defensive measures by English attackers including Francis Drake, who was knighted in 1580 for his attacks on the Spanish colonies before he assumed command of the fleet opposing the *Gran Armada,* the Spanish built forts at points such as what is now Hilton Head, South Carolina, first in 1566 and restored in 1577. The English, dominant at sea after the defeat of the 'invincible' Armada, granted a patent to Sir Robert Heath for a region between Albemarle Sound and the St Johns River in 1629–30. By 1665, 200 Spaniards and Indians were said to be 'in hiding' in St Augustine, and in 1668 English pirate James Davis raided it. In 1672 a stone fort – still a tourist attraction – was begun at St Augustine.

The Spanish, menaced by the French on the west when Pierre le Moyne Sieur d'Iberville founded a French colony at what is now Biloxi in 1699, continued their perceived task of converting the Indians into the seventeenth century, building missions from St Catherine's Island to what is now Miami and from St Augustine to what is now Tallahassee. Coping with and trying to convert the Indians must have involved some difficult linguistic tasks, although few treatments of the matter seem to have been written. The name of the Caloosa Indians, for example, is taken for a 'corruption' or 'deformation' of Carlos by Jonathan Dickinson (1697: Appendix), who says that the tribe is 'so called from their sixteenth cacique, Calos or Carlos, who supposedly took his name from that of the emperor Charles V, king of Spain'. Early maps show *Calos* or *Catos*, the latter usually taken as a mistake (Lowery 1959: 436). There are traditions that the first element of the place name Charlotte Harbor represents a kind of compromise between the name of Carlos V of Spain and the Calusa tribe of the area (Harder 1976) and that the presence of the French in the area influenced further change.

It has even been suggested (Read 1934) that Suwanee, the river known more in song than in geographic actuality, was an Indian version of San Juan, although what the English came to call St Johns was another river nearby. It is more conventional that Key West comes from Cayo Hueso by folk etymology, but a special variety without final /-o/ (see below) would make the process (/wes/ being taken for *wes'* and 'expanded' to /west/) a little simpler. By 1702 the English were an important force in East Florida. Governor James Moore of the Council of South Carolina laid siege to St Augustine in that year. In 1728 Palmer devastated north Florida; Oglethorpe did approximately the same thing in 1740. When the British took Havana in 1762, the Spanish were so eager to regain that city that they traded Florida to England for it in the Treaty of Paris of 1763. Thereafter, although the Spanish attacked and recaptured West Florida in 1779–81, the territory was governed by English speakers.

Denys Rolle, MP, started a settlement on the St Johns River in 1765, and leading Tory families came to the territory during the period of the American Revolution. According to Troxler (1989: 567), St Augustine in the last quarter of the eighteenth century 'became a nest of schemers against the revolutionaries in the South and remained so throughout the war'.

The polyglot nature of St Augustine, however, may have made difficult the establishment of any variety of English by the Loyalists. Later, according to Troxler (1989: 563), 'the British government considered buttressing East Florida and pairing it with Nova Scotia as a place of settlement for Loyalists leaving the rebellious colonies.' Furthermore, by 1783 East Florida had come to symbolize both British protection and the availability of land. In terms of Loyalist population, East Florida – probably with the notable exception of St Augustine – in the late eighteenth century was comparable in some respects to Canada. There do not seem to be enough linguistic data to determine whether that comparability extends to dialect. In 1812 a Republic of Florida, somewhat like the later Republic of Texas, was a kind of ally of the United States against the Spanish and French to the west. In 1819 Spain sold its claim on the territory to the United States, and in 1845 Florida became a state. In order to balance Iowa under the prevailing compromise, Florida was admitted as a slave-holding state.

Escaped slaves from Georgia and South Carolina, running away to join the Seminoles, had formed a part of the population through much of the period referred to above. One 'older' Seminole chief had the interesting name Mulatto King (Martin 1944: 228). Able to join the Seminoles on an equal or even superior basis, some of the escaped slaves had themselves become slave owners. There is abundant evidence (Dillard 1972: 150–5) that slaves transmitted a contact variety – probably in a pidgin stage – of English to the Florida Seminoles. As will be seen below, however, other important contact factors entered into the language of the area. In economic terms, the indigo production which caused Turnbull to import 'Minorcans' (among whom were 500 Greeks, Italians and Corsicans), in the then significant number of 1500, and the cattle trade were early activities which linked East Florida to other areas along the Gulf Corridor. The production of the indigo establishes common ground for Florida at the east of the Gulf Corridor and Louisiana at the west. According to Holmes (1967), indigo was being produced in Louisiana by 1729; by 1800 the crop was no longer really successful and as much indigo was being imported as exported. Its production in Florida was apparently somewhat later, but it was a major factor in Turnbull's bringing the Minorcan colony to New Smyrna in 1767. That same group, after many privations, moved to St Augustine, and thus into contact not only with English but with a still strong use of Spanish. There were some problems of loyalty for the group (Quinn 1975), but they kept Catalan in addition to English and Spanish (no mention seems to be made in the records of Italian or Greek), retaining some form of their Mahonese dialect until the present time (Rasico 1986). Later movements of the population, as to Farragut, outside Knoxille, Tennessee, are not well known. It was at St Augustine, still a relatively important port, that Williams (1837) reported the use of 'lingua frança' [sic].

Although evidence is scanty, this maritime variety may have been virtually identical to that of the fishing fleets discussed in Chapter 1; the whaling fleets of the Basques had joined themselves to the Spanish carrying gold to the strait between the Bahamas and Florida at a much earlier date (Axtell 1988: 147). The likelihood that there was some kind of (maritime) continuity with the sailors' varieties discussed in Chapter 1 seems, therefore, very strong. The archetypical Lingua Franca (Sabir) itself was in some ways a kind of trader's Latin (Harvey, Whinnom and Jones 1967) and Latin itself was used as a Lingua Franca a little further west (see below). The maritime linkage, even if Williams was not strictly correct, would be assured; the Catalans are well known as sea-going traders, and Turnbull's mixed group of Greeks, Italians and Minorcans had spent months on the island before proceeding to Florida. At the very least, there was what Malkiel (1976: 586) calls 'the mutual rapprochement . . . convergence' of 'long divergent speakers of Romance'.

There was argument against Williams' report. Rasico (1987 and personal communication) considers that Williams was simply unable to make an accurate evaluation of the communication situation where Spanish and a dialect of Catalan – and English by this time – were involved. Brinton (1859) had earlier presented an unfavourable picture of Williams' linguistic knowledge. Brinton, however, garbled the name of Williams' home town: Picolata. It seems possible that Brinton (and perhaps others) considered the name (*pico lato* – 'broad peak' in standard Spanish) to 'lack agreement between noun and adjective'; suspension of gender agreement is, however, commonplace in Lingua Franca/Creole situations (compare hispanizing Papiamentu *vaca gordo* – 'fat cow'.)

Rasico's presentation of the Catalan/Spanish situation in St

Augustine is impressive, and only minor rebuttals can be offered. Lingua Franca, if it was present as the Williams reference would seem to suggest, would have had only a slight effect on the Minorcan community – the focus of Rasico's interest – and probably none of his conclusions about that community would be in any sense weakened. There are, however, some counter arguments to consider. The 'Minorcans' brought to Florida were first recruited among Greeks, to whom were added Italians. The entire group remained on Minorca for several months, long enough for romantic attachments to be made (Quinn 1975: 24). The distinctiveness of the Greeks and Italians was recognized as late as 1786. Minorca, as a Mediterranean Island, could easily have participated in the functions of the Lingua Franca, especially with so multi-ethnic and multilingual a group as Turnbull's. Rasico (1986: 274) indicates some problem forms which do not appear to be either Catalan or the Spanish of relevant periods. Even if a Spanish- or Catalan-based koiné developed, as Rasico postulates, as the Lingua Franca for the group, late use of the more international contact variety in the port of St Augustine – and elsewhere – would not thereby be ruled out.

Gulf Corridor texts found so far range from broken (somewhat pidgin-like) Spanish used by Florida Indians in Jonathan Dickinson's *God's Protecting Providence* of 1696–7 to Dion Boucicault's *The Octoroon, or, Life in Louisiana* of 1861. The latter was written by an Irishman who himself played Wahnotee, the Indian who spoke 'a mashup of Indian and Mexican' which contains phrases like

No tue Wahnotee 'Don't kill Wahnotee'

where French vocabulary (*tuer* – 'kill') is clearly mixed with a negative marker and other elements which are not French.

Between Dickinson and Boucicault, and possibly a little further south in Louisiana than the latter, Bossu's *Nouveaux Voyages* (1762/1777) contains obvious examples of Louisiana French Creole, which would of course use *pa (pas)* as negator. The postulated 'partly Romance lingua franca' would not be identical to 'Gumbo' French Creole (known by many of its speakers as *Mo couri, mo vini* from the expressions meaning 'I go, went', 'I come/came') but would be similar in many respects. It may well have been a kind of common denominator – useful for trade if not for complex communication – between its speakers and Spanish in some areas and French or French Creole in others. In the area approximately between Lake Charles and Alexandria, Louisiana, the Lingua Franca and Gumbo French Creole may well have crossed paths.

Gumbo would have been spoken primarily by plantation field hand slaves; the other variety by a multi-ethnic (and multi-native-language) highly mobile population. The latter would have been – and remained – an auxiliary language to all its speakers. (This is one point against the accuracy of the fictional Wahnotee.) In the absence of any proof of the retention of West African languages, we would have to assume that French Creole soon became the first language of plantation field hands in Louisiana (essentially the situation described in George Washington Cable's short story 'Bras Coupé').

The Gumbo French Creole of the southern Louisiana plantations seems to have had little influence on the English even of that area. Babington and Atwood's (1961) Louisiana forms like *shivaree*, *armoire* (pronounced like *armor*) and even *lagniappe* seem to have come from other varieties of French. *Lagniappe* fits the pattern of Gumbo but would also be a likely candidate for the partly Romance Lingua Franca. French Creole speakers have, in fairly recent decades, moved into Houston and Beaumont, Texas. That would seem, however, to be a quite recent development, and the influence on English speakers is very little if any. The even stronger possibility is that special maritime forms – if not a maritime variety – were in use in the port of St Augustine and elsewhere along the south Atlantic coast. These forms of this variety, however the final formulation goes, enter into the picture of the Romance language(s) used along the Gulf Corridor and over into Texas and the cattle trade.

The existence of an international maritime-based *parler des îles* (Chaudenson 1974) or *Lenguaje de las islas* (Guitarte 1983) is an intriguing possibility. Where the islands are the West Indies, lexical innovations like *barbecue*, *chigger* or *chiggoe*, *hammock*, *hurricane*, *papya*, *potato*, important to the development of American English, are known to have taken place, most of them attested earlier in Spanish but taken into English from insular or maritime sources. (A late twentieth-century term like *couch potato*, as American as *television time-out*, would be impossible without the Caribbean/Spanish/maritime borrowing.)

Insofar as Spanish-transmitted innovations are concerned, the terms seem to have been borrowed during the time of the *conquistadores*. When French and other languages involved in the European conquest of the Americas come into play, what was used may have been related to Lingua Franca. Pontillo (1975) suggests that Lingua Franca may have been involved even in Columbus's discoveries.

By the third quarter of the eighteenth century, Spanish was certainly in use in both Florida and in the Mexican territory which is now Texas. It may, however, be one of the major distortions of the history of American English that the influence of Spanish upon the English of the two areas has been separated and linkage along the Gulf Corridor ignored. Bowman (1948) objected – rightly, I think – to the limited viewpoint, starting with Friederici (1926)[1] and Bentley (1934), which restricted the Spanish terms borrowed around 1775–1825 to the South-west. There are possibilities not only of transmission from Florida (or even further away) to Texas but also of independent borrowing. When international and multilingual factors are taken into account, surprisingly complex relationships emerge. *Boudin* was apparently borrowed independently from French in the more northern states and in Louisiana, with slightly different meanings. *Charivari* (*shivaree*) not only was borrowed in all the regions of the United States that were once under French influence but has a history going back to a Gallo-Romance designation for a Jewish tradition (Kahane and Kahane 1986: 292).

The economic activity associated with Spanish importations into English in the South-west is, of course, the cattle trade. According to Crosby (1972: 88), the increase of cattle was 'one of the most biologically extravagant events of that [the sixteenth] biologically amazing century'. Cattle were first brought to Mexico for breeding purposes in 1521; it was nearly three centuries later that 'Anglo' Americans crossed into what is now Texas and began learning the Mexican style of cattle herding. A great deal of language learning went with that acquisition of herding practices. By the standard viewpoint, in which a straight-line migration of English speakers results in acquisition of vocabulary from another language already occupying a given territory, an almost 'ecological' model of diffusion seems to work (see Chapter 6). There are, however, some linguistic complications which cast doubt upon that simplistic model.

Although it is beyond doubt that a great deal of learning about the herding of cattle and a great deal of the vocabulary concerned therewith came to the Anglo Texans from the Mexicans, Jordan (1981) pointed out that a cattle trade and some of its terminology developed quite early in the South Carolina area. The cattle trade, with Spanish cattle procured in the West Indies (Mealor and Prunty 1976: 364), developed early in Florida and across the Gulf Corridor, with some input into place names at least. Wacra Pilatka ('a ford or place where cows might be driven across') was translated by the English into Cowford and then later renamed Jacksonville by the Americans after General Andrew Jackson. Pilatka ('ford') remains the name of a small town in north-east Florida.

Among the language forms established in the seventeenth century in the South Atlantic region was *crawl*, from 'colonial Dutch' *kraal* according to *DARE* I but ultimately from the same Iberian source as *corral*, an enclosure filled with salt water in which turtles were kept in the 1682 attestation. The term gained some local importance in Florida, as in the *Crawl Keys* where there were pens for the turtles before they were sent to market.

Although not necessarily developed in the area, the term *cow pen* has a special meaning in early East Coast and Gulf Corridor texts, referring to a larger area than the more recent farming term designates. It is about the same meaning as in Lady Nugent's *Journal of Her Residence in Jamaica from 1801 to 1805*, dating there from the seventeenth century (Wright, ed., 1966: 12). From around 1688 the verb *cowpen* meant 'fertilize land with manure by penning cattle on it'. Darby (1821) referred to the practice in Florida at a somewhat earlier period.

A later term of questionable provenience but perhaps some historical significance is *cracker*, conventionally held to be from the British English term meaning 'boaster'. *DARE* I calls the term 'chiefly S[outh] A[tlantic], Georgia'. The next *DARE* I citation, 1836, deals with the cattle trade and is not entirely inconsistent with the derivation from *whip cracker* (Israel 1970). *Cracker cowboy* developed by around 1850 and was popularized in 1895 by Frederick Remington's painting of that title. Schoepf (1788) cites the term 'for back-woodmen, from the noise, it is said, which they make with their whips when they come to town with their teams'. Highly critical British visitor Captain Basil Hall, by 1828, had become familiar enough with the local vocabulary to call an 'anonymous Georgia squatter' a 'Cracker' (Boney 1990).

The 'Anglo' and Spanish cattle herding practices began to mix in South Carolina and Florida in a manner that anticipated the much greater mixing in the South-west. Very early on, Sir John Hawkins, a slave dealer given to force in acquiring customers (Lowery 1959: 89) and 'a *buccaneer* with cattle raising experience in the Caribbean' (Arnade 1961: 118, emphasis added), had pointed out the potential of raising cows in Florida, even though it was raiding by Englishmen that destroyed the substantial cattle industry that had developed by 1700. It is certain that non-Hispanic practices came to the Gulf Corridor at a fairly early stage. Herds were replenished between 1763 and 1783, when the English were dominant again in Florida.

McWhiney (1988: 70), quoting Jordan 1981, refers to the Anglo practices as

. . . the use of open range, unrestricted by fences or natural barriers . . . the accumulation by individual owners of very large herds, amounting to hundreds or even thousands of cattle . . . the neglect of livestock . . . the marking and branding of cattle . . . overland cattle drives to feeder areas or markets along regularly used trails . . . the raising of some field and garden crops, though livestock were the principal products of the system . . . .

Jordan (1981) shows how the use of cattle dogs was an 'Anglo' characteristic of the Gulf Corridor cattle trade which was supplanted by Mexican techniques. Nevertheless, the term *bulldog*, to describe a technique invented by Black cowboy Bill Pickett, has persisted. Pickett's 'bulldogging' actually involved the biting of the lip of the steer as a dog would, in order to bring it down. When other cowboys abandoned the use of the teeth, they still called the manner of bringing down the steer *bulldogging*.

McWhiney (*ibid.*) stresses that these characteristics 'were traditional in Scotland, Ireland, and Wales long before they were practiced in the South'. The whole matter of the 'Celtic' South is a controversial one; the linguistic evidence, at least, offers virtually nothing in support of that hypothesis (see the discussion in Chapter 4).

Perhaps the chief competitor for Celtic influence, maritime activities were responsible for a great deal of English vocabulary acquired in the New World from various languages, like *filibuster* – from Dutch but not without some special contact language influence on the phonology (Dillard 1985: 99). Among the words derived from Spanish with phonological irregularities would be *stampede*, cited by Schele de Vere (1872) from a Western source. This word is supposedly from Spanish *estampeda*; there is, however, no very good reason why English should reduce Spanish /est-/ to /st-/, considering that English has numerous /est-/ words like *esteem* and *estrange*. An 'irregularity' more generally

distributed in the cattle trade and the area is the representation
of Spanish /o/, in virtually any non-initial environment, by
English /uw/ within a domain or two of the borrowed vocabulary.
Words like *maroon, doubloon, octaroon, picaroon* and *saloon*
would be included. A fuller discussion of this phonological
development follows below.

There are very many irregularities in the conventional
Spanish–English borrowing picture, as well as a much wider
geographic range than that indicated by the designation South-
western. So many 'irregularities' may well add up to one
*regularity*, a 'partly Romance lingua franca of the Gulf Corridor
cattle trade' (Jordan 1981: 250). For various reasons, Romance
background is necessary to account for this variety, and that
beyond the mere fact of vocabulary borrowing.

This variety would have passed through northern Florida –
having had at least some input from South Carolina – thus being
consistent, in its Spanish component, with Bowman's (1948)
concept of double borrowing. Such a variety would explain some
of the apparent inconsistencies in the phonology as well as the
agglutinative morphology of the English cattle trade borrowings.
It would also be consistent with Jordan's (1981) revised picture of
what the cattle trade itself was like.

Where the vowel change /o/ to /uw/ is concerned, a representative form would be *buckaroo*, which has acquired many
meanings in American popular culture.[2] Bentley (1934) traced
the alteration of the final vowel to the influence of the pejorative
suffix *-eroo*, a kind of self-cannibalization because that suffix
itself is sometimes said to have been modelled on the last two
syllables of *buckaroo*. Mason (1960) objected to the traditional
derivation from Spanish *vaquero*, perceiving through the great
variety of spellings in attestations that something special in the
phonology was going on. Mason also made use of the novel (at
that time) discoveries of the importance of Blacks in the Western
cattle trade. He could, however, come up with nothing better
than a highly doubtful derivation from Gullah *buckra*. As a
borrowing of the pre-South-western period, still from something
besides Spanish but with the phonology of a special maritime
variety, the word can be understood in terms of the best of
Mason's insight without the shaky Gullah/'African' derivation.
Related terms can easily be shown to have been in use in the
West Indies at an earlier period and to be different from the also
occurring *buckra/bakra*, which again had a wide distribution in
the United States (see Chapter 3).

The West Indian use of the term seems to have had a trace

already of the pejorative semantic associations of the South-western term which partly motivated Mason to look to *buckra* for a source. Maduro (1961: 32) quotes a text from 1639–40.

> . . . que de donde se probeen de dicha carne es de la a de Buynare [Bonaire] que est a barlobento de Curasao [Curaçao] ya para matar las rreses ba la fragata del capitan Gaspar a la dicha ysla de Buynare a hazer guardia a los baqueros [glossed by Maduro '*veejagers*'] . . . .

Only a few years later, I. deLeon (1654) reported his expedition's experiences with the *boucanniers* of St Domingue. There the French ship took on water and its crew bought food from these hunters, eaters and sellers of island beef. This report describes the *boucanniers* – although not, note carefully, as pirates – as thoroughly immoral *(des gens desbauchez,* p. 157), without religion, and given to expending the proceeds of their trade quickly *(d'argent qu'ils mangent)* before going back to their 'savage' lifestyle.

A very similar statement is found in a Dutch text of only a few years later, Exquemelin's De Amerikænsche Zee Rovers, which has hardly been utilized except as a source for the history of piracy: 'the hunters of cattle *(Stieren)* were called *Boeckaniers*' (my translation). These *Boeckaniers*, like the *boucanniers*, are not pirates as we conceive them; Exquemelin's terms *zee rovers* and *kapers* (below) come closer to their meanings. These buccaneers were named from Tupi *boucan* ('dried meat'), a term brought from Brazil to the West Indies as early as the sixteenth century and used in Nicholas de la Salle's description of the Cavalier de la Salle's discovery of the Mississippi in 1682 (Margry 1875–86, I, 560), as well as in Pénicault's roughly contemporary accounts *(ibid.* V, 390). It was applied by Exquemelin to those who hunted wild cattle, prepared the beef and sold it to ships – much as in the quotations above. They kept slaves whom they treated with extreme cruelty, hunted with fierce dogs, kept aloof from decent society, and indulged in periodic bouts of dissipation, 'so that the bartenders and prostitutes made ready for the coming of the *Boeckaniers* and *Kapers*' (Exquemelin 1678: 22, my translation).

In the very free English translation made in 1684 from an equally free Spanish rendering of 1681, *planters* replaced *Boeckaniers* as hunters of wild cattle, keepers of slaves and social pariahs. In maritime Spanish, at least, *vaqueros* ('veejagers') seems to have replaced the derivative of *boucan*; I can find no mainstream Spanish derivative of the last term in the dictionaries.

The 'language of the islands' seems to have had at one time a varying *vaqueros/Boechaniers*.

By the time of Raynal (1780) the pirates were known as *buccaneers* because of their staple diet of *boucan*. Even earlier seems to have been the concept of '[wild] cattle hunter', on Hispaniola as well as on Bonaire and Curaçao. It is interesting, in this connection, that among de la Salle's company of twenty men in his last journey was Heins, 'a surgeon, and formerly a buccaneer' (Yoakum 1855, I, 34) A little later a Tunica Indian in the Mobile, Alabama area was called *Le Vieux Laboucanier* (letter from Puzan to Périer, 29 December 1731).[3]

In the last example, *boucanier* possibly means 'buffalo hunter' (the name of an associate is Bride les Boeufs – 'Controller/Manager of Cattle/Buffalo'); it almost certainly does not mean 'corsair'. The agglutinated article *la* is feminine in French as in Spanish but occurs here in a variety in which the features [masc] and [fem] are apparently neutralized in some environments (see the place name Picolata above).

Bossu (1777, reporting from about 1762) reports the same association of *boucanier* with 'hunter', in this case with *coureur de bois* from what is now Louisiana. The Florida terms *cowhunt* (Tinsley 1990: 44) and *cowhunter* come closer to this meaning than does *buckaroo*. The timing for the transmission to the South western cattle trade, in or just before the last quarter of the eighteenth century, seems just about right.

On the grounds of regularity of sound change alone, the Spanish/Romance-influenced English of the Gulf Corridor states, up to and partly including Texas, might most parsimoniously be looked at in terms of two varieties.

|     | Variety I | | Variety II |
| --- | --- | --- | --- |
| (1) Spanish /-a/ | /-ah/ | | /-0/ |
| (2) Spanish /-o/ | /-ow/ | | /-uw/ |
| (3) Spanish /-on/ | /-own/ | | /-uwn/ |

Under (1) for Variety II would come *lariat* from *la reata* (also involving the agglutination rule), *stampede* from *estampeda* (also necessitating some rule for deleting /e-/) and perhaps *mott* from *mata*. Maritime familiarity with such a rule is suggested by Barlow's journal (Lubbock 1934: 79) of 1659–1703, which contains the forms *Min-york* for *Minorca* and *May-york* for *Mayorca*. Barlow also calls 'the best sort of red wine' *tent*, presumably from [*vino*] *tinto*, which would seem to point both to loss of /-o/ and neutralization of /e/ and /I/ before a nasal.

Variety I would include the derivations rightly made by Friederici (1926) and Bentley (1934) as well as by their many followers. Here, final /-a/ is retained even when there is considerable 'distortion' in the pronunciation, as in Texan /meheya/ for the town of Mexia. Gender-marking 'inflectional' /-o/ is retained as /-ow/ even in the town name of Refugio, which is /riyfjuriow/ to residents. It would be valid for the Texas borrowings, and possibly for some of those in Florida, pending further investigation.

Variety II would be earlier than at least the South-western contact because of its maritime pre-history, but would have some influences perceivable even in present-day cattle trade usage. Spanish final /-o/ became /-u/, which would regularly become English /-uw/, in maritime Spanish dialects, at least passing through the Canary Archipelago as early as the fifteenth century (Álvarez Nazario 1972: 65). *OED* traces -*oon* from Romance -*on* to maritime usage in the eighteenth century, which probably accounts for (3) in Variety II. Tuttle (1976: 611) asserts that the suffix 'has strong assocations with the Spanish main'. Catalan has some features like (1), (2) and (3) in Variety II; the distribution, however, is not a good match, and the Minorcans tended to turn to seafaring occupations rather than to the cattle trade when they left Turnbull's indigo plantation. There is little evidence that the Minorcans spread far enough west during this period to account for the transmission. Minorcan contribution to both innovation and spread is an intriguing possibility, but unfortunately not a very strong one.

The suffix /-un/ (English /-uwn/) occurs as a late sixteenth-century rendering of the Romance suffix -*on*, which represented a conflation of French -*on* (*dragon* $\rightarrow$ *dragoon*) and Italian, with complex interrelationships within the Romance languages. New World usages, however, tend to come from hispanisms in *ón*, e.g. *cerser-oon* (1545, 'bale, package of exotic products'; Tuttle 1976: 622) from Spanish *serón*; *doubloon* (1622) from Spanish *doblón*; *mar(r)oon* (1666, initially 'runaway slaves on Caribbean islands') with an earlier variant *symeron* (1626) from Spanish *cimarrón* ('wild'); *picaroon* (1624, first used as 'pirate, sea-robber, corsair') from Spanish *picarón*; *quadroon* with a variant *quarteroon* (1707), nearer the source of Spanish *cuarterón*. The latter term, along with less frequent *quinteroon* (1797) from Spanish *quinterón*, doubtless provided the model for *octer-*, *octor-oon*. (Also in this context, compare *barracoon* [1851] – 'rude hut, slave quarters' – from *barracón*.)

Another feature of Variety II would be apparently agglutinated historical articles (ignoring, for these purposes, problems of derivation from Latin and from *Proto-Romance). Some of the forms involved include *Laboucanier* (immediately above); *lariat* (traditionally from *la reata*, but with spellings like *larriett(s)* which may indicate that the writers, in using a kind of gallicized orthography, meant to indicate that they thought the word was from French); *alligator* and its variant *gator*, with maritime usage according to *OED* changing from *lagarto(s)* to *alligator* between 1568 and 1591;[4] and *lagniappe* (see below). Place names like *Lavaca* (originally French, probably *Lavache* according to Harder 1976 and, as often during the period, referring to buffalo rather than to the domestic cow), and numerous Caribbean forms would fit the same pattern. According to Maduro (1962: 30), Dutch *lequan* may have resulted from *e nomber spaño o su deformación iguana*. Something like the following tree, where the branches are unabashedly historical and do not necessarily have grammatical validity, might differentiate the varieties.

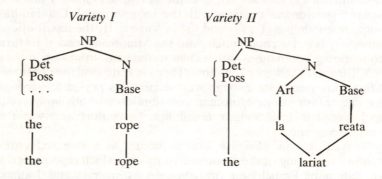

(Final /-a/ deletion and the change of /-o/ to /-uw/ would apply to the right-hand tree, but not to the left-hand.)

The right-hand set of rules would produce numerous Creole forms (Holm 1989: 97) and *lariat*, *Lavaca*, *Laboucanier*, etc.; the left-hand tree would produce English (and, probably gratuitously, French and Spanish) Determiner + Noun sequences. On the other hand, certain rules relevant to standard Spanish, French and other Romance languages, like noun-adjective gender agreement, would not have applied to the 'partly Romance' stage of the development of these forms. The 'lack' of agreement is involved in, for example, *Picolata* and *Laboucanier*.

In the case of *callibouse* (variously spelled) and its relationship to *calabozo*, the phonological rules (which are relational rather than derivational in these cases) of /uw/ for /o/ and 'dropping' of final -a would both apply. Geographically, also, *callibouse* is in the beginning a South-eastern rather than a South-western term. The earliest citation in the dictionaries, including *DARE* I, is from Mobile in 1792; Baily (1797/1983) reported it from Natchez, Mississippi, in 1797. Ingraham (1835, I, 59) wrote of the 'famous Calaboos or Calabozo' in New Orleans. Williams (1837: 207) reported a prisoner's having been committed to 'the calabosa [*sic*]' in Pensacola in 1819. Again, the question of William's observational competence is critical; *calabosa* is intolerable as a rendering of Spanish, but quite possibly accurate in an environment in which the [masc] [fem] features have been neutralized. With numerous later citations from maritime sources, as in Melville's *Typee* of 1846, and some use in Hawaiian Pidgin English in the twentieth century, the term is both earlier and more widespread than its use alongside Spanish *calabozo* in the South-west would indicate. *DARE* I calls it 'scattered, but chiefly S[outh], West', ignoring the international distribution.

Less widespread but similarly prior to the period of South-western borrowing is *cavvyard*, listed in *DA, OED*, and *DARE* I as first from Texas in 1821 but occurring in Anthony Glass's journal for 19 August 1808, from Natchez, Louisiana (John 1983). It is there spelled *cavillard*, a not unexpected orthographic variant. As a doublet for the Spanish *caballada*, it was carried on into the South-west. So, quite possibly, was *cabras*, a 'corrupted' or 'deformed' version of *cabestro* ('halter'); spellings like *cabrass*, *caboras*, *cabris*, *cavraces* and *cabaros* are attested between 1821 and 1848. The dictionaries have it from 1805, which is earlier than Glass's entry, but from a source which is neutral with regard to geographic distribution and in any case earlier than the real Mexican influence on the Anglo cattle trade.

Almost the state word for Louisiana, *lagniappe* provides suggestion of a post-*conquistador* variety of international scope. *Ñapa*, without the agglutinated article, is widely distributed in the West Indies, and *lagniappe* had wider distribution in the South-east at an earlier period (Gillat 1939).[5] Despite Santamaria's (1942) attempt to establish it as an Africanism – with no suggestion as to African source, even of any specific African language – the source in Quechua *ñapa* has no real competitor in the word's etymology. Like the place name Chunchula, Alabama, which Read (1934) traces to the Quechua word for 'intestines', possibly '[cattle] tripe', *la ñapa/lagniappe* suggests a strongly international flavour to the early Gulf Corridor variety.

In Louisiana proper (the state which now bears that name),

which alternated between French and Spanish rule before being sold to the United States by Napoleon in 1803, there was considerable resistance on the part of French speakers to the use of Spanish. (There is a possible parallel here with the linguistic experience of the St Augustine Minorcans, who exhibited a somewhat comparable language loyalty.) Surprisingly, even Louis Juchereau de St Denis – after long interaction with the Spanish governors to whom he professed allegiance, and even a stay in a Mexican prison – used Latin in at least some of his correspondence with the Spanish governors (Hackett 1931, III, 514). In fact, such use of Latin – as might be expected, non-classical in many respects – turns out not to have been infrequent in language contact. Holmes (1965: 110) reports one such use of Latin between an educated Virginian and Governor Gayoso in Natchez in 1796.

The path of the Gulf Corridor cattle trade's contact language apparently ran north of St Martin parish where Gumbo French Creole has been in use since at least as early as 1730. The two shared some structural features, and there may have been some overlap in the Opelousas-to-Alexandria area of Louisiana. French Creole mixed with Cajun French, and there is confusion over whether some linguistic and cultural features (for example Zydeco, the accordion-dominated music indigenous to the area) are Cajun or Creole.

Slaves were first brought to Louisiana in 1719; by 1724 they were almost as numerous as the Whites. The version of French which they brought with them or soon acquired had great resemblance to the Pidgin French in use in the general maritime trade as in slavery. Morgan (1972) pointed out that the Gumbo speakers still use *haler* ('pull') and *tirer* ('milk'). By the time Morgan began fieldwork in the late 1950s, the language was strongly calqued by both Cajun and English. Phrases like /ãrilif/ from English *on relief* and /peyeãtã/ from *pay on time* were used by native speakers to each other, even to family members. Idioms modelled after standard French *avoir envie de* and *avoir besoin de*, although not historically creole, were equally as widely used.

A different variety of French, usually called Cajun (or, very formally, Acadian) came into Louisiana as early as 1757. The best-known sections of the population involved came from Nova Scotia, but there were elements from other parts of the French-speaking world and populations of German, Italian and Spanish speakers were absorbed into the Cajun community at an early period. (One lady of my acquaintance, named Hernandez, stoutly maintained that hers was a Cajun surname. It happened that her Christian name was also originally Spanish but probably reflective of typical exoticism by which many Southern girls are named Anita or Juanita, rather than of direct transmission from Spanish.)

Movement of American English speakers into the Gulf Corridor area must have almost swamped the remnants of French and Spanish in the period between slightly after 1803 and 1870. Laird (1970: 154–5) says that the back country people from the south Midlands 'skirted' the older French and Spanish settlements in Louisiana, after moving 'sparsely' into Alabama and Mississippi. According to him, the lowlands people, who moved later, were first blocked by the Choctaw and the Cherokee but eventually filled the coastal 'flat lands'. The Federal Writers Project on Mississippi, however, says that in the land boom after the Louisiana Purchase of 1803 'people began pouring into Mississippi from the eastern areas, including New England'. Writing of Natchez, Mississippi only, Rothstein (1989: 92) says: 'In 1830 . . . [the population of Natchez was] augmented by a steady flow of migrants from every part of the seaboard.'

Other contributors to Polk (1989) stress the impact of Kentuckians who came down the river in flatboats with their crops and goods; so does Daniels (1962). Aside from the homey terms, there appears to be little evidence that the Gulf Corridor English-speaking population was dominantly from the eastern coastal lowlands.

Giving way to the English-speaking population was a slow process; when one looks beneath the surface, the process often does not seem quite complete even in 1990. The Minorcans of St Augustine held out in the use of their own language, being reported to use it by William Cullen Bryant in 1850 and still knowing some of it when Rasico investigated in the 1980s. Other small groups, like the *isleños* of south Louisiana, the French Creoles of St Martinville and that area (Morgan 1959, 1964, 1972) and the Cajuns have retained their historical languages to some degree to the present time.

The French of Louisiana put up some of the most stubborn resistance to domination by English, making necessary bilingual court cases and other such considerations until the 1860s. Ingraham (1835, I, 117) wrote of an 'olio of languages' in New Orleans. Reporting his tour in the 1850s, Olmsted, bound eastward across the Sabine River, wrote (1854/1953: 317ff) of how the 'gruff Texan bidding' at meal-time – 'Set up, stranger; take some fry' – found a 'smooth substitute' in '*Monsieur, la soupe est servie.'* In the same area, near Opelousas, he found an eastward- ('on the perara [prairie]') born slave who spoke English 'much better than [his Cajun] master', although 'with a slight accent', a master's wife who spoke it 'better'n my mass'r', and a 'Varginny'-born slave who had no 'accent' (from Olmsted's quotations, Black English phonology) at all .

There seems to be some possibility that slaves were agents of the transmission of English into the Louisiana French community. George Washington Cable, in his famous 'Creole Slave Songs' of 1886, calls *plunder*, used as a translation of French Creole *butin* ('personal property'), a usage 'by the Negro' – thus extending to virtually universal dimensions the attribution of the word when all the statements are taken into acount. The transmission into Texas might also have come through slaves, although in this case there is less evidence.

Ditchy (1932) asserted that Cajun was the language of three-quarters of the inhabitants of south Louisiana before 1861, but that the soldier, the labourer and the artisan had been 'Anglicized' by the Civil War. Cable's stories, and to a lesser degree those of Lafcadio Hearne, give evidence of the fight that the Louisiana French put up in giving way to the gradually dominating English. Many French speakers remain, especially in south Louisiana, but French-dominant speakers are extremely rare. CODOFIL's television programme *En Français* on Louisiana Public Broadcasting feature speakers who are obviously English-dominant.

Atwood and Babington (1961) and LeCompte (1967) give good evidence of the survival of French vocabulary in some parts of Louisiana. Some, like *pooldoo* (*poule d'eau*, 'coot' and *bagasse* ('waste from sugar cane') are strictly localized and make good diagnostic forms for Louisiana-born speakers, although probably not all of them know the words. (They are analogous to some extent to *olicook* for the Hudson Valley; probability of occurrence may be higher in dialectology textbooks than in ordinary conversation.) *Bisque* ('a thick, rich soup') spread from Louisiana through much of the nation during the recent vogue for Cajun food. *Coonass* ('a Cajun'), from an obscene French dialectal source metanalysed into a different kind of English obscenity and euphemistically replaced by *coonie*, is not represented earlier than Atwood (1962), but that citation deals with the transmission of the Louisiana terms into Texas.

The status of the French-influenced words and expressions of south Louisiana are not well dealt with in the historical dictionaries. A term like *banquette* ('sidewalk') is not listed until

1841, although Baily (1797: 165) locates one in New Orleans. Baily also identifies *levee* as 'a raised bank'; *DA* lists the word first from a French text in 1719, then from English texts in 1766 and 1851. The French-derived forms obviously characterized Louisiana well before they characterized Louisiana English; the transfer into English must have begun soon after the Louisiana Purchase, but it is a different matter to say just when they became English vocabulary.

It is equally over-simplying to specify the present status of the French terms by citing specific places and dates. Some, like *lagniappe*, which is commercially obsolete, are kept alive by appeal to a picturesque past and for the tourist trade. *Let the good times roll*, as well as its source for translation, *Laissez les bons temps rouler*, is sure to occur anywhere anything resembling a Cajun revival takes place but would seem awkward in most ordinary conversations. In the relatively southern parts of the state, expressions like *it looks to you* ('it's up to you'), *get down* ('get out of a motor vehicle'), *pass a good time* ('have a good time'), *stay still* ('remain still'), *wash the* [i.e. rather than *one's*] *head* ('shampoo one's hair'), *die a light* ('put out a light'), *make dinner* ('cook dinner'), *throw oneself on the bed* ('go to bed'), *make groceries* ('do the shopping'), *catch the rain* (French *attraper la pluie*), *catch a bridge* (French *attraper le pont*, Edmonds 1984) and others like the emphatic repetition ot the subject pronoun (*I do that me*) may find their way to north-western Louisiana, away from any large community of Cajuns, but they show little sign of leaving Louisiana.

In Natchitoches, which is very conscious of its historical significance as the site of Juchereau de St Denis's settlement in 1714, bilingual historical markers have been posted for some years. Around 1988 the French word *rue* (pronounced /ruw/, thus making it aurally indistinguishable from the culinary term *roux*) was reintroduced into street signs. Demeziere Street and St Denis Street became Rue Demeziere and Rue St Denis, but Church Street remained Church Street and Front Street underwent no change. Re-gallicization of this superficial nature is not accompanied by any real spread of French. It is doubtful, furthermore, that the citizens would want to remember Ingraham's (1835, I, 279) account of the 'Spanish and Indian mongrel breed . . . vagabonds, almost to a man' in the area.

Indians of the South-east had a strong tendency to retain their own language, along with French or Spanish in many cases, until fairly recent times. The Chitimacha and the Houma virtually abandoned their native languages for French, although some old persons can remember some texts in the Indian languages. Calques from the Indian languages were probably frequent in early times; Drechsel (1979: 151–2) tells how more than 200 years ago some of them greeted Frenchmen with *'te voilà, mon ami'*, a translation of their own greeting *ichla [esla] mongoula [mɔgula]*. Choctaw in Jena have made some attempts to revive the language, but without great success because the children, who are the crucial group in any such endeavour, could not be interested. The Choctaw-based trade language Mobilian Jargon had a wide currency until quite recent times (Drechsel 1979), but now only a few old people remember a few words. The 150 or so Choctaw of Jena have, according to my own fieldwork, perhaps 50 relatively fluent users of Choctaw who are, however, definitely English-dominant, and perhaps two or three who are Choctaw-dominant. Awareness of English is so strong that the Choctaw word for 'turkey', which resembles an obscene English word, is avoided; the Jena Choctaw avoid even *turkey* in their English, preferring to avoid embarrassment by calling the fowl *ugly head*. The usage extends very little beyond the Choctaw community. On the other hand, *Bayou*, a competitor for *lagniappe* as the best-known Louisiana localism and traceable to Choctaw *bayuk* ('creek, stream') with transmission through French, appeared in an English text of 1766 in which it is clearly a new term to the recorder, and soon spread northward and westward in slightly different meanings. *Bogue*, as in the place name Bogue Chitto ('Big Stream'), is typical of more direct transmission from Choctaw (1814) and is known primarily as a place name.

The designation of a breed of horse, *appaloosa* – 'Perh[aps] from a Louisiana Indian tribal name' (*DARE* I) – is first cited from a German text in 1845 and in English in 1857. Like many other words in American English, *appaloosa*, although not to the same degree as *bayou*, has spread to the east against the settlement pattern as well as to the west with it.

Pidgin English certainly was in use in the area, and a Koasati (Coushatta) speaker of my acquaintance once used the sentence, 'We no see too much [ordinary English *very many*] goose [*geese*] down dere'; he makes traditional Indian toys, among them blow guns which he regularly refers to as *blew guns*.[6] *Numerous Louisianians with antiquarian interests quoted to me the term pickum up truck as the older Louisiana equivalent of pickup truck*. Scattered attestations of Pidgin English in the literature are approximately as numerous as they are for the Eastern Seaboard, although they tend to be in the nineteenth century rather than in the seventeenth and eighteenth.

The slaves who were among the first to bring English into the area had at least some of the phonological features of the Black English Vernacular, and in my own fieldwork, basilect-type Black English has been especially typical of speakers who also use Gumbo French Creole. A small group of Blacks who claim Choctaw ancestry in Clifton, Louisiana, seem (from my own brief fieldwork) to lack any of the linguistic features of the other Choctaw group and to share in general Black English usage. Older Black speakers, even in the more northern part of Louisiana, have the emphatic . . . *me (I don't do that, me!)* which is shared with Cajun English. Black/white differences are clearly perceptible, from the use of *be V-ing* (see Chapter 3) to phonological features like /ant/ for *aunt*, where the white speakers use /ænt/ (Pippin, Dillard and Jones forthcoming). Groups of supposedly mixed bloods, called Redbones, are represented in literary sources (Tillery 1950) as having a very heavy concentration of non-standard features. The term *redbone* may by now, however, simply refer to a person of extremely rural background and non-urban speech.

With increasing Anglo-American dominance, most parts of Louisiana came to be dominated by populations generally speaking some version of Southern or South Midland, which came in especially after the Civil War. North-western Louisiana is part of the region called the Ark-La-Tex and the prevalent speech is generally indistinguishable from that of north-east Texas or south-west Arkansas, although a few Cajun tendencies are recognized. This is not to cast doubt upon *DARE* I's report that *banquette* ('sidewalk') is used in 's[outh] L[ouisian]A and occas[ionally] e[ast] T[e]X[as]'. The term is a rare one, however; even in central Louisiana, elderly people will offer as exotica the information that '*banquette* means "sidewalk" in New Orleans', and it is very doubtful that the term is in everyday use even in that city.

From the twentieth-century viewpoint, the contacts described in this chapter seem to provide only a few provincialisms, quaintly interesting but not especially significant. Looked at from the standpoint of history, however, they can come to appear more important. Contact with Spanish and French continued as the nineteenth-century United States acquired territories and then new states all the way to the Pacific Coast – and, in the case of Hawaii, beyond. Features of the special contact varieties continue to appear in the records, and it is doubtful that American English would have developed into what it is today without them.

## Notes

1 See, however, the comment on Columbus's Spanish in Friederici 1926: VII.
2 The popularity of the quasi-lullaby 'My Little Buckaroo' (composed by M.K. Jerome with lyrics by Jack Scholl ) from the 1937 movie *Cherokee Strip* may be partly responsible for the fact that even some graduate students in English in a class of mine thought that the word meant 'a small child'. The popularity of Buck Owens and His Buckaroos on the television programme *Hee Haw* may well lead some Americans to think that the term means 'country musician'.
3 Rowland, Sanders and Galloway (1984: 114) read the third word *Laboucanie* but refer it to *boucanier* ('smokehouse'). My own reading of the manuscript is *laboucanier*. William A. Read (1963: 82–3) and the context suggests meanings along the lines of 'beef/buffalo hunter'.
4 The number of changes required to make Spanish *el lagarto* into *alligator* – change of two vowels, metathesis of /-rt-/ into /-tr-/ and loss (or repositioning) of final /-o/ as well as agglutination – has been ignored, apparently, by the tradition. All four changes have historical precedent, but it is doubtful that there is much precedent for the concentration of all four in one word. It is beyond the scope of this study, but there is interesting material on *lagarto* itself in Elcock 1940 and Corominas 1972. The maritime varieties, which are the undoubted source of the English word, inherited the results of an extremely complicated process of change. *OED* records forms like *lagartos* from 1568, with no form recording all the changes indicated until Shakespeare's *Romeo and Juliet*. Since Shakespeare's strong point was not maritime activity (witness *The Tempest*), the term must have been fairly well established in British English usage by the time he adopted it. Variant forms continue to be attested from nautical sources for some time. Captain William Dampier's *Voyages* of 1675 records *Rio de la Gartos*.
5 On *ñapa* in the West Indies, see Dillard 1985: 140.
6 The tribe of some 300 at Elton, with a reservation of their own, retain their Indian language much more completely than do the Choctaw, with general English/Koasati bilingualism.

# Chapter 6

# Westward, not without complication

What General Ethan Allen Hitchcock called the 'border defects' of American English would seem to have had an open field once English speakers made their way through the Cumberland Gap beyond the Appalachians and out into the Great Plains, especially if those speakers included Southerners straying from the rigid paths of migration sometimes retrospectively laid out for them. From the puristic point of view to which practically everyone gave at least lip service, there was nothing to impede the spread of 'bad' English to the west except the trivial and probably futile factors of the Lyceum, the Chatauqua and the occasional schoolmarm. These agencies would have little effect in constraining the special varieties developing on the frontier. There was, on the other hand, the continuous growth of 'ungrammatical' structures and prestigeless vocabulary until there is accuracy to (part of) Mark Twain's contention in the 'Buck Fanshaw's Funeral' episode of *Roughing It* (1872) that 'each adventurer had brought the slang of his nation or his locality' with him producing a situation in which 'Slang was the language of Nevada.'

It is important that *of his nation* not be left out of Twain's report. It is essential that the contact with the other languages (American Indian) which were already in the Great Plains and the West, and the European languages (mainly French and Spanish) which were there as soon as or earlier than English not be left out. That the occupational vocabulary ('jargon' or 'slang') of the Great Plains and the West took a great amount from occupations practised elsewhere, especially that of the seafaring men, is too easily left out. What is also often overlooked is that, in addition to heading for 'the mines of California in the "early days"', as Twain asserts, the 'slang' of many nations and localities turned round and headed back east.

In the simplistic diffusion model which has been used for American English, such west to east (or north to south, south to north, one direction and then back again) movement has hardly been allowed to be possible. It is relatively easy to trace out the essentially west to east diffusion of vocabulary like the elaborate terminology of poker, faro and other diversions and vices of the frontier and the West. Otherwise, the simplistic straight line has been constantly asserted even without any special evidence being offered.

This movement is held to have been channelled – practically controlled – by the physical geography of the continent. Statements are very familiar in the dialect literature. Writers such as Wolfram and Christian (1976: 13) assert that at some unidentified point in our history 'natural barriers' separated unnamed groups; 'discontinuities' are held to be traceable to either social or geographic patterns, although precedence seems to be given, where possible, to the latter.

Human beings are too complicated for this kind of diffusion model, which can provisionally be called the 'ecological' model.[1] In such a model social factors are allowed, but usually limited to stratification. The Linguistic Atlas of the United States and Canada notoriously allowed for only three social groups, with Class I – uneducated, untravelled and generally unsophisticated – the basis for dialect patterning. But human beings have shown (in very many studies, most of them conducted outside the United States) patterns of variation in terms of age and sex grading, ethnic group membership and loyalty, religious affiliation and occupation. Pickford (1956) showed that sociologists had found the last to be more important than region of residence in American social affiliations. But Americans – and human beings in general – who identify with their occupations can change jobs and can change religious or educational status. It is the merest truism that they change age grades, although aggressive persons often change more rapidly than others. And in the twentieth century even sex change has proved not entirely impossible.

Simpler organisms can be more easily subjected to such limitations. If human beings are too complex for the ecological model, bees are the kind of creature that is not. Coming to the New World not too long after the human settlers (c. 1621), bees depended entirely upon the environment for their migration patterns. Since they found an environment to their liking, they multiplied prodigiously and spread at an impressive rate.

Bees had a symbolic function already in the colonies. Wood (1634: 55), dealing with the necessity of repulsing the Spaniards, wrote: 'and when the [English] plantations are growne noted in the eyes of the comon foes for wealth, it is hoped that when the Bees have Honey in their Hives they will have stings in their Tailes'. On the frontier they had a fairly important semiotic function. Indians who found a swarm of bees in hollow trees knew that the tribe would soon have to go further west. The 'English flies' or 'white man's flies' generally formed an advance guard 100 miles or so ahead of the European human frontier. With the White man would also come horses, gunpowder and smallpox, but the bees were often the first warning sign; along with white clover (the 'white man's foot'), another importation, the bees gave warning (Furnas 1969: 38–9; Crane 1983: 127).

Melville, in a fit of relativistic righteousness, could inveigh against the 'Anglo-Saxon hive' which had 'extirpated Pagans from the greater part of the North American continent' and had 'extirpated the greater portion of the Red race' (1846: 276 ). Confronted with the notion that the White colonization of the continent was a simplistic one having animal (or insect) rather than human characteristics, Melville might, in such a mood, have agreed. In more serious moments, however, no one could make a literal application of such a metaphor. The apian colonization was no more the same as the human than the bee dance is on a conceptual level with human language. A diffusion model which fits bees – or horses, or cattle – is certain to be too simple to fit human beings.

It is not that bees, like other creatures simpler than human beings and other patterns simpler than human language, were unimportant on the frontier. The Indians collected honey from the hollow trees, although they did not in general keep bees. For backwoods frontiersmen, 'Honey and maple syrup seem to have been particularly important because they supplemented the standard diet, with high-energy food at a sensitive and vulnerable time of the year, the spring . . . Some Missouri pioneers were said to subsist largely on "animal food and wild honey", and bee-tree lore was abundant' (Jordan and Kaups 1989: 231). That lore produced, or transmitted, a number of compounds. A type of frontier outcast was called a *honey hunter* or a *bee hunter*. There were other compounds like *bee gum* ('hollow tree or log used as a beehive', attested in 1817), *bee gum hat* (1880, in Joel Chandler Harris's *Uncle Remus*), *bee bird* ('kingbird', 1862), *bee catcher* ('robber fly', 1859), *bee bread* ('red clover', 1889).

Attempts are constantly made to derive the cooperative

working term *bee* (1769, from Boston) from some other source.
Later, and primarily on or close to the frontier, it developed into
*breaking bee, chopping* . . ., *painting* . . ., *paring* . . ., *apple-
cutting* . . ., *roofing* . . ., *shingling* . . ., *quilting* . . ., *sewing*
. . ., *husking* . . ,, *spelling* . . . from whatever source was actually
the true one. *DARE* I resorts to a far-fetched 'alteration' of
'*been, bean* var[iant] of Engl[ish] dial[ectal] *boon*' but admits that
there may have been an 'allusion to the social behavior of the
insect'. The practices, if not the terms, may have received some
input from native Americans. Axtell (1988: 119) points out how
'Iroquois clan matrons led workbees of women into the
cornfields' without, of course, suggesting an Indian etymon for
the term. *DARE* I allows *put the bee on* ('demand from or
attempt to extort from') to be a reference to 'the bee's stinging
and to *sting* to cheat, defraud'. It also sees the insect in the child's
concession to those not 'caught' in the game of hide and seek:

Bee, bee, bumblebee
[who] all['s out can] come in free.[2]

*DARE* field notes record this call – in the truncated form
indicated above – from North Carolina in 1966, but children in
East Texas in the 1920s and 1930s used the extended form.

Westward spread of '*bee* words' had taken place much earlier,
and much more extensively than the '*lamb* words' treated in
Chapter 1. Utah, nicknamed the Beehive State, was almost
named Deseret for a word in the *Book of Mormon* meaning
'honeybee' instead of its eventual naming after an American
English version of the name of an Indian tribe. There was a
Beehive House in Great Salt Lake City by 1858.

A more simplistic type of westward movement could hardly be
imagined, but the kind of spread the *bee*-words represent is
unusual in this westward movement. The only other approximation of the ecological model of change, in American English at
any rate, is provided by the adaptation of names for plants and
animals (*robin, buffalo* . . .) not really identical to the European
animals whose names were carried over, and by adapted,
mispronounced and folk-etymologized loanwords from Indian
languages (*skunk, woodchuck, persimmon* . . .). If such differences were all, Mencken would hardly have been motivated to
write of 'the American language'. Collocation and compounding
of those terms, on the other hand, contributed considerably
more. *Buffalo* contributed to *to buffalo someone* (1896, 'to
frighten or bluff another'), *to skunk* came to mean 'to shut out in

a game', and a *shif(t)less skunk* was a totally useless person. *That's a huckleberry over my persimmon* was used in frontier Tall Talk perhaps in allusion to the incomprehensibility of polysyllables in other contexts.

Moving out into the Great Plains, the frontiersmen were quickly exposed to the language of a fur trade which was perhaps earlier French than English. Notably, French *médecin* had taken on a special significance among the Indians, and it was the Indian meaning that the frontiersmen picked up. What painter and Indian enthusiast George Catlin (1973, I, 71) reports for the term – 'a trite saying of the country, "That man lying down is *medicine* to the grizzly bear" [after a female grizzly has sniffed around their mattresses without harming the sleeping men]' – is almost equivalent to what Melville reports, not too much later, for the Pacific-derived *taboo*. As Catlin (1973, I, 35) put it, '[among the Indians] the word "medecin" has become habitually applied to everything mysterious or unaccountable.' Catlin uses *white man's medicine* (his gun and pistols, *ibid.*, p. 36), *medicine men* (p. 35), *medicine bag* ('personal charm or talisman of the Indians', p. 36), *forming his medicine* ('walkabout experience of young Indian boy') and numerous other such compounds. The *OED* traces the term to the early nineteenth century, starting with Zebulon Pike's *Sources of the Mississippi* (1807) and including George Catlin among the relatively early citations.

The terminology spread widely on the frontier and in the West. Rollins (1922: 79) reports references to 'Indian customs, beliefs, or terms' like *making medicine* ('preparing for a journey' or 'planning an enterprise'), *good* (or *bad*) *medicine* depending upon the sufficiency of the preparation, and *breaking the medicine* [of a rival] ('thwarting [the rival's] attacks or efforts').

On the frontier, as in later American English, compounds appear to be the most important development. Phrasal compounds or 'collocations' (in the terms of the late British linguist J. R. Firth) may have been even more important than the lexically simpler two-word (often noun-noun) compounds. Students of the frontier who comment on the language are regularly motivated to write of 'metaphors and figures of speech'. Clark (1969: 225) includes examples like *staked and ridered*, *slick as elm bark*, *caught with his britches down*, *dull as a frow*, *fastened his nuckles to the ground*, *stumped* and *shooting shy of the mark*.

The collocations or 'metaphors' of various occupational groups contributed to the vocabulary differences of the West. Teamsters among those moving westward through Indian territory used *all set* ('Everything is ready; let's go', 1844), *catch up* 'catch and harness horses or other draft animals', 1843) and *stretch out* (1862), the last obviously a call to proceed on the way.

Perhaps something besides occupational collocations, metaphors or 'jargon' entered into the vocabulary creation – especially the innovating of phrasal compounds – of the West. Foreman/ Marcy (1939: 32) reports *seeing the elephant* – 'a slang expression, one of the commonest heard among the California emigrants'. Hulbert (1931: 41) thought that the expression 'might have arisen from the inquiry of a person who had gone to a circus'. In spite of the known reluctance of scholars to allow for pure innovation, imaginative creation seems to have played some part in the vocabulary innovating of the frontier and the West, particularly in the much-discussed Tall Talk. In new and different surroundings, and in at least some contact with a number of strange languages and special varieties, those moving westward must have come to think of phrase innovation as something like the ordinary course of things. (See Dillard 1985: 154–5 for an example of direct translation from Indian sign language.)

One of the major factors in the frontier's unreconstructed diversity, insofar as language went, was the persistence of Pidgin English, or of some maritime contact variety. As has been pointed out over and over again, pidgin languages fare best in coastal or insular areas, or on ships, where our map-making methods serve them poorly. This had apparently been the case in the early colonies, where New Englanders heard a vast amount of what was or was to become American Indian Pidgin English (AIPE) from an early period. Perhaps because of the special nature of the contact, AIPE spread inland and across the continent to Arizona, Nevada and California. Along the way, and perhaps especially in those areas, it met, interacted with and had reciprocal influence on several other contact varieties.

The claim that the frontiersmen used pidgin is as old as James Fenimore Cooper's *Redskins* (1846: 148). For the cowboy, Rollins (1922: 78) reports:

> Pidgin-English contributed its quota of words and phrases. Its 'long time no see 'em' [elsewhere *long time no see*] conveniently set forth the status of a searcher for some lost object, while its 'no can do' [elsewhere in the affirmative *can do*] definitely expressed personal impotence.

Brandt and McCrate (1979) reported, from a study primarily of documents, the use of Pidgin English

> . . . especially for the Chinese, and [the research] also shows

the presence of numerous other ethnic groups in Arizona drawn together by developing mining activity or military service. The presence of sizeable numbers of Black soldiers and cowboys, and the attested use of Pidgin English by Native American groups, ethnic miners, and soldiers of both races all interacting together, necessitates the use of a commonly understood code.

Stuart (1925: 54–5) reports a miner named John Bidwell who had 'about twenty Indians working for him . . . during the years 1848 and 1849' and a Samuel Neal, who had come into California with Fremont in 1844, who 'also had about twenty Indians working for him'. Stuart reported great mining success for both employers of Indians.

In their dealings with these Indians, the white frontiersmen apparently took with them terms like *papoose*, *squaw* and others of provenience from further east. According to Clark (1969: 465–6), 'Most of the history of the American frontier is colored by the white man's relationship . . . with the Indians', and terms reflecting both fear and hatred were used by frontiersmen about the Indians: *savage, red devils, dogs, niggers, friends, bucks, and squaws*.

Catlin is among the first to give evidence of the Indians in the Far West. (Lewis and Clark had preceded him by a quarter of a century and had heard from their cook Charbono some of the French used in the area, like *boudin*, but it would appear that Pidgin English had not reached that part of the West before their arrival.) Working among the Dakotas (Sioux), Mandans, Mohegans, Oneidas, Cherokees and others, he has a great deal to say about their languages and actually includes a comparative list of about 300 words from Mandan, Blackfoot, Riccaree, Sioux and Tuskarora (1973, II, 262–5). He refers frequently to interpreters, and probably depended upon them for most of his communication with the Indians. There are indications, including the report that at Camp des Moines 'I was called a "*Grande Capitaine*"' (II, 142), of his use of French in an area where their language operated for some time before there were English speakers. (There are also some indications of bad French – along with inaccurate zoology – when Catlin quotes a guide as saying '*voilà sa* [sic] *mari*' of a bear!) On the divide between the Ouachita (*Washita* in Catlin's orthography) and Red Rivers, Catlin reports a talk in which a Spaniard 'we luckily had with us' acted as interpreter to 'Camanches [sic], who spoke some

Spanish' (II, Letter No. 41, p. 56). In the same letter, Catlin (II, 54) cites *stampedo*. (For discussion of this form, see below and Chapter 5.)

Among the Dakota, Catlin documents – one of many from the period – the use of the traditional 'How' ('How, how' 'How, how, how') at Indian meetings. This usage has been travestied by films and bad novels, and there are many who object to its attribution to Indians. Catlin, however, was a strong opponent of the stereotyping of Indians. In a classic statement, DeVoto (1947: 396) establishes Catlin's paintings as the first counteraction to the stereotypical Indian portrait: 'in the costume of a Mohawk (which two centuries had made familiar) and posed either in a Cherokee cornfield or an Ojibwa canoe'. In his description of the 'cruel' and 'appalling' sections of the Mandan initiation ceremony, when the 'demon of terror of vulgarity' is conducting an apparently sexual rite as part of the initiation of the boys, Catlin (I, 168) uses two long quotations in Mandan – apparently where the material is not suited to be printed in English. Catlin does not tell how he arrived at these Mandan quotations – or, indeed, how he devised the orthographic system for them – but it is likely that he was aided by an interpreter. Nowhere is there any indication that Catlin learned the languages of the many Indian tribes with which he dealt.

Catlin concerns himself with the English abilities of a few of the Indians. Among the Mohegans, 'the remains . . . of the once powerful and celebrated Pequots of Massachusetts', now located near Green Bay, Wisconsin, Catlin observed : 'John W. Quinney . . . in civilized dress, is a civilized Indian, well-educated – speaking good English – is a Baptist missionary preacher, and a very plausible and eloquent preacher' (II, 103). The contemporary chief of the Oneidas was known as Bread, was well educated, and was observed as 'speaking good English'. No examples are given directly; whether the Pidgin English examples quoted immediately below exemplify such 'good English' remains a matter of conjecture.

In a kind of philosophical reflection upon the meaning of his experiences with the Indians, but apparently talking about Sioux (Dakotas), Catlin quotes the Indians in English:

> You, white man, where you come from? (From England, across the water.) How white man come to see England? how you face come to get white, ha? (II, 230)

> Among white people, nobody ever take your wife – take your children – take your mother, cut off nose – cut eyes out

> – burn to death! . . . Then *you* no cut off nose – you no cut
> out eyes – *you* no burn to death – very good

> . . . . the Indians' Great Spirit got no mother – the Indians
> no kill him, he never die. ( II, 241)

Such use of pidgin was not confined to the West. New England itself
– or at least select parts of it – was re-exposed to Pidgin English at
various points. In the early nineteenth century a Hawaiian convert
to Christianity had travelled extensively before he came to Connecticut, was converted and became a model of piety. Here is part of his
reported speech (Beecher and Harvey 1818).

> Owyhee gods! They *wood*, burn; Me go home, put 'em in a
> fire, burn 'em up – they no *see*, no *hear*, no *anything* . . . We
> make them – our God . . . *He* make *us*.

The quotation comes from the international missionary journal
*The Religious Intelligencer*, which, for the period of the early
nineteenth century, indicates something close to worldwide
distribution of conversion experiences and expressions of faith in
clearly pidgin English. Attestations are widespread and have
been widely printed (e.g. Dillard 1985: 12–25).

In a frontier area like Texas, rather early Pidgin English
attestations can be found. A letter of 14 February 1846, written
by Josiah Pancoast tells how an Indian 'come out to him and said
you man, you lost your Horses me sorry for you Indians steel
[*sic*] them me (good) Ingon [*sic*] . . .' (Chabot, ed., 1940).

The precise nature of language contact phenomena – both the
languages (pidgin and other) and the pragmatics of the contact –
has always been rather difficult to establish. Political considerations have always made some commentators reluctant to ascribe
'bad' English to the native Americans; even observers like Catlin
tend to use a highly elevated style which apparently represents
the interpreters' rendition of Indian speech, giving examples in
AIPE only coincidentally and to a restricted degree.

The practice of Catlin, for example, is about like that of
Granville Stuart, who records a great deal of material about
communication with the Indians in essentially his own variety of
English and gives one example of an Indian's actual speech, in
Montana around 1886 (Stuart 1925: 112).

The language is complex, involving subordination by parataxis
where *spose* (*suppose*) is also used.

> Wild turkey hard to kill. Indian break some stick, turkey
> stop one second, say maybe Injin [*sic*], Injin be good hunter
> he get shot. White-tailed deer, he hear some little noise way
> off – say Injin – W-u-zz he gone, Injin no get one shot.

Whatever the limitations of Stuart's transcription practices, there is evidence of Pidgin English structures like negation with

NP no V

and copula forms like

NP be NP

Citations like these, apparently substantiating James Fenimore Cooper's claim that Pidgin English was the frontier lingua franca, are superabundant in the literature of the nineteenth-century West. Beginning in the seventeenth century up until the early twentieth, ranging from New England to the Pacific North-west, in something of the extremely rough (with frequent discontinuities and retrogressions) progression involved in the generally accepted east to west dissemination of dialects of American English, the Pidgin English forms tend to precede any that can be reliably assigned to dialect regions. Insofar as any straight-line progression goes, the pidgin forms tend to move along with the advancing frontier. At least part of the general unwillingness to acknowledge the presence of Pidgin English may be associated with our general reluctance to deal with the frontier as it actually was.

The unfortunate social effects of frontier contact must have had considerable influence on that limitation of direct reporting. Although Catlin has been called 'Rousseauistic', his deprecation of the 'drunken, naked, and beggared state of Indians on the frontier, given to all kinds of excesses' in contrast to the 'prudency and self-denial of tribal life' (1973, I, 123) has the value of first-hand observation. Elsewhere Catlin attacks those who judge Indians from 'the poor, degraded, and humbled specimens which can be seen along our frontiers'. He complains about 'this blasting frontier'. The extensive use of Pidgin English is likely to have been more usual along such a frontier than where the tribes had little contact with Whites. Whatever the judgement about such matters – frontier contact and frontier use of Pidgin English – both seem to be unalterable facts of history.

Whether or not pidgin-transmitted, vocabulary borrowed from the north-eastern Indians went along to the Great Plains and further west. Catlin himself uses squaw, with cognates in Naragansett and Massachusetts, 'with related forms in many other Algonquian dialects' (OED), and sachem (1973, I, 186), first attested from Bradford (1647); Catlin referred to a leader of the Minatarees who lived eight miles above the Mandans on the banks of the Knife River, a tributary of the Missouri. The same term, extended in semantic range, was used of (White) higher-ups in the Tammany Society of New York by 1890 (*OED*).

Other kinds of diversity came from varying directions. Even during the period (approximately 1720 to 1790) of extreme levelling of American English, approaching the status of a koiné, the ports of the East Coast and the ships that arrived at them were the loci of very different dialects. There are many references in the historical sources to the special varieties used by sailors. But some of the maritime forms came from the other direction, seldom with the approval of those reporting. Dana, off the coast of California, in 1835 saw it in a negative sense: 'an Englishman of about six and twenty years', whose knowledge of French could be accounted for by his years in the smuggling trade between France and England, neverthless puzzled Dana because 'his cutter education would not account for his English . . . for he . . . spoke with great correctness'.

There are many indications that maritime usage was considered the opposite of that 'correctness'. It included, but was not limited to, maritime Pidgin English. It soon exerted its influence on the diversity of the frontier, but in some ways it was also important in the language of the East Coast.

During the War of 1812, the 'coasting trade' carried on with horse-drawn wagons, especially to the southern states, was slowed down so much that nautical accounting methods were recommended and even adopted. It was proposed that owners should name their vehicles 'as in the case of ships' (McMaster 1895, IV, 22) and that logs apparently on the maritime model should be kept as to their points of origin and destination, date of departure and arrival, etc. Naming the wagons was proposed, and was carried out with some apparent humour. Among the names were 'Neptune Metamorphosed', 'Mud-clipper' and 'Don't Give Up the Ship'.

A little later on the East Coast, one of the seemingly minor influences but one with a surprising continuity and spread in American life was the developing game which became baseball. The frontier itself apparently did not nourish sport – at least, not in the sense of physically competitive games which required permanent installations like playing fields. (For the importance of card games on the frontier, see Dillard 1985: 167–72.) But the Eastern cities soon developed, out of a complex of British games, what became the American 'national pastime'. The early teams were in Boston and New York and in other eastern cities where the ports were of primary importance: 'baseball . . . began to fan out from New York, and interest in the new sport was felt in such

neighboring cities of the Atlantic Seaboard as Philadelphia and
Baltimore' (Glieb 1950: 25).

The regionalism *cowhanded* ('awkward'), from a Gaelic and
Irish source is attested first in 1834 and seems to have remained,
in a sense, specialized to a baseball grip, in the state of New York
until about 1931 among sandlot players. (The grip, called *cross-
handed* elsewhere, was not used by really proficient players and
possibly never among professionals.) Early attestations of the
terms have not so far been found, but it seems significant that
going around Cape Horn was important enough to a Yankee
clipper (a shipping term which seems eventually to have provided
the nickname of San Francisco-born New York Yankee centre
fielder Joe DiMaggio) for *around the horn* to become part of
general American phraseology. According to Albion (1939), the
development of the Cape Horn route coincided immediately with
the development of New York from fourth to first place among
American ports. In baseball, *around the horn* refers to the
longest of double plays – usually third to second to first. It
functions also in lumbering (McCulloch 1958) and police work
(Goldin, O'Leary and Lipsius 1950). Dana (1841) did not include
it in his list of seaman's terms, just possibly because he took his
list from sailors on the West Coast where it was not in use. But
Willard (1828) pointed out that sailors' talk frequently referred to
Cape Horn. At his time, Cape Horn was usable as a metaphor
for extremity.

More certainly, maritime terminology abounds in baseball.
Batters are *on deck* when batting next and *in the hold* (made into
*hole* when nautical associations were forgotten) when second on
the waiting list. Batted balls were *fair* or *foul*, terms familiar at
sea for successful or unsuccessful manoeuvres. In 1856, a pitch
out of what we would now call the *strike zone* was *foul*; the
attestation is from New York, as is the 1865 citation of *fair* for a
pitch that would be a strike if the batter did not swing. The term
*foul*, in the present-day sense of a batted ball that does not go
inside the playing field, is first attested from Chicago in 1844.
Balls struck soundly became *line drives* or *liners*, like ropes
(lines) at sea. An adaptation into baseball of the nautical term
*larrup(ing)* from *lee rope*,[3] which came to mean 'especially good'
(M. I. Dillard 1980), is a logical source for the nickname of
Larrupin' Lou Gehrig, whose line drives were the antithesis of
team-mate Babe Ruth's towering flies. Even *strike out* may have
nautical associations; an early nautical use meant 'to hoist from
the hold and lower to the dock' (*OED*), and *to strike* ('lower [a
flag]') as a term of defeat was common.

Baseball remained an East Coast sport until after the Civil War, when the game began to 'spread north, south, east, and west' (Glieb 1950: 37). Its terminology spread with it, and it became important in casual American speech in the twentieth century, when phrases like *get to first base* and *score* developed widespread usage in other domains.

But even in the relatively unathletic West, nautical terminology became important, perhaps naturally because the kind of long-range migration the pioneers were undertaking had only maritime precedents within usable memory. The wagons on which the pioneers travelled were called, perhaps not without some reference to the humorous appellations of the wagons in the coasting trade, *prairie schooners*. *Caboose*, from the term for the ship's kitchen ultimately going back to Dutch, became the term for the supply wagon, heavily loaded and likely to proceed slowly and to be the last in the train. The transfer to the last car on a railway train, used for living and eating by the train crew members, gives the word its best-known meaning in American English, although not in British English (Jensen 1981: 155).

The term for a camp cook, *coosie*, which Ramon Adams (1944) wanted to trace to Spanish *cocinero*, has the usual phonological problems with the stressed /-o/ (see Chapter 5). It may be from maritime *cusina*, from Italian *cucina*, which Kahane, Kahane and Tietze (1958: 20) specifically compare to what was otherwise called *caboose* at sea.

Forms like *chuck* (in *chuck wagon*) may well have been nautical. *Chuck* ('food, grub') has been known in (British) English since 1850, but an 1864 attestation refers to 'chuck, used by sailors for biscuit', and the earlier citations are non-commmital as to terrestrial/maritime provenience and usage. *Chuck* gave rise to *chuck wagon* (1890), *chuck line* ('places where a cowboy can get a free meal', 1903) and *chuck line rider* (1928), as well as *chuck wagon chicken* (1944), although the general cultural background would lead one to expect earlier occurrence for at least some of these.

Like many other Western terms (*cow)hand* has obvious nautical parallels and probably a source therein. Schele de Vere (1872: 343) pointed out that *bear a hand* was borrowed from the sea phrase and that 'even in the Far West' it meant 'to be active and not to delay'.

Railroad terminology, as Farmer (1889) pointed out very early, took a great deal of its terminology from its predecessor, water travel – especially ocean transportation. Terms like *bill of lading, all aboard, freight,* and others became familiar through the railroads to Americans who did not know the nautical source forms. According to Pyles (1952: 135), in his boyhood railroad conductors were given the title *captain*, although Pyles says 'this custom seems to have died out in most parts of the country'. Pyles ties this usage to 'the American attitude toward titles' – even phony ones (1952: 134) – and makes it ultimately a matter of American 'turgidity', but *DARE* I establishes it as 'by ex[tension] from *captain* of a ship, first to "a stagecoach driver" (1835) and then to "a railroad conductor"' (1867) and it may simply be a typical adaptation. Pyles indicates that the usage was general (i.e. non-regional) before it began to 'die out'. The timetable of changes – ships to railroads – fits an important pattern in the developing commercial life of the United States and in the development (or exploitation) of the West.

There are others. Slumgullion Pass, in the Rocky Mountains, seems likely to have whaling associations. Sprague (1964: 339) points out that 'some seafaring New Englander noted the splotched yellow fold which reminded him of slumgullion, the refuse draining from the cutting up of a whale for its blubber. The name was applied to Slumgullion Pass'. Mark Twain's use in *Roughing It* (1872), the first recorded in the dictionaries, deals with something that 'pretended to be tea'. By 1887 it could mean 'a muddy deposit, a mining sluice' (*OED* II). In this respect it may be significant that ships, including whalers, which pulled into California around 1848 were in danger of losing their crews, who preferred to run away to the gold region than remain on board. There is still a kind of poor man's stew called *slumgullion*, first listed from 1902 by *OED* II.

Colloquial American terminology – not always distinct in these respects from British usage – shows a large amount of this maritime influence; circumstances, although not in all cases clear attestations, favour its coming in during the early-to-mid decades of the nineteenth century with the frontiersmen and pioneers. A vessel which got its *clearance papers* had *cleared out* (Chase 1942). In Krio of Sierra Leone the term means 'Go away, esp[ecially] as an exhortation' (Hancock 1971: 116). Hancock also observes that the expression is 'first recorded in England as nautical'. In colloquial American English, my own intuition is that 'clear out!' – an order, and not a respectful one – is more normal than the *OED*'s first American citation (from Thoreau, *Letters*, 1961): 'The doctor . . . tells me that I must "clear out" to the West Indies or elsewhere' – although of course Thoreau could have travelled only by ship to the West Indies. Had Thoreau chosen – or known – *light out* in approximately the same meaning, he could have used another phrase with maritime associations. It is found in Dana's *Seaman's Friend* (1841) and Mark Twain's *Letters from Hawaii* (1866).

By about 1850, cases like Melville's Captain Bildad would not have been rare: 'Something of the salt sea yet lingered in old Bildad's language, heterogeneously mixed with Scripture and domestic phrases' (Melville 1851: 85).

A mere reconstruction from modern meanings does not always reveal the import of those 'salt sea phrases'. Hayford and Parker (Melville 1951: 226) point out that *tell it to the marines* connoted, in Melville's time, the special credulity of the marines in maritime matters. Melville used a similar phrase in *Typee* (1846: 298)[4] 'says the nautical sportsman, "Talk taboo to the marines. . ."'

If the bee provides the closest example of a stoichastic immigration paradigm for the early period, perhaps the horse does so for a slightly later one. Introduced (or, geologically, reintroduced) by the Europeans, the horses found as good an environment on the plains as the bee had in the forests, and the mammals proved more useful and more important than the insects to human beings. There should therefore be much more horse lore and many more horse terms than bee terms.

Wild horses multiplied on the plains. As is well known, they tended to transform the lives of Indian tribes. Catlin (1973, I, 142) reported the Indians on the upper plains riding wild horses that had strayed from the Mexican border as far as 3000 miles north to Lake Winnipeg. They were so plentiful that an individual man might own as many as twenty of them, and they were taken with a leather thong known as a *laso* [*sic*], a term which was also *lassoo* with the familiar /-uw/ for /-o/ among some horsemen and cattlemen. As late as 1945, the pronunciation was available to rhyme with *Sue* in the popular song 'Sioux City Sue' by Roy Freedman and Dick Thomas, although it served to contribute to the quaintness which was the primary gimmick of the song.

Even before Catlin, horses of this type had been called *mustangs* – the word itself one of the earliest, and most problematic, of the South-western borrowings from Spanish. Whether by imitation of the Indians or the Mexicans or for some other reason, the cowboys adopted the practice of having a *string* of horses: circle horses, roping horses, cutting horses, and perhaps even a bronco. The last, according to a late source (1946), needed only to be cowboy broke; the name was taken from a Spanish word with an interesting history tracing back to a broken branch, according to Corominas.

The tradition, especially beloved of movie cowboys, of one preferred and faithful mount had some basis in fact. Granville Stuart (Phillips, ed., 1957, II, 183), reporting on Montana in the 1880s, wrote : 'Each cowpuncher owned one or more fine saddle horses, often a thoroughbred, on which he lavished his affections, and the highest compliment he could pay you was to allow you to ride his favorite horse.' The string of five or six horses, on the other hand, was usually supplied to the individual cowboy by the owner. Because of proprietary pride among the cowboys, taking away one of a string – *breaking the string* – was an insult. The term spread to other domains, so that a 'string' of victories by an athletic team may be 'broken' by a loss – with a loss of pride perhaps equivalent to that of the cowboy who lost one of his assigned horses.

The language of the cowboys was strongly influenced by Spanish, and in this contact the already strained ecological model would finally break. Considered historically, these terms – insofar as the historical dictionaries portray an accurate picture – present an unexpected complication. Perhaps the simplest of the myths to be exposed for what it is would be that of Texas origin. A few words are first attested from outside the United States. *Corral* has an *OED* II citation from 1582 and nineteenth-century attestations in South America before its 1842 appearance in Texas. (See also *kraal* and *crawl* in Chapter 5.) *Olla*, with a Portuguese as well as a Spanish derivation, is found in the maritime literature of the 1620s. *Frijoles* ('pinto beans') is attested in the sixteenth and seventeenth centuries; its first North American attestation, 1759, is from California; Dana found it still along the California coast in 1840. Metanalysis makes the singular not *frijol* but *frijole*, a form recorded by Ruxton around 1845 (see below). *Tank*, often assumed to come from *tanque* with a problematic loss of the final vowel (see Chapter 5), would have to be differentiated from *tank* ('a pool or lake'), with a very different derivation and attested as early as 1616. *Lasso* is attested by *OED* II from South America (in an English text) as early as 1768, not in the United States until 1831, and then not from Texas. *Rodeo*, perhaps the king of all the stereotypical Texas cattle trade words, is attested from Darwin's *Voyage of the Beagle* for 16 August 1831, before any attestation in Texas. It is not recorded that the *Beagle* touched on any Texas port.

*Vaquero* (1826 according to *OED* II) is the unique example of a borrowing in Texas between Stephen F. Austin's leading in of Anglo settlers and Texan independence in 1836. *Hacienda* is attested too early for that move – 1808 – and from Zebulon

Pike's experiences with officials in New Mexico and Chihuahua. Others are attested later than the date of Texan independence. *Remuda* (1842), *chaparral* (1845), *pilón* (1883) and *lariat* (1842) are first attested from Texas, but rather late to be the vocabulary of learning the cattle trade and its environment from the Mexicans.

Judging from the historical dictionaries again, a number of forms like *pinto* (1860, California), *hackamore* (1850, California), *bronco* (1868, California or New Mexico) come from further west. So did *adobe* (1759, California); it is reported from New Mexico in 1844 and from Texas in 1892. *Mesa*, attested by the *Dictionary of Americanisms* in 1759 from California and by *OED* II in 1775 from Florida, apparently converged on the Texas lexicon from two directions. Additional South-western Spanish words like *canyon* and *burro* appear to have been borrowed in New Mexico, Arizona and even further west before being transmitted to Texas. Schele de Vere (1872: 120) apparently thought of *alamo* and *alameda* as Texas borrowings, but earlier attestations come from Arizona and elsewhere. As in the case of Florida for some of the terms discussed in Chapter 5, California seems to have been the locus for much of the Spanish borrowing. But the dictionaries do not exclude – in fact, they seem to document – first borrowing in New Mexico or Arizona, progression to California, then movement back east to Texas.

Thus, despite the frequent statements to the contrary, the Texas area seems to have been the recipient rather than the originator of the Romance/Spanish terminology now known as 'Southwesternisms' (Bentley 1934). Movement came westward from Florida and eastward from New Mexico, Arizona and even California.

The contact between Spanish and the advancing 'Anglos' had been a long and complex one, ultimately perhaps more complex and even more important than the also lingering contact with French, although in places not so neatly separated out as one might think. Zebulon Pike had apparently used French with Mexican officials in New Mexico and Chihuahua in 1807 and 1808 to make up for his limited Spanish and the only sporadic availability of interpreters into English.

Austin, on his way to Mexico City in 1822 when accosted by a band of Comanches, went up to the chief and spoke to him 'in Spanish and the few words of Indian he knew' (Carter 1963: 253). Austin managed, in this one case at any rate, to surmount the multilingual difficulties of the time and the place. But it cannot be assumed that either the Comanche chief or Austin was fluent in Spanish; during the same incident the Spanish grammar that Austin carried suspended at the saddle bow, that he might study it as he rode along (Carter, *ibid.*) was lost, and its chance recovery by others led to the rumour that Austin had been killed by the Indians. Hatcher thus reports Austin as a user, in contact situations, of one kind of Spanish – in this case probably a beginning student's rather than *cowpen Spanish*, a term that later writers at least used to describe the English speakers' efforts in the South-western contact situation.

The 'bad' Spanish of the Anglo-Texans at times may have involved something more sophisticated than simple English interference or linguistic naivety. When Colonel William Barret Travis, the 'martyr' of the Alamo who liked to make entries in his diary in Spanish, wrote about his *inamorata* twice – 20 and 21 March 1834 (Turner 1972: 63–4) – he almost seemed to be drawing on some past, if probably brief and superficial, exposure to Italian. Fellow 'martyr' James Bowie moved in among early Cajun speakers in Louisiana in 1802; the children of his family studied Latin. Earlier use of Latin with Mexican officials has been dealt with (Chapter 5). In a context where English, French and Spanish speakers were trying to establish their own language without giving anything like official status to either of the other two, the use of something Romance but not clearly Spanish or French could have had a very important function. For the Indians, *coureurs de bois*, and others more completely separated from the European educational system and the traditions of the use of Latin, the practical communicative value of such a variety – without reference to the traditions of 'high' culture – could have appealed even more strongly. This communicative need seems to have been met, in the cattle trade at any rate, to some extent by the 'partly Romance lingua franca' (Jordan 1981 and Chapter 5 above).

Austin himself and later Anglo-Texans must have learned more Spanish, but the nature of it cannot be determined simply by looking at a modern list of South-western Spanish borrowings. The 'Anglos' who proceeded under Austin's leadership after having been brought to the Los Adaes (near modern Natchitoches, Louisiana) area by Moses F. Austin, after the adventures of Philip Nolan and after considerable pondering on the part of the Mexican government about how to balance the need for immigrants against the obvious danger from the expansionism of the United States, were subject in the beginning to Mexican rules. They had to become at least nominal Catholics, for example, and they were forced to learn a version of Spanish. It has been assumed that the terminology of the cattle trade was basic to what they learned. The historical dictionaries do not bear out that assumption. With independence, much of the enforced Spanish may have been dropped and the 'aloofness' from Spanish influence that Sawyer (1959) detailed for a later period may have begun developing.

In the cattle trade itself, it seems unnecessary to invoke the 'partly Romance lingua franca' for some of the Spanish terms – the eastward side of the convergence on Texas. It is not that these terms are 'deformations'; deviations from Spanish patterns are represented in familiar processes. *Wrangler* from *caballerango* and *chaps* from *chaparreras* are familiar enough as 'clipping' of polysyllabic words. *Dolly welta* (or even . . . *welter*) from *dar la vuelta* ('turn', with derivatives *dally* and *dally man*) and *hoosegow* from *juzgado* are normal English spellings representing regular phonemic substitutions for the Spanish words. What is special about the words moving westward towards Texas is that they fit the patterns described in Chapter 5, whereas other borrowings from Spanish do not.

Interestingly, the examples of normal English interference in the borrowing of Spanish words are attested quite late. Except for *chaps*, with an 1844 citation in *DA*, they come at the end of the great cattle drives, not at the beginning or at their height. There is no citation for *wrangler*, for example, earlier than Theodore Roosevelt's of 1888. *Hoosegow* is not attested until 1911; the variations on *dar la vuelta* from the 1930s. *Wrangler* (1892) has an apparent back formation *wrangle* from 1899. Unless one assumes yet undiscovered attestations, these terms seem to belong to the period of almost complete independence from Spanish cattle-tending instruction and of 'aloofness' from Spanish influence. One might almost say that they come over as parodies of Spanish terms. Etymological consideration of *hoosegow*, for example, gives birth to the familiar South-western folklore that one brought into a Mexican court was 'jailed' as soon as 'judged' (*juzgado*), but it seems impossible to base historical conclusions on good stories which have circulated in fairly recent times.

Even before the undoubted South-western terms, and coming from the east, were the 'article agglutinated' nouns, *mustang* with its impossible blend derivation or 'corruption' ('combination' of *mesteño* and *mostrenco* according to Bentley 1934: 171), and forms like *cabestro* (and perhaps its near-doublet *cabras)*. Mixing of west- and east-moving forms produced doublets like *buckaroo/vaquero*, and *callibouse/calabozo* (treated in Chapter

5), *ranch/rancho* and *caballada/cavvyard*, the last *calf-yard* by folk etymology in Nebraska according to van den Bark (1931: 241) *Stampede*, with its problem simplification of Spanish /est-/ to /st-/ in a language which had numerous words like *estrange* and *estuary*, certainly went along, although its origin is not as simple as Bentley and others make out.

When the cattle drives of 1866–86, which expanded to a degree that dwarfed the not insignificant South-western beef industry of 1845 to the Civil War, began along the dozen or so routes from Texas like the famous but not necessarily dominant Chisholm Trail to destinations such as the equally famous but not necessarily most important Dodge City, they began the northward and north-westward transmission of lexical items which had converged on Texas from both east and west. The observers of the time and even later experts such as Ramon Adams (1944/1968), still felt that the cattle trade and its terminology came from Texas, in spite of all the complications just noted. Stuart (1925), basing his observations on the 1880s, reported that 'more than one half of the Montana range cattle were driven over that [the Texas] trail and almost every cowboy that worked on the [Montana] ranges made one or more drives up the trail'. The trail in question started at the Rio Grande and crossed the Colorado at San Angelo, then went across the Staked Plains (*Llanos Estocado* [*sic*, without plural marking on the adjective, in Stuart]) to the Red River at about the site of Amarillo. Thence it ran north to the Canadian River and crossed the Arkansas River at Dodge City; then it went to Ogalalla and crossed the North Platte at Camp Clark. It followed the Sidney and Black Hills stage road north to numerous rivers, creeks and streams, and it crossed the Yellowstone just above Fort Keogh. The end of the trail was at the Musselshill River, down Lodge Pole creek from the continental divide. All this way, the cowboys used their 'intriguing, half-Spanish lingo' (Hulbert 1929: 135).

There apparently was some romanticism – even sentimentality – in making it the Texan who carried all the language, customs and manner of working all that distance. The hard evidence from the historical dictionaries suggests rather that the lingo was formed all along the route and some of it – like perhaps even *dogie* – transmitted from the North-west back to Texas.

However that may be, the language had its accretions along the way beyond what has been discussed above. For example, *crease* ('to stun [a horse], especially by a shot in the "crest" or ridge of the neck', called 'U.S.' by the *OED*) came into use as a method of acquiring a wild mount by stunning but not maiming it. This term is first attested rather far to the east by Zebulon Pike and was also used by Catlin in 1841, where the animal involved was a buffalo and probably not desired for a mount. *Taking the top off a horse*, periodic gentling, was more to the average cowboy's taste than *bronco-busting* (Clark 1969: 638). Large unbranded animals, especially calves, were *heredics* in Florida and *hairy-dicks* in the West (Adams 1944). Smaller calves were *dogies*, a name about which there are almost endless possibilities for etymological and transmissional dispute.

A primary activity of the *round-up* (a translation of *rodeo*, perhaps, but first attested in Wyoming in 1873 and having a nautical predecessor) was *branding* the cattle. The word *brand* in the sense 'mark indelibly, as proof of ownership' had been used in English for centuries, but the cattle-raising activity specialized it to a degree that it meant 'to burn one's mark of ownership on to a cow', and the noun *brand* regularly and predictably referred to such a mark. (It is doubtful that, if a cowboy had happened to read Hawthorne's 'Ethan Brand', he would have been any more likely than the average reader to discern the symbolism of the name.) *DARE* I, which does not list this *brand*, has several rather late compounds designed as 'West': *brand artist* (1934), *brand blotter* (1910), *brand burner/brand burning* (1926) and *branded in the hide* ('uncompromising', 1965)

An unbranded steer or calf with an ear mark (a design cut into the animal's ear to designate ownership) was called a *sleeper*. *OED* gives the first occurrence of the term as 1910, but Owen Wister used it in 1893. An entry in the *OED* for a 1918 occurrence suggests that a *sleeper* might be 'something taken for something else'. In that sense it may well be the source for one present usage meaning a play or film, book, athlete or politician that unexpectedly achieves great success. Another show-business term, *stinker*, may also be borrowed from Westerners. Among buffalo hunters, an unskilled hand would be given the repulsive task of skinning the freshly killed animal. Because of the blood, intestines and other parts of the buffalo that adhered to the skinner, he was an obvious 'stinker'. The extended usage takes off from this meaning of a strong smell, but it later developed other (perhaps stronger) associations of selfishness, untrustworthiness, etc.

A cow or calf that had no brand and could be claimed by anyone was known as a *maverick*, from the family name of a prominent Texas rancher who either lost a lot of cattle because he refused to brand his own or gained a lot because he had a propensity for latching on to the unbranded property of others, depending upon variant stories. The term has been widely used since for a non-conformist, especially in politics. In the 1970s the Ford Corporation made it the name of an inexpensive automobile model, apparently one designed to appeal to teenagers and others who might be attracted by the fairly mild rebellious connotations of the name. It is now the name of the Dallas team in the National Basketball Association.

As suggested above, the cowpuncher's contacts with the Indians had some influence upon his communication, although not so much as that from the Spanish speakers – possibly because of the more transitory nature of the contact. Rollins (1922: 59) reports that the cowboy would signal acceptance of an offer by 'giving an Indian sign, usually that for medicine, or that for good or that for peace'. But Rollins specifies that 'only such of the cowboys as are brought into intimate contact with the Red Men' used much of the sign language, most limiting themselves to a few signs of great utility.

The cowboy is perhaps more important to American English for symbolic reasons than for his quantitative contributions to the language. There are those who feel that the cattle business typifies American business. The free-wheeling, improvisational (but grounded in non-traditional learning from more sources than immediately met the eye) character of the cowboy was typical of the direction American business was to take in the late nineteenth and early twentieth centuries. It may be more than local pride that the Dallas Cowboys have been known as 'America's team'. (Only an elderly wag would remember that the minor league baseball team once located there was somewhat embarrassingly denominated the Steers.) It is characteristic of American English vocabulary that *cowboy driver*, for a user of an automobile noted more for his mobility than for his caution, developed. *DARE* I calls it 'chiefly n[orth] East', but more than one term from the cattle trade has made its way out of its original habitat.

Notably, the terms which were transmitted along the cattle trails were occupational terms, not the homey terms from the Old South. Perhaps cowboys on the trail drives had no use for either *counterpanes/counterpins* or *bedspreads*. They seem to have carried *frijoles/frijole*, however derived, along with them but to have had no need for *snap beans*. *Barbecue*, even though ultimately from outside the North American continent, had more of a place in their vocabulary than the Old Southern *souse*. The home and farm terms by which regional dialects have been traditionally mapped out somehow seem to be excluded from even the most important of occupational activities – as the cattle trade certainly was in the third quarter of the nineteenth century. In terms of dialect phonology there has apparently never been a suggestion that 'Old Southern' forms made their away along the cattle trails. Somehow, the occupational terms came to be circulated as far as Wyoming and Montana within or slightly after the cattle drive period. Insofar as dictionary documentation goes, some of them may have originated (in English) there.

From the beginning, even in the pre-Civil War drives, the cattlemen would have found other complex linguistic situations further north. George F. Ruxton, who spoke excellent Spanish having served in Spain before coming to Mexico and then the western frontier, reported around 1845 the existence of a 'puchero-like jumble' of English, French and Spanish by a French Canadian trapper, 'one of many who are found in these remote settlements, with Mexican wives':

> *Sacre enfant de garçon . . . voyez-vous* dat I was nevare tan pauvre as dis time; mais before I was siempre avec plenty café, plenty sucre; mas now . . . I not go à Santa Fe' . . . and mountain men dey come aquí from autre côte, drink all my café. Sacré enfance de gârce, nevare I vas tan pauvre as dis time . . . I not care comer meat, ni frijole, ni corn, mais widout café I no live. l hunt may be two, three day, maybe one week, mais I eat nothin; mais sin café enfant de gârce, I no live, parceque me not sacré Espagnol, mais one Frenchman.

Ruxton (1973: 250) reports the interesting interaction of French and Spanish in the '[place name] Pickatwaire of the mountaineers. The full Spanish name was *Las Animas Perdidas en Purgatoria*, which French trappers shortened [and translated] to Purgatoire'. Somewhere along the way, Bois Brûlé became Bob Ruly; Terre Bleu, Tarblue; St Joachim, Swashing (Creek); and Embarras, Ambrosia (Meredith 1930). A section named Bonne et Fidèle, in Portsmouth, Ohio, became Boneyfiddle; almost predictably, local legends tell of a thin ('bony') person who played the fiddle.

In Ruxton's time the majority of mountain trappers and hunters were (French) Canadian, along with some St Louis French 'Creoles'. These hunters used terms for slaughtered buffalo titbits like *boudin*, a term paralleled in Louisiana French[5], and *dépouille*.

From other Western activities, like logging, the vocabulary spread is west to east generally, against the settlement pattern.

*To drag one's feet, skid row (road), grease the skids* (Dillard 1985: 147–9) are part of that pattern. The growing importance of mining from the Gold Rush of 1849, replacing the fur empire which was 'definitely on the wane after having exerted its influence on national expansion' (Clark 1969: 569), was the agency by which a term like *gold washings*, attested in North Carolina in 1832 (*Dictionary of American English, DA*), found its way to California at the very beginning of the Gold Rush, 1849 (*DAE*). It is a fairly safe bet that the term spread by the occupation of mining and not through the migration of a group of North Carolinians to California.

Nor were international factors absent, from the gold rush. Carver (1987: 211) reports the use of *jerky*, ultimately from Quechua through Spanish *charqui*, which 'entered American English in California around the time of the 1849 gold rush and spread from there throughout the West'.

The gold rush also started *prospector* (1851), *strike it rich* (1852), *pan out* (1851, acquiring the general sense of 'be successful' by 1873) and *stake a claim* among others in the same domain. All of the mining terms except *gold washings* seem to have gone west to east, not in the more publicized direction.

*Claim* was, of course, not an 'Americanism' in the narrow sense often required in the branch dictionaries, but expressions like *jump a claim* seem to come from mining. The use of *claim* to mean 'a plot of land to which one has a right', as in the plaintive pioneers' song 'Little Old Sod Shanty on my Claim', seems to have begun with a 1792 reference in the West (Clark 1969: 225). In more modern usage this expression – like many others – exists primarily in a figurative sense. A 'claim' is as likely to be 'jumped' by a girl attracting another's boyfriend as by a conniving prospector. A commercial scheme is as likely to 'pan out' as gold from a stream – more likely, in fact, in view of recent changes in the technology of mining.

Chinese being brought into the mining camps to do the dirty work at coolie wages was far from unknown, as even the poems of Bret Harte bring out. Although exploited and regarded with suspicion, they were sometimes given *a Chinaman's chance* to dig in a mine the Whites considered to be worked out. The negative form [*one] hasn't got a Chinaman's chance* had a real vogue among sports and other columnists around 1940. Bobo Olson, a reasonably good middleweight boxing champion who really went out of his depth when he scheduled a fight with outstanding light-heavyweight champion Archie Moore on 22 June 1955, was a target of the phrase in a column by Walter Winchell, who reported that 'those in the know' didn't give a 'Chinaman's chance' to Olson. Unfortunately for Olson, the victim of an early knockout which virtually ended his career, 'those in the know' were strikingly correct. *DARE* I does not include *a Chinaman's chance*, but *Chinaman gets it* ('nobody wins'), attested from 1968–9 and 1981 from California, looks like an adaptation or at least a survival of the same basic idea.

Large numbers of Chinese coolies were used in building the two big transcontinental railroads in the nineteenth century. There were so many in Arizona that a Chinese Exclusion Act was enacted in 1882, and another law prohibiting those who left the country from returning was passed in 1888. Unwanted by Whites, who regarded them as too competitive for labouring jobs, the Chinese were more at home with the Indians. Forbes (1967: 63) records how 'The Indians would then say as they left them, "Go straight to Chinatown – travel fast."' Both Indians and Chinese used Pidgin English, and it is regrettable that we do not have fuller records of the interaction between the two groups. Unfortunate but necessary participation in opium selling and in prostitution also fell to the lot of many of the nineteenth-century Chinese (Asbury 1938). Not being accepted by settled, main-stream America, the Chinese of the period threw in their lot with the more nomadic groups.

Like those groups, they contributed to the distinctive vocabulary of the country perhaps as much as or even more than their more fortunate co-inhabitants. It was probably the Chinese, after Schele de Vere (1872: 155) 'the Canton jargon of the Anglo-Chinese', who brought *chop* and *first chop*, an alternative to *first rate*, cited by *DARE* I from 1810 and in 1844 in the contrasting variant *common chop*. *DARE* I traces the word *chop* itself to 'Hindi *chāp* "stamp, brand" trans[ferred] from trade usage'. This may be true in the strictest etymological sense, but transmission by sailors from Pidgin English is clearly indicated. Existence on the East Coast (*DARE* I's only regional indication is 'Boston, MA[ssachusetts]' with an 1882 citation from Howells, *Modern Instance*) could have come from the late eighteenth-/early nineteenth-century China trade (Dulles 1930); later (Western) usage from the Chinese of the gold rush and later. *Joss-stick*, cited by Schele de Vere (1872: 157), must have come with the gold rush group, like *joss-house* ('temple') and *joss-pidgin* ('religion').

Cowboys, loggers, miners, and ill-treated minority group members – all these were nomads not content to follow the settlement patterns of the farmers. Such familiar phrases as *deal*,

*pass the buck*, *on velvet* , *hock, in hock* and *hock shop*, *put one's
cards on the table, deal from the bottom of the deck, cash in one's
chips, ace in the hole, [aces] back to back, [ace] up one's sleeve*
and many others have come into general American usage – and,
in many cases, into British and even worldwide usage – from the
American West rather than from the East. Harry Truman's *the
buck stops here*, with what must be thousands of humorous and
quasi-humorous parodies and imitations, is associated with the
White House and Washington, even though Truman may well
have used it while in the Senate or even while a Missouri
politician. Or one could cite the most nomadic of them all, the
hobos, who originated or familiarized *hobo jungle, flop, flop-
house, mulligan, slave-market, main stem, drag* (a section of a
town), *mooch, handout, panhandle, ride the rods, bughouse*
('crazy'), *barrelhouse* and *rustle a meal*, as well as possibly
*hangout* and *out of sight*. Other highly mobile groups like blues
and jazz musicians are only partly traceable in any coherent
geographic pattern of migration; Jelly Roll Morton travelled to
California before he went to Chicago and then to New York. The
simplistic view of the history of American English, which may
work fairly well for farmers, simply does not work out for several
groups which have had a great influence on our vocabulary, if not
on the other aspects of our language.

The cattle trade, if not the other occupations concerned, was
strongly affected by the moving of the farmers into the Great
Plains and the closing of the open range. The mobile and wide-
ranging, if not exotic or romantic in anything except fiction,
cowboy began to give way to the farmer. In theory at least, the
half-Spanish lingo of the former was replaced by the homely
terms the latter brought from the East. In most direct contrast to
the wandering cowboys were the farmers, moving much more
slowly but in a more nearly direct line from the Atlantic Coast to
the Pacific. Fairly exact tracing of their migration has been
performed by using terms like *worm fence* (1652 and 1724, both
in Virginia). The term has been called (Laird 1970: 148) 'a
Midland expression, occurring with high frequency and almost
exclusively in New Jersey, Pennsylvania, Delaware, Maryland,
and West Virginia'. Jordan and Kaups (1989: 105–7) trace the
fence type itself, however, if not the expression back to Finnish
settlers and state that the seal of the General Land Office of the
state of Texas, not at that time regarded as part of the Midland
dialect area, depicted such a fence.

Actually, the rail fence and the worm fence had little impact on
the economic life of the Great Plains and were no real obstacle to

the dominant cattlemen who drove the trail herds. *Paling fence* and *picket fence* were competing terms, but none was of much utility in restricting the movements of rangeland cattle. When barbed wire was invented in 1873, however, right in the middle of the cattle boom of 1866–86, the situation changed. Often pronounced as though it were *bob war*,[6] the new type of fence was a formidable obstacle. According to Kraenzel (1955:130), 'Barbed wire meant that the homesteader – the farmer – could settle the plains'. At least hypothetically, the terms for the wooden fences could have retreated back into restricted locales as barbed wire replaced the fence types themselves. Others (Higbee 1958: 234) stress the importance of steel ploughs and railroads in allowing the Corn Belt to take shape in the late 1850s, but the actual entrance of the farmers into the Great Plains came rather late.

Another homey term given prominence in such studies is the South or South Midland *bucket*, contrasted with the Northern *pail*. Even this distribution is not without complication; *DARE* I's first attestation, from 1622 in Massachusetts, refers to a single object as 'an English Paile or Bucket', and overlapping of the terms has continued at least into the 1980s. Samuel Woodworth, born in Scuitate, Massachusetts, wrote the well-known song 'The Old Oaken Bucket' in 1818; it was published in Boston in 1834 and the words were set to another tune in 1870. Actually, a lot depends upon context: *Bucket of Blood* is appropriate as a name for a tough bar, and has certainly been so used in one motion picture or another; *Pail of Blood* would be ludicrous. *Bucket of beer* also probably goes better than *pail of beer*. With *milk*, on the other hand, and *water* (since almost everyone knows the nursery rhyme 'Jack and Jill'), *pail* seems quite appropriate. In baseball, which was still a Northern and Eastern activity as the sport developed, a certain stance is called *foot in the waterbucket;* . . . *waterpail* would be unathletic. (Among even slightly younger informants, the habit of drinking water from a common receptacle has been forgotten and the expression is *foot in the bucket*.) Only in a restricted context or two can this homey term be used to trace the putative contrast split westward.

From settlements to the north and west of Delaware Bay and Yankees from western New England, farmers began to expand towards the Ohio Valley along the course of the Miami, Wabash, Kaskaskia and Illinois rivers. They were joined by frontiersmen and backwoods people from the upland South (Reed 1977: 41–3). Restricted to use of homey terms, linguistic traces of these movement groups are not easy to find in literature. One approach is to say that the Midlanders and Southerners lacked the aggressive personalities of the other groups and, 'as typical frontiersmen . . . stood a good chance of losing their identity among their Yankee neighbors' (Reed 1977: 42). Or, as a social dialectologist might put it, the purely physical factors involved in dialect formation and transmission were almost always subject to social – even personal – modification. An almost casual phrase *typical frontiersmen* may yet tell the most important tale about the westward spread; losing the more easterly roots, including the indices of dialect, was one of the strongest effects of what Catlin called the 'blasting frontier'.

The much-discussed Scotch–Irish from Pennsylvania were joined, after 1795, by Germans in the 'checkerboard resettlement' (Reed 1977: 42). It should be remembered that the French were still relatively strong in some of these areas. This is the region in which, and not far from the time when, Beadle (1878) proposed his composite 'Hoosier dialect'.

The westward-moving group is traced southward through the Appalachian mountains and Ohio valley (Laird 1970: 156–7; Reed 1977: 42) down to Texas in the South-west. These would be joined by more southerly migrating groups which bypassed the Mississippi River delta in the New Orleans area where French influence was paramount. Texas and the South-west, where contact factors like those with French and Spanish have been acknowledged even in the most conventional treatments, received the dialect mixture eventually resulting from these patterns.

Atwood 1962, considered a monumental reaffirmation of the settlement pattern hypothesis at the time of its appearance, bears out most of these conclusions in terms of the vocabulary selected for test, classifying (1962: 98) 'all of Texas and an indeterminate portion of the surrounding states as a major branch of General Southern, which I will label *Southwestern*'.

Atwood bases his conclusion primarily on the distribution of homey and farming terms like *counterpane* or *counterpin* ('bedspread'), which *DARE* I identified as 'chiefly S[ou]th, S[ou]th Midl[and]' today but shows as attested first in 1836 from Maine and in 1917 from Kentucky; *surly* ('bull', with the accompanying ideas of avoiding 'indecent' terms); *pond* or *pool* ('pool of water'); *plunder room* ('room for storage'); *shed* ('tool house, wood house'); *salt meat* ('salt pork'); *souse* ('pressed pork loaf'); *gallery* ('porch'); *turn (of wood)* ('armful of wood'); *harp, mouth harp, French harp, mouth organ, hamonica* ('harmonica'); *low* ('noise made by a cow'); *snap beans, snaps, green beans,* ('beans in the pods'); *mosquito hawk, dragon fly, snake doctor* ('dragon fly'); *whinny, nicker* ('noise a horse makes'); *redworm, earthworm, worm* ('earthworm'); and *tow sack* ('big burlap bag'). What combinations of dates and places are available suggest that these are later arrivals in the Texas area than the Gulf Corridor cattle trade terms discussed in Chapter 5 and elsewhere in this chapter. A number of the other Spanish terms discussed above are treated and even asserted to be more persistent than some of the (partly archaic) old Southern vocabulary of Texas (Atwood 1962: 109). Atwood relies, although not without some reservation, on statements like one made by Richardson in 1958 that, before the war between the states, 'ninety percent of white immigrants to Texas had come from the Old South' (1962: 6).

If it is true that these terms – and others to be discussed below – came with the group described by Richardson, then the Old Southern vocabulary must have arrived in Texas between about 1830 and 1860. Carver (1987: 228) considers 'yet a fourth subregion' of Texas along the Red River valley and northward to have arisen in this period, with settlers from Arkansas, Kentucky, Tennessee and nearby areas.

Citations in the historical dictionaries confirm this relationship between settlement patterns and regional vocabulary in only the roughest terms. Neither is it overwhelmingly convincing that especially Southern plantation forms, remembered by informants in their sixties and seventies around 1960 – who, however, could not themselves have taken part in the migration of over a hundred years earlier – support such a contention. A form like *croker sack* ('chiefly Gulf States, S[ou]th Atl[antic]' according to *DARE* I) is not attested before 1895, and even that was in western Florida. *Chittlins* ('chiefly S[ou]th, S[ou]th Midl[and]' according to *DARE* I) is not attested before 1841.

Louisiana forms transmitted to (eastern) Texas, largely from French or through a French intermediary, show Louisiana first attestations in 1834 (*armoire*), 1776 (*bayou* – but its next attestation, 1804, would show eastward movement towards Mississippi rather than westward movement) and 1841 (*banquette*, in New Orleans in 1841 but not attested in Texas until Atwood's list). These pattern as Louisiana French, probably Cajun influenced although *bayou* is well known to be ultimately from Choctaw.

Non-French Southernisms like *carry* ('escort, conduct, guide') and *tote* ('carry in a physical sense'), the latter quite possibly an Africanism and the former Black-associated from the earliest documents, may well have gone as far as Texas between 1830 and 1860, although documentary evidence for that conclusion is lacking. With the list of nouns above, these two 'Southern' verbs make up Atwood's perfectly orthodox case for an Old Southern basis for Texas vocabulary until the mid-twentieth century. According to Atwood and others, an influx of Midland terms had begun at about that time – perhaps just after World War II.

Surprisingly for all the importance given to farm terminology in dialect studies, there has been very little non-linguistic information provided about farming, farmers or the spread of farming practices. Note also that most of the information provided about farming vocabulary is fairly late, it presumably being assumed that the same vocabulary existed at earlier periods and historical tracing was simply a matter of following settlement patterns. Carver (1987: 60, emphasis added) concedes that 'As always in this *rurally slanted* account of American dialects, farming [in the more northern states] has contributed a substantial number of terms to the lexicon, but to a considerably lesser degree than in the South'.[7]

Scargill (1977: 37–8) apparently follows the Linguistic Atlas tradition in giving prominence to farming vocabulary far north of Texas in Canada, but without much social or cultural information. He cites *homesteading* (1891), the *Homesteader's Bible* ('the mail-order catalogue', 1965) and the *homesteader's fiddle* ('the crosscut saw', 1954) along with *back-forty accent* 'the term by which city people designated rural speech', 1958).

In the United States in general, terms like *hick, rube,* and *hayseed* were used to designate the definitely non-urban person, and the terms could be used in (hardly complimentary) phrases to indicate his speech. Melville, in *Moby Dick* (1851, I, vi, 52), expressed a combination of pity and contempt for the 'poor hayseed' who would be hard pressed to endure his first storm at sea. Allen (1989a: 89) reports that, in his fieldwork in the Upper Midwest between 1947 and 1953:

> A major change in American society is reflected in the general designation of nouns meaning 'rustic' as old-fashioned, 'no longer heard' [response by Atlas informants]. Six so described *clodhopper, country jake*, and *hick*; nine *honyock*; and 23 *hayseed* . . .

Apparently based on the same materials, Carver (1987: 60) reports that 'The relatively strong urban character of the Eastern North has often cast the farmer as an unsophisticated rube, so much so that *farmer* is used with derogatory force for any awkward, ridiculous person'. The natural association of farmers with dirt ('clods') probably contributes to the popularity of that term (1940s to 1970s) and *clodhopper* (1856 into at least the 1960s) in the same meaning.

Rural terms continued to contribute to the general vocabulary of the United States, particularly to opprobrious usage. *Haywire* ('in an emotional state, tangled, confused, crazy') is first attested from 1934 (*DA*), but *to go haywire* is attested from 1929 and *haywire* ('poorly equipped, roughly contrived, inefficient') is cited by *OED* as early as 1905. Either the historical dictionaries are missing something or the terms lagged far behind the (agri)cultural developments. According to Schlebecker (1975: 190–1), wire binders were invented before twine binders for hay but were difficult to handle. *Haywire* seems a natural term for the mess these early binders must have made. The twine binder, invented in 1874, fully replaced the wire binder by 1882. *Going haywire* would seem to belong culturally to 1870–80, although attestations do not match.

The general movement of English westward, including the acquisition of formerly French territories in the Louisiana Purchase (1803) and that of the formerly Mexican territories in Texas, New Mexico, Arizona and California, took place roughly contemporaneously with maritime spread. Westward movement reached the Oregon Territory and California fairly rapidly. In the latter, however, the dialect migration pattern runs into special difficulties. Assumptions that the numerical superiority of northern Atlantic Coast and upper Midwestern migrants to California would result in dominance of those more easterly characteristics in that western state have not been borne out (Reed 1977: 58; Carver 1987: 83, 219).

Homogeneous groups from the East did not find their way across the continent to the Pacific. One of the earliest dialect studies of the West Coast (DeCamp 1958) found that, in the formation of dialects in San Francisco, the peer group was more important than the family, and the family more important than the residential section. The dominance of the peer group is an important agent in dialect levelling, of which California today is often considered a special example (Reed 197: 59), even though its Mexican population may have been more influential than it has been given credit for in developing the 'Western' vocabulary and dialect pattern.

In effect, the same kind of imperialism that subjugated the Spanish or the South-west and California brought American dominance and American English to the Canal Zone, Puerto Rico, Cuba, the Philippines and other Pacific areas, including Hawaii. Although not literally conquered, Hawaii (early known as the Sandwich Islands) was subject to occupation by the English almost from the time of Captain Cook's landing in 1778. With the arrival of American liberal congregationalist missionaries from New England in 1820 (Lineberry 1963: 67), English-speaking groups remained significant in the Hawaiian islands up to and including statehood in 1959. It was a part of the Pacific, where many sources like Melville's *Typee* reveal the importance of Pidgin English.

Pidgin-speaking Hawaiian seamen had been working on the West Coast when Dana first arrived there around 1834. Some Hawaiians had worked on foreign ships. Dana (1845) tells of the *Ayacucho* which he observed in 1835, built at Guayaquil, Ecuador, with a Peruvian name, a Scotitish owner and a 'crew of Sandwich Islanders' (p. 45). He noted further that trade had been carried on between California and the Hawaiian ('Sandwich') islands and that most of the vessels were manned by the islanders, and reported a small colony of Hawaiians in San Diego. He records their use of Pidgin English along with a 'Babel of English, Spanish, French, Indian, and Kanaka [probably Hawaiian]'. *Kanakas* was a term for the islanders, one which in the twentieth century became fairly well known through the vogue of Hawaiian music but which was earlier established in the form *canuck*. There has been argument about the etymology of this term. Adler (1975: 158–9) points out the use of *canaque* in French and asserts that 'English-speaking sailors in the Pacific (or, for that matter, French or Canadian sailors) were doubtless familiar, early in the nineteenth century, with *kanaka*.' Melville (1846: 120, his own footnote) describes *kanaka* as 'universally used in the South Seas by Europeans to designate the islanders'. He notes that it is 'simply a sexual designation applied to the males' in the principal languages of the area, but that the natives now use it 'in their intercourse with the foreigners in the same sense'. *Typee* is also noteworthy for fairly early literary records of Pidgin English in the Pacific.

On the Hawaiian islands, Carr (1972: 4) records that 'at least two words from Cantonese pidgin had arrived in Hawaii' by 1791, having been recorded by the Spaniard Manuel Quimper, who spelled one *piquinini* in his Hawaiian journal and recorded the pronunciation *pikanele* as well as *chow chow* (spelled *caucao* and retained as *kaukau* in Hawaiian Pidgin English). Like Henry Obookiah, Pidgin English speakers in Hawaii tended to use such features as subject pronoun *me*, negation with NP no VP, and unmarked verb forms (Hawaiian Pidgin *make* for Standard English *made*) in a 'past tense' situation. (Like many other varieties of Pidgin English, Hawaiian Pidgin English can use a variant of *been*, *wen*, to mark definite past time in the relatively small number of cases in which it is really important to the discourse.) A physician's wife with the first group of missionaries in Hawaii recorded in 1820 that the Hawaiians, impressed by the slim bodies of the American women, called them *piccaninny* – 'too [i.e. 'very'] small' (Carr 1972: 95).

Complicating the language picture in the islands themselves but facilitating the use of the pidgin, labourers from other countries were brought to Hawaii in great numbers. In the periods 1876–85 and 1890–97, 46,000 Chinese were brought from South China; between 1878–87 and 1906–13, some 17,500 Portuguese workers came from Madeira and the Azores Islands. From 1886 to 1900 there were imported some 61,000 Japanese workers; in 1901, nearly 6000 Puerto Ricans; in 1904–5 about 8000 Koreans. Between 1907 and 1913 there were nearly 8000 Spaniards brought in. Largest of all, more than 120,000 came from the Philippines between 1907 and 1931 (Carr 1972: 6) A popular phrase book, *Me Speak English,* was published in 1938; presumably it helped many of the immigrants into multi-ethnic and multilingual Hawaii adjust to the local communication situation.

Pidgin English, creolized Hawaiian Creole English and Hawaiian dialect, a de-creolized version (Tsuzaki 1971) have coexisted to some degree to the present time. Hawaiians themselves use the term *pidgin* perhaps somewhat indiscriminately of the three varieties recognized by linguists, but prefer the term *da kine English*. Ethnic varieties of Hawaiian Pidgin English (Carr 1972: 81–100) make up the distinguishable dialects; only insofar as groups of the same ethnic make-up, speaking the same home or traditional language, live close together are there 'regional' varieties of Hawaiian English.

Ordinary – more or less standard – English is definitely the most prestigious language in Hawaii today, used for most formal and public communication. Tourists find it quite possible to travel around the islands without learning any Hawaiian or pidgin. *Haole* residents generally come to realize that they are *haoles* ('foreigners'), even though the Hawaiian islands were annexed to the United States in 1898 and formally made a territory in 1900. In the year of annexation, *grass skirt* seems to have been in use among English-speaking visitors; a direct attestation comes in 1937. Statehood, conferred in 1959 in answer to Hawaiians' expressed preference for that over commonwealth status like that of Puerto Rico (Lineberry 1963: 52–3) has meant perhaps some greater influx of Caucasians, who had dropped to 5.4 per cent of the population at the turn of the nineteenth century, in the influx of Asian and other foreign workers (Carr 1972: 5). The numerical minority of ordinary English speakers is linguistically dominant; nevertheless, a few expressions from Hawaiian and its special varieties of English have drifted back to the mainland.

Some of the words the *haole* resident is likely to pick up are *wikiwiki* ('hurry, hurry up'), *pau* ('finished') and *luau* ('feast'). *Kane* ('male') and *wahine* ('girl, woman') became familiar even to continental Americans during the 1930s, in the period of popularity of Hawaiian music. Melville had recorded the latter (in the form *whihenee*) from a well-travelled Polynesian in *Typee* (1846), along with *kanaka* and *ki ki* ('eat'), (Hawaiian Pidgin English [HPE] *kau kau*). The generally known *aloha* hardly needs to be mentioned, except that *DARE* I calls it 'chiefly H[awai]I[an], although recognized throughout U.S.'. *Aloha party* is more specifically Hawaiian, recorded by Carr (1972); and *aloha shirt* is also 'Hawaiian but recognized throughout U.S.'. *Aloha* and *mahalo* ('thank you') are words that even the tourist arriving by plane is certain to hear from the steward or stewardess. Everyone knows that the flowers (by now, alas, often made of plastic) draped over the incoming visitor make up a *lei*. *Luau* is well enough known for broad jokes to be developed like *Southern luau* ('a 'possum and a six-pack'). *Hula*, the word for a Hawaiian dance, was featured in numerous films of the 1920s and 1930s, and the same activity made *grass skirt* a commonplace, if perhaps not perfectly authentic, part of the American vocabulary for the life of 'exotic' islanders. *Ukulele*, from a Hawaiian word meaning 'flea', has been known since 1900 and the abbreviation *uke* has been in use since 1929 (*DA*); the term may have been given more currency by the vogues of Hawaiian-tinged Tin Pan Alley songs.

The first fad of Hawaiian-influenced popular music with pseudo-Hawaiian language began as early as 'Yacka Hula Dickau Dula' and others in 1915–16. According to Spaeth (1948: 400), 'nearly everyone tried his hand at something Hawaiian'. There were 'Hawaiian Suite' (1919) and 'Beautiful Hawaii' (1920), both by Bob King (*né* Keiser). Just before World War II, vaguely Hawaiian movies appeared such as *Waikiki Wedding* (1937), in which Bing Crosby popularized songs like 'Sweet Lelani' and 'To You Sweetheart Aloha', *Hawaii Calls* and *Hawaiian Buckaroo* (both 1938) and *Honolulu Lu* (1941). After the Japanese attack on Pearl Harbor on 7 December 1941, for quite some time any mention of Hawaii tended to have warlike significance. There seems to have been an interval before commercialization brought the *hula hoop* (1958), trading upon a child's imagination that Hawaiian-style hip movements were involved.

Continued familiarity, including that brought about by statehood, aggravated the characteristic American difficulty with 'foreign' names, so that from saying /hawayə/ for the name of the state many turned to attempts at glottal stops between at least two of the final vowels. Melville may well have had something like glottal articulation in mind for the *q's* in his *Queequeg* for the Polynesian harpooner in *Moby Dick*; if so, Peleg, who pronounced the name *Quohog* and *Hedgehog*, may have represented the first American attempts to struggle with the articulation. Statehood has made little difference; mainland Americans have little more knowledge of the Hawaiians and their language than did the movie goers and listeners to popular music of other decades.

The other non-contiguous state, Alaska, admitted to the union in 1958 and technically the forty-ninth ahead of Hawaii, was never so much the subject of popular lore. Purchased from Russia in 1867 and known temporarily as 'Seward's folly' by Americans who believed the purchase to be an unprofitable one, Alaska was known for its Eskimos, part of a group distributed from Greenland to Alaska and into the Soviet Arctic. They began to be joined by English-speaking Americans in 1889, when the gold rush to the Klondike (actually in Canada) carried them through Alaskan territory. Eskimo terms like *igloo* and *kayak* (both attested in 1662 but not from Alaskan Eskimos) and the command to sled dogs *mush!* (from French *marchons*) were known to most residents of the lower forty-eight, and some might have known *mukluk* ('large seal', 1868). There are disputes about the etymology of *hooch* ('whiskey'); Flexner (1982: 22) is one of those who would derive it from the Alaskan name Hoochinoo.

The finding of gold at Nome almost immediately and at Fairbanks in 1902 completed the picture of Alaska as a gold-rich territory. We have the word *sourdough* from the Alaskan gold rush, first attested according to *DA* from Jack London's *Daughters of Snows* of 1902. This term for a prospector, particularly an Alaskan prospector, derives of course from the necessities of preparing meals in the wilderness. *Sourdough bread*, on the other hand, has had a vogue in the 'gourmet' movement of the last three decades. Such a well-known and eventually widespread term may be balanced by *beanschew* ('bean liquor'; Warner n.d.: 10).

Little was known of the indigenous Alaskans by most Americans, not even a certain way of naming them. Tabbert

(1989) reports that there is some reluctance to use the Algonquian word *Eskimo*, which is similar to a word meaning 'eater of raw flesh', although Tabbert discards that etymology. Trying to use the more polite term *Innuit* or *Inuit*, English speakers are trying to use the modifier form *Inupiat* and the plural/collective noun *Inupiat(s)*. In Canada there is a tendency to use *Inuit* (a plural in the native language) or *Inuk* for the singular and a plural *Inuits* according to the productive English pattern. Tabbert suspects that the same pattern will come to prevail in local Alaskan English.

Otherwise, Tabbert (1990) suggests that hypercorrect *whom*, and the same kind of quibbling about it that goes on in American popular articles, is alive and well in Alaska. Mainstream American English made its way across the country, skipped across the ocean to Hawaii (and other places never technically part of the United States), and up to Alaska. But it changed on the way. Even back in the East the results of the migration are part of everyday speech.

## Notes

1  I had adopted this terminology – and rejected the theory designated by it – before discovering Lyons 1987, in which approximately the same meaning appears to be applied to the term as a sociological model. None of the alternate models discussed by Lyons, however, appears to be especially relevant to the process of language dissemination and change.

2  In this call, *bee* functions only for the sake of rhyme, to point up the critical word *free* in a call which would need to be heard over long distances, relative to children's perception at least. A trick variant substituted *climb a tree* for *come in free*; gullible ones caught by this trick were likely to become 'it'.

3  *Larrup* is derived from nautical *lee rope* in the historical dictionaries with the marginal exception of Webster's Third, which calls it 'per[haps] imit[ative]'. This point, and other factors in the American development and distribution of the term, are dealt with in M.I. Dillard 1980. In the narrow sense of the branch dictionaries, *larrup* and *larruping* are not 'Americanisms'. On the other hand, calling a baseball player Larruping Lou is hardly British idiom. Flexner (1982) derives it from Dutch *larpen*. Such a derivation would still fit in with the notion of the importance of mobility (see *plunder*, p. 100) and would certainly not exclude maritime transmission.

4  World War II sentimentality brought a different, if temporary, meaning to the phrase; in effect, 'the marines are the ones to whom you should go with your problems'.

5  The Louisiana borrowing, referring to pork sausage rather than to

buffalo tripes, is not attested before 1961 but it is hardly conceivable that it should not have been earlier in Louisiana French at least.

6 Tarpley (1970a: 127) reports *bob war* by 61 per cent of the informants, with the '*war*' pronunciation used 'outside the city, especially by the lowest educational group and by informants over 40'.

7 Carver (1987: 61): 'Rhubarb has been called *pie plant* in the North since the 1800s [*DA* 1847]. The well-known winter squash *hubbard squash* is also a favorite crop in this region. A favorite grass is *timothy grass*, first mentioned in print by Ben Franklin in 1747. . . . All three have considerable currency as far as Southern Tennessee and parts of the southern Appalachians.' Although Carver's materials on settlement patterns are impressive, the typical Atlas disregard of chronological factors (1747 and 1847 lumped together as though they were contemporaneous) reduces the value of his historical presentation.

# Chapter 7

# Regionalization and de-regionalization

No one of the contiguous forty-eight states and no other region on the continent is so easily distinguished from the others as Hawaii. The reasons in this case are inescapable: a still active (if somewhat declining) native language for the oldest group of inhabitants, Hawaiian Pidgin and Hawaiian Creole English, and the Island Dialect which is clearly related to the last two and incorporates some vocabulary from the first. There is also, however, a large group speaking aggressively mainstream American English and striking assimilation of some of the other groups to that variety. It is generally assumed that at least the pidgin and creole varieties of Hawaiian English will give way to the last tendency. In this case, the origins of regional distinctiveness are clearer than the eventual result. Almost the opposite would have to be said of the states on the continent.

There is a partial analogy to the process of regionalization in the continental states, although the greater number of groups of languages involved, the vastly greater expanse of territory and the much longer span of time make for a more complex process. Some of the same forces were obviously at work in the early period, and some of the same statements can be made. As the distinctive quality of Hawaiian English depends very little if at all on the region from which mainland speakers came, the formation of dialects of American English does not seem to be merely or even principally a function of settlement patterns from England. It would not be wise, however, to overstate the analogy.

Most of the recent insights into the nature of mainland American English have come from the study of social rather than regional factors. Compared with England, there is and has been surprisingly little regionalization in the United States. When, however, the English of the United States is placed historically in the total migrational context along with Canadian, Australian and other varieties, the striking factor is the astonishingly large amount of regionalization observable in America in the twentieth century and projectable back into the nineteenth.

Pringle (1983: 225–6) reports on New Zealand, where the colonization took place between 1840 and 1890 and which has 'one of the most aggressively egalitarian societies known' and a language 'amazingly uniform'. Pringle speculates that something similar must have happened in Australia. On Australia, see Bernard 1969; for Canada, see the discussion on pp. 194–5. The maritime and pidgin factors discussed at such length in the preceding chapters and in Dillard 1985 were perhaps even more in evidence in those other varieties; the influence from immigrants – from Europe especially – perhaps less of a factor.

Far from being what is almost automatically to be expected, the regionalization of American English is unusual enough, in its immediate context, to require explaining – or, failing in that over-ambitious purpose, at least dating. Whatever explains it, it does not appear to be the transmission of regionalisms from England; the regional indices of American English are almost completely dissimilar to those of England. Mencken's work strongly suggests that the influence (vocabulary importations, in his rather simplistic presentation) from foreign language groups was a major – perhaps *the* major – influence. Magner (1976) suggests that 'Certain languages sink into immigrant history without a significant trace, while others contribute distinctive elements to the English of their region'. The French of Louisiana and elsewhere, the Spanish of the South-west, the Germans especially in Pennsylvania and the Dutch of colonial New York and New Jersey, along with less visible groups elsewhere, have certainly contributed to that regional distinctiveness. Whether incoming groups like the Vietnamese will have an equivalent effect is a matter of speculation. A sometime creolist would be strongly tempted to credit the developing differences, with Mencken, to foreign language influence *plus* the undeniable presence of Pidgin English in the seventeenth, eighteenth and nineteenth centuries. Other contact varieties have clearly been part of the general process.

Certainly those influences have been great, and the exploration of their influence has only begun, so far as historical context is concerned. Occupational differences have also had a major impact. The differences in natural resources in various parts of the United States, with attendant differences in occupations, must have had some effect on the distribution of dialect forms, although it is difficult to account for anything except vocabulary in terms of such correlations.

When something more than mere projection of twentieth-century isogloss bundles is examined, it becomes clear that the mapping of regional distribution which has worked its way into even the collegiate dictionaries cannot have existed since the beginning. The very settlement patterns of the United States and North America make that point clear. Neither, as almost this entire book has been directed at pointing out, are the patterns clearly in germ in the Atlantic coast settlements of the seventeenth and eighteenth centuries, although this has been a kind of dream among the reconstructionists. Reed (1977: 41), even though highly orthodox in most of his dialectology, is clear about part of this: 'lines of dialect difference have only gradually begun to make themselves evident in the Middle West and scarcely at all in the Far West'.

Laird (1970: 151–8) set out to show how three areal groups of the early East Coast migrated and spread their dialects westward. Narrowing the 'early' East Coast dialects down to two groups, lowland Southern and back country Southern, he took as indices of their dialect the familiar ones of fish worms, household articles and containers.

|  | *Lowland* | *Back country* | *Other* |
| --- | --- | --- | --- |
| Fishing | fish bait | redworm | angleworm |
|  | earthworm |  |  |
|  | fish worm |  |  |
| Household | mantel | fireboard | not specified |
|  | mantel board |  |  |
| Container | gunny sack | tow sack | not specified |
|  | guano sack | croker sack |  |
|  |  | poke |  |

There is probably an east-to-west geographic distribution of these conveniently chosen words, but chronologically the early-to-late distribution simply does not work. The 'other' group's term for a worm used for fishing bait, *angleworm*, is attested in Maine in 1832, in Connecticut in 1894, in Indiana in 1900, in New York and Missouri in 1912 and in California in 1925; the westward movement may be documented, but the colonial chronology is not. *Fishworm* is first documented from 1854, in the writings of Thoreau. OED II cites *gunny sack* from 1862; *DA*, *guano bag* from 1856 in Maryland. (Cassidy, personal communication, cites *gunny bag* in the *DARE* files in 1820.) The only colonial citations in the historical dictionaries are *red worm*, cited from Virginia in 1705, and *crocus*, from 1699. A form like *ginger-baggs*, from Jonathan Dickinson's Florida journal *God's Protecting Providence* of 1696–7 apparently never figured in regional distribution at all. More modestly but less explicitly, Reed (1977) leaves the indices of geographic spread much less explicit – and much less subject to criticism.

In phonology, something of the westward spread seems to be shown by *DARE* I's Map 4 (p. 1xi), which shows the distribution of homophonous *caught* and *cot* – that is, the neutralization of /ɔ/ and /a/. Words like *sought*, *wrought* and *taught* (which thus becomes homophonous with *tot*), *hawk*, *caller* and *dawn* (thus not contrasting phonologically with *hock*, *collar* and *don*) tend to have /a/ in the area starting in Pennsylvania, spreading through Iowa and Missouri, fanning out rapidly at Kansas and Nebraska and widening further to include the panhandle of Texas, most of New Mexico, all of Colorado and most of Wyoming, all but the southern tip of Arizona, all of Utah, and all but the northern tip of Idaho, all of Nevada, California and Oregon, and all but the north-easterly parts of Washington.

Dialects having /ɔ/ in such words are generally felt, unless other evidence is present, to be 'Southern' and perhaps unsophisticated, and, as Marckwardt's (1957)[1] distinction between Chicago and the remainder of Illinois might indicate, /a/ to be urban. (Southerners and some speakers in other communities who make this particular distinction have an equally unprestigious tendency to neutralize /ɛ/ and /ɪ/ before nasals.) An Iowan of approximately my age and academic status recently corrected my /wɔk/, for the Chinese cooking utensil *wok* to /wak/ , undoubtedly feeling urban and even urbane in the process. A picture in the Portsmouth, Ohio *Times* for 12 June 1990 (Section A, p. 1) showed a demonstrator carrying a sign

BEVERLY IS GONE,
FRY VAUGHN

which is characteristically non-Southern, the rhyme being imperfect for most inhabitants of the formerly Confederate states. There does not appear, however, to be any indication of the date at which this neutralization developed.[2]

*DARE* I's materials on relevant words – and other sources which I have been able to consult – contain no misspellings, observers' comments or other evidence which could be taken to indicate the timing of this particular neutralization. *DARE* I's map (referred to above) showing spread from the East Coast westward could hardly be taken as any real evidence that the neutralization started with the first group of English speakers on the East Coast or developed soon thereafter. One possibility – no more absurd on the face of it than the one just referred to – seems to be in the area of influence from the phonemic systems of German speakers in Pennsylvania, Ohio and nearby areas. Like a number of immigrant languages, reported dialects of German would not have this contrast.

Foreign-language dominant speakers often have neutralization of the same two vowel phonemes, as for example in the English of many Spanish-dominant speakers, especially in the South-west. A student at Texas College of Arts and Industries in Kingsville once (*c*. 1958) amused me by writing 'the Corpus Christi *Collar*' in an essay on local newspapers; its name was of course the *Caller*. The fact that most 'Anglos' in the area have the /a/ /ɔ/ contrast is a small addition to the linguistic burden borne by the local 'Chicanos'. The overall problem of Spanish-dominant bilinguals is also complicated by the lack of contrast of either vowel with /æ/. There is, however, no evidence of transmission of /ɪ//i/ neutralization or any of the others characteristic of Spanish-dominant bilinguals to English-dominant speakers in the area.

Coincidental identity of Pennsylvania 'Dutch' English and Spanish-influenced varieties is observable in at least one other area. Shields (1987: 168) reported *The first time since I'm here* for more ordinary English . . . *I've been here*, with a 'recessive' distribution since it tended to be characteristic of informants without high school education and those over forty. Quite similar usage (*Is this the first time you are ever outside the States?*) are observable, especially from Puerto Ricans but also from others whose first language is Spanish. Identification of the place of residence of the speaker on the basis of language usage could very easily run afoul of such factors. On the other hand, features like *outen* ('extinguish'), *fress* ('eat too much, eat sloppily' [like an animal]), and *spritz* ('sprinkle') would distinguish Pennsylvania Dutch–English speakers from users of 'Spanglish', and probably from all others.

Features like the (restricted) neutralization of *let* and *learn* (both German *lassen*) and the (now much more widespread) Midland neutralization of *lend* and *loan* (both German *leihen*) are sometimes traced to such influence. The American use of *dumb* to mean primarily 'stupid, ignorant' rather than 'mute' is also sometimes traced to German influence. Shields (1987) cor-roborates earlier findings that idioms like *It wonders me* (German

*Es wundert mich*) and lexical items like *speck* ('fat', German *Speck*) and *smooch* (*schmutz*) ('kiss') have remained in use in the area through the 1980s. As the *DARE* I map shows, the Midland influence spread through heavily germanized areas of Pennsylvania to Ohio, where Mennonite/Amish groups have been strong since 1683. There was, furthermore, a Pennsylvania German-like contact variety involved in cross-country transmission. There was also an 1878 report of a 'Hoosier' dialect containing 'the rude translations of "Pennsylvania Dutch", the Negroisms of Kentucky and Virginia, and certain phrases native to the Ohio valley' (Dillard 1985: 97–8). Unsatisfying as such evidence is, it is as good as anything else available for dating of the dialect phonology in question.

In the examination of the indices of regional dialect which have been treated herein, it is very rare to find any clear attestation within the colonial period. In fact, it seems reasonable simply to deny that regionalization of American dialects really traces back to that period. (That some regional patterns may have developed during the colonial period and then have been absorbed into other patterns is not, of course, excluded by any such statement.) It is in fact striking how few of the regionally diagnostic features which have formed the basis of our picture of American dialects developed before 1800. On the other hand, there seem, judging from the historical dictionaries, to be rather striking clusters of such occurrences – including some of the ones Carver (1987) uses as regional indicators – around what Lingeman (1980) cites as the primary times of immigration, 1816–18, 1830–7 and the early 1850s.

Some words introduced before 1800 illustrate the principles fairly well. *Banter* ('to haggle', not the more familiar 'indulge in humorous ridicule'), appears in Massachusetts and perhaps remained in the states east of the Mississippi until fieldworkers found it in New York and Georgia in 1968. *Bad off for X* ('lacking X' – in the sense the mountain men represented much more picturesquely with *froze for X*) is attested in Pennsylvania in 1794, in Kentucky in 1821 in Rhode Island in 1852, and in Mississippi in 1893. Slightly different combinations with *bad off*, semantically related, occur in a conglomeration of times and places – although never west of the Mississippi according to *DARE* I.

There are some importations immediately after 1800. *Bore* in the now unfamiliar sense 'ridicule, humiliate, embarrass' is attested in 1800 from Philadelphia, jumps to Florida by 1836, is over in Missouri in 1923, and is obviously an old-fashioned form for a *DARE* informant in 1972. In the same vein, *bagonet* ('a bayonet', also applied to a plant) is attested in 1808, called 'obsolete or vulgar' by the *OED*, and listed by the *EDD* but given no precise regional designation. *DARE* I's first citation is from South Carolina, and no occurrence after 1899 is listed.

In 1810, also, Margaret Dwight Bell, in *A Journey to Ohio* (published 1920, p. 37), reported: 'Youns [*sic*] is a word I have heard used several times but what it means I don't know.' The indication is that the usage was relatively new, at least to Dwight, but one of the more recognizable tendencies of non-standard American dialects is to provide a plural for *you*, historically itself an oblique form of a plural extended into the singular. Kurath (1949: 67) cites a number of such examples, including *mongst ye*, 'common in the folk speech of the central part of Delmarvia' with 'rare instances . . . from the mouth of Chesapeake Bay to Albemarle Sound', but with no indication of source or date of origin. Southern Ohioans today alternate *you uns/y'uns* as a solidarity pronoun with the slightly more formal (and distancing) *you guys*.

The oft-cited and criticized American *calculate* ('suppose') is called by *DARE* I 'formerly chiefly New England, now more widespread' but is first attested from Pike's *Expeditions* (1810). The first specifically East Coast attestation is in 1828, although Humphreys' *Yankee in England* (1815) has an occurrence which might be so considered. *Calico* ('fish with mottlings or spots', 1815) is first attested from New York and is now considered characteristic of New York and New Jersey. It is one example of the metonymic use of the word for the cotton fabric with meanings like 'a woman' (1848). *Bergall*, otherwise called *cunner* ('a perchlike saltwater fish', 1815) is variously attested around New York and New Jersey until 1933; there is a possible Scots source. *Kiver* as a pronunciation for *cover* is also attested in Humphreys (1815), then from Georgia in 1837, North Carolina in 1856, southern Illinois in 1902 and back east in New Hampshire in 1907. If there was progression from New England westward with migration, it is not shown by data of this type. *Cork* ('to make tight against leakage', 1823), obviously maritime, is a special form of *caulk*. *Budge*, in the special sense 'a fit of nervousness', is first recorded in Virginia in 1824; the only other attestation is from 1904, also from Virginia. *Applejack* ('liquor distilled from apples') is attested from 1816, earlier than other meanings of the word, and is widely distributed, the only geographical limitation being apparently 'east of Mississippi'.

A larger group appears about 1830; although not perfectly well behaved regionally, it shows some tendencies toward relatively clear-cut regionalization. *Clevis* ('iron bent in the form of an oxbow') was called characteristic of New England by Webster in 1828 and was widespread afterwards, last attested from Kentucky in 1960 in a possibly archaizing collection. *Cob* ('a blow, usually to the buttocks', 1828) does not occur again until 1859, is now considered obsolete, and is assigned no regional designation. *Cohogle* ('hoodwink') is listed in 1829 from Virginia, in 1855 from Olympia, Washington, in the very different meaning 'associate', and in 1931 from Kentucky. *Brash* ('a slight attack of sickness often resulting from a digestive disorder', 1830), first occurs in West Virginia and was apparently limited to that state, Pennsylvania, and Virginia until 1899. The adjective *brash* ('hasty, rash', 1837) has early attestations in Kentucky, Indiana, Tennessee and Virginia and has apparently become more widespread in the twentieth century. Between the two chronologically, *catstick* ('a piece of kindling') is first attested from Boston but appears to have moved to Pennsylvania and Maryland by 1859 and to have become obsolete some time after 1867. *Clapperclawing* ('a fight, a beating a tirade', 1834) appears to be strictly from Tennessee; the only other citation is from 1939.

*Cowhanded* ('awkward, clumsy', 1834) has no other attestation outside baseball terminology; it apparently specialized for that originally coastal sport, but there is no detailed evidence as to the chronology. It seems to have remained in use in New York state, where its more general competitor *cross handed* was called odd in 1962. The grip, as the meaning suggests, was not used by those really proficient with the bat; professionals seem never to have resorted to it.

Andrew Jackson used the intensifier *consarned* in 1834 and the word seems to have remained around Tennessee and Kentucky for a while; dialect fiction may be at least one reason why it is, in jocular usage, much more widespread by now. *Brickle* ('brittle, crisp', 1837), called 'Eng[lish] dial[ectal]' but not narrowly localized, is characterized as 'chiefly S[ou]th, Midl[and]'; its second attestation (1890) is from Louisiana, with another (1893) from Mississippi, but the occurrences thereafter tend to fall into the Kentucky/Tennessee/Virginia/Ozarks pattern. *Blueweed*, a synonym for *viper's bugloss* (1837), is listed by the *EDD* from 1750 and really appears from the citations to have been more botanical than regional in distribution, although there is no indication of any occurrence west of Missouri.

*Aside of*, a phrasal preposition (1838), is attested from New York, South Carolina (from Julia Peterkin's *Scarlet Sister Mary*

[1928], in which the dialogue is in what the bidialectal Peterkin herself calls Gullah) and Pennsylvania. Aside from Gullah usage, the phrase was never a Southernism; the low probability of Black borrowing from Northern dialects makes one suspect that the Gullah usage and the 'N[orth]East [Black]' citation from 1970 represent development independent of White usage. Certainly such transmission as hereby indicated does not favour the familiar thesis that Black usages preserve archaic Southernisms.

The use of *bad* to mean 'sorrowful, depressed' (Marryat 1839) is later attested for New England, Indiana and Tennessee. The *bad* ('not well, out of sorts, enervated') which forms the basis for the 'chiefly S[ou]th, S[outh] Midl[and]' map in *DARE* I is not attested before 1954. According to Carver (1987: 179), *muley* ('hornless') *(cow)* is attested in New York and New England in 1838; because of an Irish or Welsh etymology, it 'probably' was in earlier use in the Pennsylvania area, but there is no documentation.

A favourite device of the dialect geographers and tracers of alleged dialect movement across the United States has been 'worm words' (Marckwardt 1958: 144–5). These, however, do not seem to deviate from the pattern set by the other terms. The *DARE* I citation under *angleworm* (1832) lists also *earth worm* and *brandling*. *Angle worm*, also called *angling worm* but not until 1933, is of "chiefly N[orth] and West" distribution. *Brandling* apparently has no regional utility and thus has no entry of its own. *Earthworm* is the national term – what would appear on television commercials if fishing worms were advertised there – attested according to Cassidy (personal communication) in 1737 with reference to use in Ireland.

A more heterogeneous distribution appears to begin with the words first attested in the 1840s. *Coggle* ('to wobble or be unsteady', 1843), a variant of the 1829 *cohogle*, lacks any narrow regional distribution. *Bug-eater* ('an insignificant or worthless person', 1840) is called 'chiefly West' but the next citation (1852) is from Virginia, from a Black. *Bamboozle*, which came in in 1842, is not listed in *DARE* I and was possibly never regional in distribution. *Conscience* ('judgment, estimation', 1843) is traced to a 'n[orth] Eng[land] dial[ectal]' origin but is attested only from Indiana and eastern Tennessee (1939). *Bussen* ('ruptured', 1845), having, as so often, an *EDD* citation but no clear British regional provenience, occurs first in North Carolina and again in Virginia in 1899. *Conbobberation* ('a disturbance', 1845) may be related to English dialectal *bobbery*. The first listing appears to be Southern, and the only other listing is from Virginia in 1852.

*Cady* ('a hat or cap', 1846) has a probable Scots dialect origin but a not very clear regional distribution except that it appears never to have gone much further west than the Mississippi. *Buck load* ('a large shot of liquor', 1846) is attested first from northern Alabama and only one more time, from Virginia in 1899. *Bore* ('an obnoxious visitor', approximately its present meaning) is first attested in 1848 and apparently never had any truly regional distribution.

In the 1850s, another concentrated group of regionalisms is introduced, insofar as the evidence of the historical dictionaries goes. *DARE* I lists *applejack* ('an apple turnover', 1852) from Virginia, with later attestations in North Carolina. *Baga* ('rutabaga or Swedish turnip', 1854) is of 'chiefly MI[chigan], WI[sconsin], and M[in]N[esota]' distribution, although it wandered down into Florida between 1965 and 1970. *Certain sure* (1856) is 'chiefly Mid[land] and S[outh] Atlantic, N[ew] Eng[land], and Ohio Valley'; that is, the West and the 'deepest' South are excluded. *Anigh* ('near, close to', 1856), is 'esp[ecially] S[outh], S[outh] Mid[land]'; the homophonous word meaning 'nearby, close by' has a more general distribution although it seems to have stayed generally west of the Mississippi. *Any more* (1859), in the positive rather than the 'natural' negative sense in which the term is found in ESL textbooks and the like, is 'scattered, but least freq[uent in] N[ew] Eng[land]'. *Catstick* ('a bat or cudgel', 1859) seems to have no regional restriction – unlike its 1832 incarnation – and is not attested after 1872 (Schele de Vere).

With a possible Scots origin, *airish* ('chilly, cool', 1878) is first attested in the West. Later occurrences are in Virginia (1912, 1918, 1947), the Ozarks (1926), Kentucky (1960) and perhaps Atlanta (1972). The Scottish-to-the-West progression would be much more convincing if there were geographically and chronologically intermediate attestations. The special use of *and* ('what with, at a time when') may be originally Scots or Irish; it is attested in 1866 (Massachusetts), 1926 (Black, without geographic designation), 1931 (Kentucky mountains), 1938 (Florida), 1942 (south-east Kentucky), 1943 (western North Carolina) and 1976 (Maryland). *All setting* ('all ready, in good condition', 1874) is attested as 'Western in usage' in 1889 (Farmer's *Americanisms*), and in 1977 is included in Watts' *Dictionary of the Old West*. In this later group of importations, the 'scattering' perceived in some of the words brought in in the 1850s is becoming still more pronounced.

Although such evidence certainly does not indicate that sharply delineated regionalization had taken place by 1818–20, the 1830s, the 1850s and later, it seems to give a rough indication that the process took place, and some idea of the chronology. It seems important here to compare the chronology proposed for the Black English Vernacular in Chapter 3. The stereotypical Black food *chitlins*, more formally *chitterlings* ('intestine, usu[ally] of hogs, prepared as food'), is first attested in 1841, from Georgia, in a definitely non-Black context. Black poverty and resultant dependence upon less desirable foods would easily explain the later restriction of the term to almost exclusively Black usage. It would be absurd to extend the denial that Southern archaism is the exclusive source of the Black English lexicon to a blanket denial that such retentions existed at all. No such claim is intended for the presentation in Chapter 3, however much atemporal *be* may have been asserted to be something other than a survival from some otherwise uninfluential English or Irish variety.

It is striking that many of the developments outlined for the South-west in Chapter 6 have approximately the same chronology, with a heavy concentration of Spanish borrowings in the 1830s. The analogy cannot be carried too far. No concentration of forms from other regions, like Arkansas which supplied many of the prospectors, in the West around 1850 is very impressive. In fact, the only immigrant group which could complete the analogy would be the Chinese who came in the gold rush. That group has been accorded little influence by dialectologists, even though they spoke a variety of the Pidgin English which can easily be shown to have been important in the West. It is also acknowledged that regionalization never proceeded so far in the West as in the other regions of the United States.

Although the pattern which emerges from consideration of this evidence is far from neat, a general picture of regional differentiation of the Eastern and Midland areas appears to begin around or just after 1800, with peaks around 1816–18, 1830–18 and the 1850s. The first is, in effect, the same period as the one in which Knight, Kirkham and others began observing regional characteristics in the speech of the American White population, along with some usages attributed to the Irish but with no attention whatsoever to the Blacks. By the evidence of contemporary observers (always excepting Noah Webster, who seemed predisposed to discover archaism in New England), the regionalization of American English began not with the movement of the East Coast population westward but with the immigration of groups from outside the continent. Quite a number of these were Scottish or Irish, and the folk traditions of

Scotch–Irish formative influence seem to have some validity. On the other hand, there are many exceptions to the observation that these settlers and their descendants proceeded along specific routes, carrying dialect forms with them.

The kind of picture which emerges from the data upon which this regionalization is based contains considerable 'fuzziness'. Regional distributions are far from clear cut where many of the forms are concerned, and even those rough indications of regional distributions are based upon words (or special meanings of words) of which a quite literate, educated American may confess himself ignorant with no embarrassment whatsoever. The words or special meanings of words which figure in this fairly early development of dialect regions may well have seemed bizarre and obscure even to the inhabitants of the region at the time. By the principle that the unusual is reportable, forms different from the commonplace have more attention called to them than what is in daily usage. The overwhelmingly greater part of the American vocabulary was non-regional from the first, and there is little reason to believe that the same was not true in grammar and phonology.

Regional data are also thoroughly disjunctive. Many years of effort have shown no relationship between the regional distributions of British English and those of American. And there is another kind of disjunction; anyone who works with the materials produced by the Linguistic Atlas of the United States and Canada must become familiar with what could be called the 'also phenomenon': any form found in one area is very likely to be also in another, usually quite some distance away. *Buckra* in the coastal South Carolina–Georgia area (down as far as Savannah in the 1830s) and in Bracketville, Texas, is an excellent example. Features are not exclusive to regions; configurations of features are necessary, and even then the boundaries between the configurations ('isogloss bundles') are extremely fuzzy.

Attempts to trace population movements by dialect features alone are also typically restricted to small, disjunctive sets of items. According to Carver (1987: 178), the origin of the Midland 'layer' in the south-eastern Pennsylvania and tidewater Virginia 'hearths' should be reflected in the histories of words. He finds, however, only *sugar tree* (= sugar maple) and *papaw* (a North American tree) coming from the latter and the bovine use of *muley* and *dousie* (= ill, sickly) traceable to the former.

Since the movement of the Florida 'Seminoles' to Bracketville, Texas is a matter of specific historical record, the one tracer *buckra* seems as strong as or stronger than the two to four items tracing the Midland layer to its hearth. This tracing involves data and distributions less familiar in dialectology, but it appears to be at least as reliable as the more thoroughly established pattern.

Although most of the observers who reported, as well as they were able, the speech of the Black slave population and of the other ethnic groups were perhaps more liable to the accusation of bias and incompetence, their evidence is much more consistent. It also tends to indicate a slightly earlier development. Nothing about these materials poses any strong argument against the thesis that Southern dialects began crystallizing around the same time as the other regional varieties, and after the fairly clear differentiation of Black speech. In the South-west, the borrowings from Spanish (ignoring for the moment the discussion in Chapter 5), which are often held to be the first indices of that regional variety, reach a kind of peak around the time of the declaration of the independence of Texas in 1836.

By the time of the local colour movement in American literature around 1880, regional characteristics, in speech as in other traits, were sufficiently pronounced to be recognizable to almost any reader and therefore usable by writers of fiction and other commercial authors. Schele de Vere (1872) simply assumed regional distributions without any perceived need of support. Ethnic dialect – especially Black English – was clearly recognized by Black authors like William Wells Brown, Charles Waddell Chesnutt and Paul Lawrence Dunbar, as well as by William Gilmore Simms, Joel Chandler Harris, Thomas Nelson Page, J. A. Page and many other White plantation novelists. These and others represented White Southern dialect quite as frequently. Lafcadio Hearn and George Washington Cable, notably, added the French-influenced dialects of Louisiana to their fiction. Mark Twain has been associated with the West in the popular imagination, but he also had his say about the speech of places as far apart as Missouri and Louisiana. Bret Harte, Joaquin Miller and Dan DeQuille (the last two at least partly pseudonyms) represented the West more exclusively than did Twain. Mary Noailles Murfree can be added to traditions of writing of Southern dialect which reached almost an apotheosis in the works of William Faulkner. Sarah Orne Jewett and Mary E. Wilkins Freeman were among those who rendered New England speech. One cannot, of course, take the literary evidence as absolute; one would conclude that New England speech underwent incredible changes between Hawthorne, who wrote about the same area, and the last two above, where the authors' different styles are clearly the important factor.

Nevertheless, there are limitations to the picture that regional distributions were clear cut by the 1870s or 1880s. Schele de Vere observes that, in South Carolina, *chair* is 'uniformly pronounced as *cheer*'. (*DARE* I reports the spelling *cheer* in North Carolina from 1774 and also reports [-i-] or [-I-] in 'folk speech, in S[ou]th and S[outh] Midl[and], scattered in P[ennsylvani]A, N[ew] Eng[land]'.) Schele de Vere makes an equivalent observation about *stairs* being pronounced like *steers*. On the other hand, he observes that *deer meat* has become *dare meat* – again in South Carolina. Since directly opposite phonological trends in the same population seem hardly feasible, it seems likely that Schele de Vere found, but did not report, different phonological processes among different groups of South Carolinians – always assuming that he was not outright mistaken.

On external grounds one could say that regional awareness in general American culture tended to reach its height around 1870–80, and it is reasonable to assume that regional distributions – cultural as well as linguistic – reached some kind of high point shortly before that time. It would seem that the kinds of general dialect distinctions roughly recognized by Knight, Kirkham and others in the first decades of the nineteenth century were fully developed in approximately the third, fourth and fifth decades of that century. Social dialect distinctions had developed even earlier, and they were not obliterated. Before, during and slightly after the Civil War, plantation (and farm – see Dillard 1985: 108–13) Black slaves – not at all freed from the plantation system by the Emancipation Proclamation (Johnson 1934) – were generally recognized as a relatively homogeneous dialect group. Gullah-speaking Sea Islanders, like Daddy Jack in Joel Chandler Harris's *Nights with Uncle Remus* (1883), were recognized to be more extremely non-standard. Freedmen, skilled craftsmen hired out in the towns and house servants stood against the field-hands in social differentiations.

One's confidence in the literary evidence is shaken, or at least tested, by the case of Appalachia, where a kind of *Ausbau* ('outbuilding', distinction-creating) dialect relationship has existed – or perhaps is even still developing. Literary figures (Brooks 1953: 11) have felt that there *should* be a specific Appalachian dialect, even though dialectologists have had a much harder time finding any unique forms or distributions there.

Brooks, who refers to the 'idiomatic, highly concrete, richly metaphoric language' of James Still, differentiates it from the Southern of Faulkner, and credits it with the 'true lilt of oral speech [*sic*]', cites (1953: xi) *mort* ('a great deal of something'), with attestation in seventeenth century England, possible Norse origin, but no American information outside Still (and Brooks); *roust* ('rout out'), called 'orig[inally] dial[ectal] and U.S.' by *OED* II but with no other indication of Appalachian associations; and *bunty* ('derived from *bunting*, meaning "swelling" or "plump"'). *DARE* I has '*bunty n[oun]. also attrib[utive]. Also buntie, bunting* [Engl(ish) dial(ectal) *bunty*], chiefly Appalachians "A tailless fowl"'. The earliest attestation in the United States is from Schele de Vere (1872), but *OED* has attestations from much earlier; if the term is more widely used in Appalachia than in any other part of the United States, as Cassidy (personal communication) assures me, the frequency relationship must have been rather late in developing. The form *bunting* instead of *bunty* is first attested 'Among the Negroes'. A nursery song

> Bye, baby bunting,
> Father's [*Daddy's* in eastern Texas in the 1920s] gone a hunting

known in Appalachia and possibly most parts of the United States, is traced to 1665 by *OED*, which calls *bunting* 'a term of endearment', is cautious about its etymology and even questions whether the word has any meaning.

Since the mountainous region is outstandingly recognizable, and since there is solidarity – a kind of defence against the outside world – among the most 'typical' inhabitants, there is a strong tendency to recognize and defend 'mountain talk' (Mary L. Dillard, personal communication, the use of the term being reported from eastern Tennessee) as a legitimate variety. Traditions of Scotch–Irish ancestry (Blanton 1985: 73), of pioneering expansion in search of freedom as soon as the Cumberland Gap opened in 1750, and of (largely voluntary) separation help to form the image of a different Appalachia. Although mobility of the group has certainly not been limited – many of the things written about the Blacks after the world wars ( pp. 219–21) would also apply to the Appalachian population – there are long-standing traditions of family groups remaining in the same area for many generations. The notion of feuding families, for example, continuing their fight for long periods of time is a specifically mountain tradition in the United States. Stories by Jesse L. Stuart provide a rallying point for the educated; more popularly, the comic strip [*Barney Google and*] *Snuffy Smith* has provided, since before World War II, a rich inventory of stereotypable and ridiculable expressions: *if that don't take the rag off'n the bresh, he's tetched in the haid, shif'less skonk.* Al Capp's *L'il Abner*, even more successful until the death of its author, provided a setting in Dogpatch, Kentucky which has influenced the creation of a real town.

More serious dialectologists like Carver (1987) make more conservative reports about the unity of an Appalachian dialect. He reports (1987: 176–8) 'a viable if small regional lexicon, perhaps a remnant of a much larger vocabulary that diffused throughout the Upper South'. The *small* and *viable* lexicon consists, so far as the evidence goes, of *spring house, poke, whistle pig*, and *lay out*; the 'much larger' vocabulary 'diffused throughout the Upper South' apparently remains only a supposition. Documentary evidence would be extremely valuable, but it either does not exist or has not yet been discovered.

Outsiders report with some frequency having difficulty in understanding 'mountain talk'. An oft-cited phrase like *I don't care to*, which is a positive response to a request or an invitation but which is likely to be perceived as negative, is, however, regarded by *DARE* I as 'chiefly Midl[and]', not Appalachian. The first attestation (1903) is from south-east Missouri, and the second (1907) from north-west Arkansas. Only the third (1931) specifies West Virginia mountains. The usage obviously occurs in the mountains and is reportable – especially noticeable to an outsider – but not Appalachian by any historical or distributional evidence.

In spite of undoubted factors of solidarity, Blanton (1985: 82–3) finds difficulty in classifying Appalachian as a dialect. In contrast, a popular version of dialects like Herman and Herman (1947) has no problems in presenting a chapter on 'The Mountain Dialect', citing *inter alia* to 'confidence' a stranger; *DARE* I, on the other hand, considers *confidence* as a 'v[erb] to trust' as 'chiefly S[outh] Midl[and]' with attestations from 1917 (North Carolina Mountains), 1931 (s[outh] Appalachians), 1933 (Ozarks), and later spreading into areas like north Georgia. In this case, the historical associations with the mountains, if not the Appalachians, seem to be confirmed. In the case of *come . . .* (a time), *DARE* I's designation 'esp[ecially] S[outh] Midl[and]' reflects heterogeneous attestations from 1908 and there is little or no confirmation of Herman and Herman's intuition. They complicate the picture further by asserting (1947: 149): 'Elements of the [mountain] dialect are heard in Fort Worth and Dallas, Texas, northeastern Oklahoma, the Delaware–Maryland–Virginia peninsula, and the Piedmont as well as in the more immediate lowland regions.'

In somewhat similar manner, the attempt to define an Appalachian culture has depended upon features which are far from uncommon elsewhere in rural America, although they may have persisted longer in Appalachia. Activities such as spinning and quilting, the particular kind of music once classified as hillbilly, herb medicines, dressing patterns with aprons for the women and overalls for the men, special types of dancing, canning and preserving, making home-made beverages, black-smithing, carving in wood, making soap, and old fiddlers' contests were far from unusual in eastern Texas in the 1930s. Dulcimer making and playing would have been strange in that environment, but home-made instruments were certainly not. For the uninitiated, at any rate, Jesse Stuart's stories read and sound (in public readings) like any other relatively sentimen'tal fiction with a rural setting.

' These examples, and considerable other information, point in the direction of a late development for an Appalachian dialect, based primarily upon late survivals rather than early differences. Instead of fulfilling the popular notion of Elizabethan or some other, more sophisticated version of Early Modern English migration, the language practices of Appalachia appear to involve retention of a number of lexical, grammatical and phonological features which were quite widespread in the early nineteenth century and have been giving way at differential rates to the influence of more mainstream American English. Loyalty to 'mountain talk', while not a trivial factor in the usage patterns of the Appalachians and possibly the Ozarks, generally means holding on to usages and pronunciations (*fla'r* for *flower*, approximate homophony of *tire* and *tar*) which are regarded as old-fashioned elsewhere.

By the final third of the nineteenth century, literary evidence tends to show that the more poorly educated and less travelled residents of the northern, Midland and southern states and a few subdivisions thereof could be rather clearly differentiated.[3] This is approximately what would be shown by a backward projection from the Linguistic Atlas materials, which rely heavily upon Class I informants who are very similar in many ways to the human subjects that the local colour writers preferred. On the other hand, social groups, like the field-hand Blacks still in the 'shadow of the plantation', the Pennsylvania Germans, certain Louisianians who also used French, and some of the Spanish speakers of the South-west, had dialects much more extremely deviant from ordinary English than the most non-standard of the regional dialect users. In all the regions and among all the social groups, some speakers were capable of speaking (and writing) a dialect of wider communication rather strikingly different from that of the main body of dialect speakers. The evidence of writers such as William Wells Brown and, later, Julia Peterkin tends to indicate that at least some of the users of social dialects were bidialectal.

Until about the time of World War II or slightly later, this dialect pattern appears to have remained relatively well in place. Migrations, like the famous one of Blacks up the Mississippi – traceable as much in terms of jazz history (Ramsey and Smith 1939 and many others) as in dialect data – to Chicago and even over to New York, almost necessarily provided the beginnings of other processes hardly studied in any depth until the 1960s. When Carver (*DARE* I: xxx) points out that the distribution of *beau dollar* ('a silver dollar') entirely among Blacks in the North and primarily among the same ethnic groups in the South 'reveals the spread of the term northward [as] the result of the migration of southern Blacks into the urban North', it is a counsel of ignorance – but ignorance we all share – to assert that this 'spread' came after World War II because the first recorded instance of the term, in *DARE*, is from 1944. We simply do not know how far back the expression goes. *DARE*'s 'probable' derivation from French suggests Louisiana origin rather than 'lumber camps along the Mississippi River', which is the guess of the first *DARE* I attestation. It is pointless to suggest a (possibly now lost) Louisiana French source for the term; we simply do not know about its history before 1944.

The dividing lines between dialects geographically considered – the isogloss bundles, in conventional terminology – were fuzzy at best. Even when the expressions are preselected, 'few regional expressions confine themselves within sharp boundaries' (Carver, *DARE* I: xxx). There is no strong historical indication that any sharper geographic dialect divisions ever existed in the United States.

The population redistributions that took place during World War I and much more extensively in World War II were influential in the further blurring of those regional distinctions. At that time, perhaps especially among enlisted men, regional dialect stereotypes and prejudices were quite strong. 'Funny' dialect pronunciations of the area in which servicemen were stationed were subjected to considerable ridicule. In the Yorktown and Norfolk, Virginia areas, announcements of buses leaving for Newport News (with [ny-] in both) led to outright complaints that the dispatchers could 'just say' the words with unpalatalized [n-]. Kurath and McDavid (1961: 174) confirm the distribution '/nu, du tuzde/ . . . current throughout the North and North Midland. In Pennsylvania, northeastern West Virginia, New Jersey, and Metropolitan New York, /u/ is universal; in the New England settlement area it is the predominant pronunciation, but not the only one', as against /nju, dju, tjuzde/. . . curren[t] in the South and South Midland'. The Atlas materials which are the basis of these statements were collected soon after the World War II period, and little change would have taken place. The sailors' reactions – even the unsophisticated nature of those reactions – are explained in Kurath and McDavid (1961: 174 ) 'In the North, /ju/ is infrequent, though preferred by some cultured speakers, as in Metropolitan New York.' The groups of sailors contained, alas, very few cultured speakers; the almost universal reaction was to attribute the /nyu-/ articulation to Southern slowness.

Sailors of about the same level of linguistic sophistication entertained each other, in 1944 and 1945, with the supposed Tidewater sentence

> There's a mouse [muws] in the house [huws], get him out [uwt].

The actual Tidewater diphthongs were, of course, much more nearly [əw] than [uw]. Many of the sailors may have known an old joke about a Scotsman who was told that a certain animal was a moose ([muws], approximately his *mouse*) and ran screaming from the area in fear of encountering a rat. Peer pressure on the enlisted men themselves certainly acted to produce the gradual, if unadvertised, substitution of [aw]. In my own case, ridicule of my 'outrageous Texas dialect' attempt to produce a German umlauted vowel for *Loew's* (the theatre chain) led to resigned production of /lowz/ – or to avoidance of the word altogether.

With the media-promoted sentimentality about returning home after the war, there may have been a temporary re-regionalization on the part of some dischargees. Dialect levelling had, however, received a great impetus from the moving about involved in World War II. More wars, migrations for the purpose of employment, increased travel in general, and a simply less narrowly regional attitude acted against dischargees' readopting their regional speech patterns. The dischargee who had vowed, in conformity to the fashion of the separation centres, to 'go back to Mesa/Amarillo/Kansas City/Hartford . . . and never leave' soon found abundant reasons to revisit some of the places he had been during the war, or to go to new places. From Texas, Oklahoma and Arkansas, for example, many relatives had migrated to work in the defence plants of California; servicemen who had been Texans or Louisianians before the war found themselves Californians immediately thereafter. Pride in describing the places they had visited soon became the fashion, rather than the opposite trend of never wanting to leave home again. The American population, which had never had much of a stable peasantry, became increasingly more mobile during the 1960s, 1970s and 1980s.

The 'undeclared' wars (Korea and Vietnam) of the 1950s, 1960s, and 1970s, although by no means on the scale of World War II and notoriously lacking the involvement of the entire nation, carried on the kind of mixing which promotes levelling. Linguistically, perhaps little came out of the Korean War except the temporary 'Bamboo English' (Norman 1955), which had a number of pidgin characteristics, and the occasional use of *just a skosh* (little) as a kind of solidarity form for veterans of overseas conflict. Vietnam produced such atrocious phrases as *body count* and the ultimately ironic *light at the end of the tunnel* for officialese, and *fragging* ('destroying one's own obnoxious leader') among the troops. According to a report from a participant, the preponderance of Black soldiers in actual combat gave prestige to some of the more recognizable forms from Black English, and White soldiers felt that the adoption of at least a few characteristically Black phrases was necessary for their survival. The National Defense Education Act (NDEA), designed as an educational response to Russia's perceived space and technological superiority, had made available graduate education to many, the great majority of them White. With the prevailing attitudes, deferment of students – again, mainly White and of a higher socio-economic level – meant that Blacks and poor Whites made up the preponderance of soldiers in combat. Recognition of what had gone on led to renewed Black protests and perhaps to Black unity, although expressions of Black solidarity were more likely to use ethnic slang than Black English Vernacular basilect.

Regional distribution in the post-World War II period may perhaps be typified by /s/ – /z/ in *greasy*. Atwood (1950) had established a distribution basically of /grizi/ South and /grisi/ North, with 'relatively narrow' transitional areas where both [s] and [z] are used 'to the west of Philadelphia' (1950: 428). Nothing is said about the historical provenience of this distinction; so far as I know, no one has claimed, for example, different origins in British dialects among the colonists as the source for this distinction. Yet Kurath and McDavid (1961: 176) could assert without fear of contradiction 'Voiceless /s/ and voiced /z/ are current in this word [*greasy*] in remarkably clear-cut regional dissemination.'

Since 1961 the dissemination has become more questionable and even the distribution less clear cut. The /-s-/ articulation has been gaining in the South. In Texas, Louisiana and probably all the southern states, younger and more nationally oriented speakers adjust themselves to the national norm; spelling pronunciation probably has something to do with it also. Among self-conscious academics, at any rate, the /-s/ articulation is now heard rather often from older Southern-born speakers. The intuition of a /-z-/ speaker is that /-s-/ speakers are puristically conscious of the derivational relationship to the noun /griys/, the verb form being at that time /griyz/ in the familiar historical pattern of *wreath* and *wreathe* or *loath* and *loathe*. It used to be an effective rejoinder to say, 'You wouldn't say /lawsiy/ for /lawziy/, would you?' However, in recent years an increasingly large number of speakers seem to be using /-s-/ in *lousy* as well. In Pennsylvania, as Shields (1989) reports, the boundaries between the variants 'of *greasy* have shifted . . . specifically, the fricative /s/ has now attained near universality, except in York County'. No one would be greatly surprised to find that much the same development is taking place in many other areas.

In other matters of dialect, the not unexpected results can be observed. Hartman (*DARE* I: xlix) put it about as conservatively as it could be put: 'Young speakers, especially socially mobile ones, appear to be breaking with local speech patterns in favor of broader regional and perhaps even newly developing national ones.' Among the tendencies Hartman specifies are 'continued loss of marginal contrasts' like /ɔ/ and /a/ or /o/ /ɔ/ before /r/ and 'reinstatement' of non-prevocalic /-r-/ (noted for New York City, in more formal contexts, by Labov 1965). Many do struggle to eliminate their neutralization of /ɛ/ and /ɪ/ before nasals, perhaps with less success. It is quite easily perceptible, also, that certain regional expressions are giving way to the national usage. The fad for the use of the suffix *-teria*, which produced seemingly endless innovations around the 1950s, appears to be over, leaving only the original *cafeteria* and a *washateria*, sometimes stigmatized as Southern in contrast to the more prestigious *laundromat*.

In Canada, and especially in its cities, de-regionalization may have gone further than in the United States, if there ever was any development of dialect regions in Canada. (Interference from French in zones with a heavy French-speaking population is, of course, excepted.) Pringle (1983: 231) reports:

. . . despite the wavering over tomato, lever, schedule, etc., Canadian English is . . . at least in the cities, remarkably uniform: indeed, English Canada has been described as the most uniform speech area of any world language. Thus there is usually no possible way to localize a Canadian urban speaker within Canada.

Even the long-stressed ambition of underprivileged groups to speak the regional standard began to prove old-fashioned – or non-existent. Lambert and Tucker (1969) found that Black freshmen at Tougaloo University in Mississippi far preferred Network Standard to the speech of educated White Southerners. In fact, the last variety proved lowest in the scale of attitudes of the Black speakers.

Under really close examination, dialect history is seldom so simple as the trend toward homogeneous usage. McCrum, Cran and MacNeil (1986) probably give the argot of the 'valley girls' of California more attention than it really deserves, but even relatively trivial variation of this type can show that the 'California homogeneity' so easily invoked is a relative term. Earlier, the description of 'boontling' (Adams 1971) gave an extreme example of how local fashions in speech can produce radical, if perhaps temporary innovations.

Yet some pronounced trends have been observable, usually among other than regional groups. The *beat generation* or *beatniks* of the 1960s, children in a sense of the veterans of World War II and college under the 'GI Bill of Rights', tended to become *dropouts* in a very different sense from the later use of the term; that is, in the 1960s 'dropping out' was a favourably regarded withdrawal from the repressive institutions of society, which might include school, whereas later it came to designate the process of not acquiring enough education. The dropouts of the 1960s in some respect duplicated their veteran parents' delay in proceeding from high school to college and then into the conventional world of work.

The youngsters of the late 1950s and the early to mid-1960s replaced the area with the generation as a focus of loyalty. One was not to trust anyone over thirty, and older people talked sadly of the *generation gap*. There were linguistic correlates for the youngsters. All over the country, a general superlative was *the most*. The supreme accolade was 'You're beat', with later replacement among adolescents by ' . . . a freak' or 'freaky'. Young men, very unlike their fathers, reacted favourably to the idea of wearing flowers in their hair, being called 'flower children' and supporting 'flower power'. Letting the hair grow long was a more permanent part of the movement and more universally observed. Favourite greetings were 'Peace' or 'Peace and love'. An 'in' conversation opener was 'Like . . .'. There was the joke about what a Beatnik says in an emergency: 'Like . . . Help!' Jack Kerouac, whose claim to have adapted the term *beat* from *beatific* is not well substantiated, made *On the Road* (1957) a favourite manifesto for youngsters who refused to be identified with any one place, although San Francisco did acquire prestigious status.

To some extent these young Americans were equivalents, in a less intellectual framework generally, of Britain's *angry young men*. They were proud of being the *counter culture*. Samuel Beckett became a familiar name and *Chianti* and *existentialist* everyday words for youngsters who had never been to Italy, had hardly ever drunk wine, had not read a word of Kirkegaard or Sartre and probably had never heard of Gide or Camus. There was, tragically, the even more pronounced spread of the terminology of the drug trade among their successors, the hippies, who soon fell into the *drug culture*; the term *hippie* became well known to Americans who knew so little about jazz and the Black culture behind it that they still preferred *hep* to *hip* as the adjective form and probably did not recognize the relationship of the noun form to the ghetto *hipster*. The influence of that trend spread even to bilingual Puerto Ricans (Llorens 1968).

Jazz for the early beatniks was replaced by rock and roll for the hippies, with later 'disco' and 'rap' for a comparable generation group. Purely regional loyalties and associations remained at most subsidiary. Even the 'Sun Belt' associations of the popular music of the 1980s represent more nearly what some anthropologists call *dramatic low status assertion* – identification with low-status segments of the population – than any kind of re-regionalization.

Impressionistically, de-regionalization is the strongest force in American English today. One is not surprised any more, after speaking to an older man with a strong local dialect and to a younger man with virtually no trace of one, to be told that latter is the former's son. My own experiences of this type include a case where the father had a strong Charleston, SC accent and the son was a virtually perfect Network Standard speaker, and another in which the father was himself apologetic about his Georgia/Louisiana background and its effects upon his dialect, the mother had clearly identifiable east Texas/Louisiana features, and the two sons – who grew up in the Philippines and Puerto Rico, among other places – were often asserted to have a New York accent, even though they had not even visited that city or state.

Regionalisms like Louisiana Cajun terms may be spreading but primarily in food terms and usually only in *Cajun* itself as a component of a food name; *blackened redfish* is hardly a 'Cajun' expression. *Let the good times roll* (from *Laissez les bons temps rouler*) may have achieved some national distribution through the fad for Cajun music roughly accompanying the vogue for Cajun food. With new, if not uncontested legitimacy for Spanish, a few South-western Mexican terms (*macho*, for example) may be becoming better known. *Chicano*, a term for a South-western Mexican, is not listed by *DARE* I and may have become non-regional by this time, although it seemed to spread from the South-west beginning around the 1950s. *Pachuco*, indicating a person of more rebellious 'Latin' abstraction, may never have gained much currency outside the South-west. Even during the period of aloofness from Spanish in Texas (Sawyer 1959), Mexican (often asserted by people who really knew Mexico to be 'TexMex' in actuality) food terms like *tamales* (*hot tamales* in the east Texas of the 1920s and 1930s), *enchiladas* and *tortillas* were generally known. *Sopapillas* came in later and possibly has not yet gained as wide a distribution. In spite of the widespread Puerto Rican presence in the United States, especially in the eastern cities, *alcapurria* and *lechon asado* do not seem to be gaining much currency.

Yiddish terms (*maven*) seem to be spreading primarily among better-educated residents of the cities, and those in the hinterlands who read their writings. Phrases like *So what else?* and *Don't ask* (/ɛsk/) are probably more familiar to Northerners and North-easterners than to residents of other parts of the United States.

Divergence from standard English (or from local non-standard, predominantly White dialects) is said to be taking place among Blacks in the inner city (NWAVE 1987). While it is debatable whether this is divergence or an age-grading feature, since the analyses are based upon studies of contemporary generations and the records of the past are treated in cavalier fashion, it is clear that the social factors in divergence – if that is what it is – are stronger than the geographic factors. Or, since people of one ethnic group (now, anyway) are ghettoized into certain parts of the inner city, the social/geographic distinction has perhaps finally collapsed. No one can doubt, however, that the social factors (ethnic solidarity, recognizability, etc.) are stronger than the geographic factors in this development.

Certain generalizations of features at one time or another regional in some sense are fairly easy to trace. For example, the Black English Vernacular in its Southern, rural form has in the past frequently been used for the kind of folk tale which ends with a traditional tag:

> I stepped on a pin (/tin),
> The pin (/tin) bend
> The story end.

With many variants, this ending formula probably comes from the English 'nominee' formula:

> Be bow bended
> My story's ended.

There have, however, been many changes, grammatical, phonological and lexical, in the transmission of this formula. (For a fuller account, see Dillard 1977: 129–34.) It is at least as old in the West Indies as in the continental United States (Herskovits and Herskovits, *Suriname Folk Lore*, 1936: 142–6), and its very variability seems to show how close the cultural ties of the West Indies and the Black population in the United States are – or at least were at some time. The formula is recorded fairly early in the South (Fauset 1927), and its transmission up the Mississippi as far as Benton Harbor, Michigan (Dorson 1967) is traceable. With its constant function as ending tag to trickster tales (Brer Rabbit in the US, primarily Anansi in the Caribbean) in an African–American community, this tag is obviously 'the same' through all its variations.

It is hard to draw the same conclusion about *be [too] slow to catch the itch* (*DARE* I, under *catch v[erb] phr[ase]*). *DARE* I, which places no regional label on the expression, cites examples from North Carolina, Arkansas, Florida, Missouri, South Carolina and Oklahoma. A variant is *too slow to catch a cold*. As a child in Texas, I was exposed to something similar in this form:

> A: Which is faster, heat or cold?
> B: I don't know.
> A: Heat is, stupid. Anyone can catch cold.

It is certainly open to question whether this is a transmitted bit of folklore or the type of bromide which anyone with a (small) degree of punning skill can innovate. It may be accidental that

only examples from the South and South Midland are immediately available to me.

Uncertainties seem to be almost inherent in language history,
and the closer one is to the language the less certainty there
appears to be. There are certainly a number of mere probabilities
in this presentation (see *around the horn*, [p. 148]; *tote*, pp. 102,
114; *buckaroo*, pp. 124–6; *dogie*, Dillard 1985: 134–5, and
others). On the other hand, no other presentation seems to do it
much differently, although the assumptions are often not stated.

For an illustration of the historical problem, consider the
example of *blinky* ('Of milk, beginning to go sour: chiefly W[est]
Midl[and], Plains States, S[outh] W[est]' – *DARE* I). Intuitively,
as a native speaker of whatever dialect it is that uses the word, I
can corroborate a feeling for its regional nature. However, my
intuition would place it in east Texas, where I grew up. Some
north-west Louisiana speakers (in the region known locally as the
Ark-La-Tex) know it, even some in their thirties, but hardly
anyone under twenty anywhere, at a guess. Students in
dialectology class in New York City and Puerto Rico are
impressed with the 'esoteric' nature of the term but amused by its
naivety and rural quality – perhaps the typical reaction to a
regionalism by someone who does not use it. The old-fashioned
nature of the term probably also enters into that reaction.

The reaction 'old-fashioned' is confirmed by Tarpley (1970) as
to milk's becoming *blinky* or turning into *blue-john* in a short
period, before advances in refrigeration. *DARE* I shows *blue-
john* to be less widely distributed than *blinky* ('chiefly S[ou]th,
S[outh] Midl[and]'), although recorded over a greater period of
time and from a greater variety of sources.

It is the history of *blinky* which illustrates the point about lack
of certainty. *DARE* I records no attestation earlier than 1902,
although etymologically the adjective is linked to '*blink v[erb]* Of
milk, to turn sour', which in turn is linked to an adjectival *blink*
attested from 1883. The source is said to be (unspecified) British
dialectal *blink*, 'Of milk: to turn sour [From *blink* to exercise an
evil influence, bewitch, hence to sour]'. This *blink* is attested only
from 1905. Again, it should be emphasized that there is no
argument with the data presented. But there is a rather large
time as well as a space gap – the 1902 attestation is from north-
west Arkansas. It is a quite reasonable assumption that this, and
many another homey word came over from England with earlier
settlers, followed the migration pattern along the South Midland
area (see pp. 176–7) and was present over fairly great stretches of
time and space without being recorded in any easily accessible

source. It may also be assumed that documents may eventually be discovered which confirm the hypothesis. But it remains a hypothesis, not an empirical demonstration. Isogloss maps, however impressive, tell us relatively little about the historical relationship.

Technology – the improvement in refrigeration and in dairy practices in general – may well have had an important part in the near-disappearance of *blink/blinky* and of numerous other words of the same type. One might also say that the socio-economic change, which is not necessarily improvement, by which the rural or small-town family which owned its own cow and had its own milk gave way to the urban dwellers who abandoned the cow and got their milk first from a bottle ('Milkman, Keep Those Bottles Quiet', a popular song during World War II, on the theme that a 'swing shift' [late night] worker needed his/her rest and could be disturbed by the milkman), then from a carton and finally from a plastic container, contributed as well.

Commercial terminology and national distribution help, perhaps, to explain the shift to *cottage cheese* from *smearcase, clabber cheese* ('chiefly S[ou]th, S[outh] Midl[and]' according to *DARE* I) with occurrences from 1904 to 1973 (according to Allen, *Linguistic Atlas of the Upper Midwest*) and *bonnyclabber cheese* (*DARE* I: 'N[orth] East *somewhat old-fash[ioned]*' attested from 1941 to 1949).[4] *Clabber* itself represents a process technologically at least obsolescent – unless of course the product is marketed under the name of *yogurt*. An aging acquaintance of mine, with a farm background, had plain words for (un-sweetened) yogurt: 'just old clabber'. The American consumer, however, pays a great deal of attention to the name.

This is just one more example of what Reed (1977: 63) observed: 'Dialect fusion in itself further complicated by literary influences from specific occupational sources.' Looked at from another perspective, these 'literary influences', which perhaps inhibit an announced programme of discovering regional differences, are as legitimate a process of change in twentieth-century American English as any other: the elimination of rural, homey or regional terms by the influence of a generally urban but geographically hard to localize tendency. Commercialization and the ubiquitousness of advertising 'literature' is one part of that process.

That this influence should be strongly linked to occupations is no surprise. Pickford (1956) inaugurated the criticism of the purely geographic approach with her observation that sociologists were finding that Americans identified primarily with their occupations rather than with their areas of residence. Evidence of generalization into the American vocabulary of occupational terms tends to suggest, although not with the precision that would be possible if there had been sociological studies in the eighteenth and nineteenth centuries, that the identification pattern has been the same almost from the beginning.

Occupational and interest groups have 'tracers' of their own. One who uses the phrase *catch 22*, for example, is likely to be an academic in one of the literary disciplines or an associate of such academics. The term *catch* ('unexpected and unfavourable eventuality') goes back to 1855. When Joseph Heller used *Catch 22* as the title of his 1961 novel, he was emphasizing the tiresome repetition of such 'catches' in the armed services. Some members of the academic and literary community (apparently British as early as American) picked up the phrase and now describe a restrictive and unpleasant eventuality as a *catch 22*. The number adds nothing to the meaning of the noun; in a purely semantic sense the phrase is verbose. There is, however, as usual, a function: the user of the phrase identifies himself as a reader of Heller's novel and a sympathizer with the attitudes expressed therein. As an interest-group identifier it has a solidarity function; it may also serve as a putdown to an unliterary person and as an antagonizing device to one who does not share Heller's socio-political views. As a tracer the phrase identifies its user as one who entered the liberal community around the 1960s (*OED* attestations range from the *Atlantic Monthly* in 1971 through a few other magazines and newspapers to a book on psychoanalysis) quite as well as any other tracer identifies geographic movement of a population.

Among academics the pronunciation of the final vowel in *premises* is another such identifier. In the beginning it seems to have been a kind of hypercorrection, a pronouncing of the word by analogy with the pronunciation of Greek-derived plurals like *theses*. An administrator at a small college wishing to show solidarity with erudite members of the faculty may well adopt the (false) etymological pronunciation. Some members of the faculty, especially those with a little Greek, may retain the traditional plural pronunciation as in *promises*. Still a third group, perhaps with some course work in modern linguistics, may reject the middle group and identify with the 'erroneous' pronunciation on the principle *les extrêmes se touchent*. Much the same can be said for the realization of *vis à vis* as /vɪz ə vɪz/. All of these last three examples appear to be specific to a social/occupational group (college faculty members and others, like clergymen, of academic inclinations) with variation according to attitudes and loyalties within that group, but there seems to be no more specific geographic correlate than that any of the usages would be rare between Pecos, Texas, and Lordsburg, New Mexico.

The presidents of the United States within the second half of the twentieth century illustrate the de-regionalizing tendency rather well. Franklin D. Roosevelt was the essence of North-easternism and almost stereotypically a graduate of Harvard. Harry S. Truman, the first president of the post-World War II era, was almost as stereotypically a Midwesterner – and subject to snobbery from Eastern columnists and political analysts. Truman's famous successful campaign in 1948 over New Yorker Thomas E. Dewey was almost a triumph of Middle Americanism over Easternism. Eisenhower, associated with Kansas and almost accidentally with Texas, was remembered more for his European campaign and little objection was raised to the slight Midland traces in his speech. John F. Kennedy, another quite visible Harvard graduate, had a recognizable New England accent which was imitated – and admired – just as much as it was typically exaggerated; on one LP record of his speeches Kennedy used linking /r/ in only a third of its potential occurrences. Yet Americans thought of him as always saying 'Idear of it' and 'Cubar' and generally cherished the object of their own hyperbole.

With Texan Lyndon B. Johnson, on the other hand, it was quite a different story. Stereotyped as a Texas political boss type because of his association with Samuel Rayburn, and superor-dinated beyond having to change his dialect, Johnson became in his first and only term (after finishing that of the assassinated Kennedy) not only the wrong man at the wrong time but 'from the wrong place'. His sometime assistant Bill Moyers, who eliminated at least most of the stigmata of his Texas accent perhaps partly through study in Scotland, was never subject to the same kind of dialect prejudice and continues to function on television with no special criticism.

Johnson's successor, Richard M. Nixon, a Californian with a law degree from Duke and a rather widely variant background, began a period of presidents with notably levelled regional accents. The press was often at odds with Nixon, even when he was governor of California, but never over the issue of regionalism. Even when most of the nation believed Nixon guilty of the cover-up at Watergate, the term *credibility gap* was not used about him as it had been of Johnson. Nixon's temporary successor after his resignation, Gerald Ford, born in Nebraska but active primarily in Michigan, was considered 'klutzy' by many but was not criticized for his dialect.

Perhaps the most unfortunate experience was that of Jimmy Carter. His Georgian accent, although actually rather slight, attracted unfavourable comment, as did the other Georgians who accompanied him to Washington. While the satirists of *Saturday Night Live* had portrayed Ford as a disorganized stumblebum with speech full of *non sequiturs* but not especially dialectal, they specifically caricatured Carter's Southern accent. His disastrous 'my daughter Amy' speech in a crucial television debate with Ronald Reagan compounded the 'folksiness' associated with his dialect and probably contributed to his defeat.

Reagan, the 'great communicator', had had a brief career as a radio broadcaster before becoming a movie actor and then governor of California, and was a master of Network Standard. It seems quite possible that his lack of 'dialect', along with his camera presence, aided him in maintaining a high level of popularity with the American public at a time when critics had little trouble finding flaws in his political and economic policies. To the more critical he was known as the *Teflon* president; nothing would stick to him – certainly not a regional label.

George Bush continues the Reagan tradition in most respects. Attempts are made to characterize his speech as an improbable mixture of Texas and New England, but those efforts seem to be based more upon known facts about the history of his residence than upon his usages and articulations.

It is doubtful that television, with which no one can interact on a peer basis, is productive of the changes going on in de-regionalization any more than the radio which preceded it. Nevertheless, Network Standard remains a fairly accurate descriptive term for the prestigious dialect of American English. It is 'r-ful' in non-prevocalic position, unlike some of the older aristocratic dialects of New England and the South. While the importance of this feature has been exaggerated, it is what most Americans think of first when they seek to characterize dialects. A seminal socio-linguistic study like Labov 1965 made perhaps its most telling, and certainly its most quotable, point in showing how /r/ production varied among New Yorkers, with upwardly mobile lower-middle-class speakers leading the trend to adapt to national norms.

Dating this spread of non-prevocalic /r/ is partly an impressionistic matter, but personal experiences agree with statements by socio-linguists. My own 'r-ful' speech was objected to by New York City-derived speakers around 1953–5 (they took it as a marker of my Texas origins, whereas I assumed it to represent adaptation to the national norm). Labov (1968: 42) refers the development to 'recent decades'.

Southern, the most stigmatized regional dialect with the possible exception of 'Brooklynese', is often said to be disappearing, although there is popular controversy about the matter. Atlanta *Constitution* writer Dick Green took reprisals in 'The Woim Toins: Southerners Stage Linguistic Counterattack' (New York *Times* News Service, 18 December 1976) against alleged attacks on the dialect of president-elect Carter. The familiar theme is that New Yorkers, for example, speak 'worse' English than Southerners, the assumption being that there is a canon alongside which anyone's English can be measured and in comparison to which most varieties are found wanting. More quietly, but perhaps more effectively, regional dialect speakers tend to do what Erskine Caldwell described in 1963 (*Around About America*, p. 83). He says that a 'girl with a Southern accent that was a shade too thick' would enroll as a speech major at a local university, especially if she desired to become a radio announcer or a 'disc jockette'.

Exceptions remain even in the most urban areas, especially in the working class, as Labov (1965) established. Those exceptions are still strongest among Black speakers. Labov (1980), while detailing how some older Blacks retain features of a given city's working class phonology, refers to the striking uniformity of the great majority of ghetto Blacks in different cities. The trend towards uniformity has accompanied a national trend to urbanization, but even the cities – given the social conditions productive of differences – can be the scene of extreme variation.

## Notes

1 Marckwardt (1957) found approximately this distribution for the vowels of *foggy* and *hog*:

| Ohio and Indiana | Illinois (except Chicago) | Michigan and Chicago |
|---|---|---|
| [ɔ] | usually [o], frequently [ɔ] | [a] |

2 A Puerto Rican tourist publication, *Qué Pasa in* [sic] *Puerto Rico*, in 1960 recommended a tour of the Phosphorescent Bay in a 'lunch' (obviously a launch), where lack of /a/ /ɔ/ contrast in Spanish is clearly involved.

3 A resolution of the disputes even among dialect geographers as to the exact regional divisions is far beyond the scope of this work. The list in

*DARE* I: p. xxxii may represent a kind of consensus, but even a cursory reading of the dialect literature will show many differences.

4 *DARE* I traces *bonnyclabber* to 'Ir[ish] *bainne clabair* "thick sour milk"' and calls it 'chiefly N[orth] Atl[antic], somewhat old-fashioned'. It is attested first from Maine in 1731, then from Philadelphia in 1807, from New Jersey in 1883, from Maine in 1903, from Virginia in 1904 and from Maryland in 1925.

Kurath (1949: 41) called it 'still common in the Philadelphia area . . . in Eastern New England (except for Rhode Island, the New London area, and the greater part of Maine) . . . also in scattered fashion in central and western Pennsylvania and from there Southward to North Carolina, an area in which it has been largely replaced by other terms'. Note the term *scattered fashion* in Kurath's account. That the term was spread to areas where Irish immigrants were an important (dominant?) part of the population and then was gradually replaced by other terms as other groups achieved dominance is of course a possibility, but other possibilities are not excluded.

**Chapter 8**

# Deruralization: the small town, the city and the suburbs

The processes which tend to eliminate or reduce the use of *blinky* and *blue-john* and to replace *clabber* with the more modish *yogurt* have developed away from the rural areas where the terms of the farm and simple home life were appropriate. The regional patterns most easily demonstrated by rural terminology have become a lesser factor in American English. If the relative urbanization cannot be identified with certainty as the cause, it is quite clearly a correlate.

Beginning with the later decades of the nineteenth century the American trend has been away from the rural and the isolated. Especially during World Wars I and II, even very ordinary Americans gained a certain awareness of the rest of the world, including England. The vocabulary of England (*Chemist's*, *petrol*, *lorry*, *tuppence*) became familiar. German loanwords (*flak*, *panzer*, *Luftwaffe*) became a part of the daily American vocabulary of the 'hot' war of 1941–5 and *sputnik* an early part of the 'cold' war lasting nearly forty-five years more. (In 1989 *glaznost* and in 1990 *perestroika*, from Nobel prizewinner Mikhail Gorbachov's new policies for Russia, attained a currency for which the limits and extent can hardly be yet known.) A greater international movement and awareness correlated to some degree with a greater national awareness. Yet it always seemed that the foreign terms were recast in the American mould. *Blitzkrieg*, once a terror-inspiring term for the capacities of the Nazi war machine, shortened to *blitz* and specialized to mean a routine defensive manoeuvre in the game of football; the wartime meaning was virtually forgotten.

Equally forgotten were some of the attitudes to other parts of the country prominent during the wars. Soldiers, sailors and marines who otherwise might never have seen the larger cities were stationed in them, usually proclaiming the superiority of things 'back home'. So did rural and small-town workers who moved to the cities to work in armament-producing ('defence') plants, where round-the-clock production schedules put many of them on *swing shifts* and forever broke up the rural 'early to bed, early to rise' pattern. Many of them decided that they didn't really want to go back 'home', and a movement pattern already in progress was intensified. Many of the historical phenomena associated with American English had to do with movement of the population from rural areas to the city.

The wars only intensified and sped up processes of urbanization which had begun during the latter part of the nineteenth century. Urbanization during the late nineteenth and the twentieth centuries was perhaps the greatest factor of all in vocabulary change (Wood 1970: 47), and the generally slower elimination of rural-associated phonological and grammatical patterns was certainly not unaffected.

Although virtually everything has been called *the last frontier* or *a new frontier*, the frontier became primarily a nostalgic factor, useful mainly in advertising. (One need only consider the names of certain automobile models – Bronco, Mustang, Pinto, Charger, Colt, Thunderbird, Falcon, Cougar, Wildcat, Bobcat, Maverick, Hornet, Rambler – and to contrast them with the equivalents among Japanese imports: Accord, Sentra, Civic . . .) Nevertheless, the people of the United States had long continued to be primarily a rural and small-town population. When the cities grew at their fastest rate during the 1840s and 1850s, with an increase of 92.1 per cent in the 1840s and of 75.4 per cent in the 1850s, more than double the growth rate of the nation, the population of the United States changed from 10.8 per cent to 19.8 per cent urban. Two groups accounted for the change: farmers and other rural persons moving to towns of 2500 or larger, making up most of the slightly over 6 million urban residents of 1860 and immigrants from other countries, some 5 million of whom arrived between 1835 and 1860; (McKelvey 1969: 50–1)

Small-town America was an intermediate stage between the essentially rural and the urbanized nation, with comparatively little linguistic output. Yet the small town is the natural habitat of the Chamber of Commerce, with its junior ('Jaycee') affiliate and the near-adoration of business as a way of life. The movement of the ambitious, aggressive small-town boy to the city is one of the prevalent motifs of American popular fiction. It was in the context of the change from small town to metropolitan emphases that *booster* ('one who supports [especially his own town or in-group] enthusiastically') and *boosterism* developed; *OED* calls both originally US, dating the first to 1890 and the second to 1926. The opposite term, *knocker* ('one who criticizes'), equally American in origin, is attested from 1900. The latter perhaps met some competition from *knockers* ('female breasts' – 'vulgar' according to *OED* II), beginning around 1941. *Booster* also has a possible meaning of 'burglar, shoplifter', which may have helped to eliminate the term from some vocabularies. Sinclair Lewis, especially in *Babbit* (1922), made satirical capital of the 'booster' mentality, although the word had been around for some time before he used it. Lewis's *Arrowsmith* (1935), almost sophomorically idealistic in its portrayal of the seeking of 'truth' by Dr Martin Arrowsmith and the idealized scientist Dr Max Gottlieb, achieves some of his better touches when the booster, now a 'Live Wire' (Lewis's own capitals), as unschooled educational employment agent tries to enlighten Professor Gottlieb as to the realities of the academic job market in America.

Writers like Sarah Orne Jewett, Thornton Wilder (*Our Town*, 1938) and even, in their earlier works, Lewis and Sherwood Anderson (*Poor White*, 1920) contributed to the relative idealization of the small town. Lewis's Gopher Prairie in *Main Street* (1920) was part of the beginning of a kind of revolt against the dullness of small towns, but even there the satire is not so biting as that on Zenith in *Babbit*. According to Clapin (1902), the city name was first used of Duluth by 'the great humorist' James Proctor Knott, governor of Kentucky from 1883 to 1879. Lewis's longer-remembered use of the name may in its own time have been an allusion to a temporarily familiar speech, much as Richard Nixon's 'Checkers' remained available for satirists and supporters throughout most of the 1980s.

With the development of urbanization, the use of terms like *hick* – and parody of rural, small-town and pretentious urban usage – grew. Damon Runyon's Ethel Turp, proud of being from Brooklyn even though its dialect was one the media felt free to use and abuse, refused to be intimidated by a 'hick cop' from Washington, DC, somewhat to husband Joe's embarrassment. New York *Daily Mirror* and syndicated columnist Walter Winchell, proud of his position and influence in New York City and especially on Broadway, ran a series of definitions of a 'hick town' during the late 1930s and early 1940s, one of the more familiar ones being that a hick town was one in which a motorist could ask a gasoline station attendant to put in two gallons without being asked whether the driver were trying to 'wean' the car.

The use of a breast-feeding reference in connection with a mechanism like an automobile would probably not be possible in the United States of the post-World War II period. Mechanization made many changes in lifestyle, although there does not seem to be a good study of its effect on the lexicon. Rather representative of the change in emphasis is a book with the revealing title *A Cow Is Too Much Trouble in Los Angeles*, written by Joseph O. Foster in 1952, significantly about a Mexican immigrant family trying to adjust to the increasingly mechanized city.

With radios replacing phonographs, which had in turn tended to replace pianos, in almost every American home, national and urban speech became at least a model accessible to small town and even rural residents. A diffidence, amounting to feelings of inferiority in some cases and to defensiveness in others, was a more immediate result than real mastery of prestige forms.

Trading, probably unconsciously, on this national attitude, the media used accents and dialects for effective comedy purposes, especially in the period just before World War II. Fred Allen's filibustering Senator Klaghorn from *somewhere* in the South, Eddie Cantor's Parkyakarkus, a stereotypical Greek, Jack Benny's Eddie 'Rochester' Anderson, who reportedly had to learn to speak like a Black in order to get the part, and Mr Kitzell, with a broadly Jewish accent, had enormous followings. Mrs Nussbaum, in 'Allen's Alley' on the Fred Allen show had a 'thick Jewish accent' (Dunning 1976: 223). Groucho Marx used some Yiddish-tinged expressions in the Marx Brothers' movies, but his brother Chico spoke a stage-Italian dialect and Harpo chose not to speak at all. Comedian and bandleader Ben Bernie's speech 'suggested the influence of Europe, Brooklyn, and the Old South' (Dunning 1976: 60). Freeman Gosden and Charles Correll continued to play Amos and Andy in Black dialect, even appearing in blackface in movies, up to the time of television.

Marion and Jim Jordan did 'Fibber McGee and Molly' from Wistful Vista, a broadly satirized small town from (probably) somewhere in the Midwest. Their speech, except for a few elements of stage Irish on the part of Molly, was apparently meant to represent Midwestern America and dialect comedy was not notably a part of the programme, but a character named Gildersleeve (played by Harold Peary, born Harold Jose Pereia de Faria and of Portuguese descent) featured a speech style obviously meant to represent a political ward-heeler.* George Burns and Gracie Allen depended upon Gracie's illogical statements and comical tones of voice (a style close in most particulars to that of Dumb Dora and the early Blondie), pitted against George's exasperated seriousness, without utilizing any recognizable dialect, although 'Señor Lee', with a stage Spanish dialect, was on the programme for a while.

Popular reading material, especially the comic strips, exploited the same attitude toward language. (Eye dialect writers like Artemus Ward and Mr. Dooley were the most probable models.) Al Capp's *Li'l Abner* and Billy DeBeck's [*Barney Google and*] *Snuffy Smith* in the comic strips exploited a kind of 'mountain' dialect; movies and radio programmes struggled to exploit their popularity but with an almost complete lack of success.

More successful for the sound media was Chick Young's *Blondie*, presenting the 'average' suburbanite couple of the 1940s and 1950s with one income, a one-family but two-storey house, two children, a dog Daisy (with puppies which materialized when needed for comic effect but were not around enough to be inconvenient), comical neighbours, and a postman who somehow managed to be on his rounds early in the morning when Dagwood rushed out of the house late on his commuter's schedule.

Bryce (1921, II, 108) had described the American city just after World War I as a huge expanse of ground

> covered with houses, two or three square miles appropriated by the richer sort, fifteen or twenty, stretching out into the suburbs, filled with dwellings of the poorer. They were not members of a community, but an aggregation of human atoms, like grains of desert sand, which the wind sweeps hither and thither.

By the 1930s an almost exact switch was beginning to take place, as urbanization of the working class and suburbanization of the middle class gradually developed.

Sentimental representations of the small town and of the farm remained, but the United States came more and more to visualize itself as urban for work and suburban for residence. That such a lifestyle as Dagwood, Blondie, Alexander (earlier 'Baby Dumpling') and Cookie Bumstead maintained was not accessible to those earning the national average income hardly occurred to the readers. Yet the comic strip bore out the observation of a Report

---

* Small-time, marginally-honest politician.

of the Social Science Panel (1974: 55), quoting Gans, *The Levittowners* (1967: 288–9): 'The crucial difference between cities and suburbs then is that they are often home for different kinds of people.'

Suburbia as represented by the Bumsteads reflected an ideal of long standing. Blondie herself was originally a *flapper*, like many others starting in the 'Jazz Age' of the 1920s and chronicled by more serious writers like F. Scott Fitzgerald. (The term, 1888 according to *OED* II, is not originally American, but the American flapper was more nearly exhibitionistic than 'immoral' according to *OED* II's British definition.) Her only aim was to be pretty, to be normal – even if a bit 'jazzy' for a time – and to catch a husband and provider, an ambition for which a young lady could easily appear to be too clever. In this respect she resembled Dumb Dora in the comic strip of the same name, which often ended with the tag line 'She's not so dumb.'

The Depression that succeeded the Jazz Age had slight influence on such popular fare, although *Blondie* for a time had to share the comic page with *Apple Mary*, who sold apples on a corner until the Depression was over and then turned into an affluent *Mary Worth* and then into *Mary Worth's Family*, and with *Pete the Tramp*, who lived in a *hobo jungle* (a term which, according to Flexner 1982: 314, had been current since 1910 but which had not been called to the attention of many of the more fortunate), looking for a *handout* (1832, but with some of the same qualifying circumstances) in a country in which hunger was the result of maldistribution rather than under-production of food, and *riding the rods* (under a railway compartment) in a nation in which poverty never greatly reduced mobility. The tramps virtually disappeared with wartime prosperity. An occasional ragged beggar who says *youse* has for decades occasionally appeared at the Bumsteads' front door looking for a handout, but either dialect or the awareness that the whole world doesn't lead the suburban lifestyle hardly penetrates this 'American institution'. The drug problem and its vocabulary (e.g. *crack house*, a usually tumbledown residence converted to the sale of a cheap variety of cocaine), AIDS, abortion, the divorce rate, homeless people, the environmental issues are not found in the comic strips and hardly on 'prime time' television.

The radio programmes and popular reading materials like the comics prepared the way for the television programme. Many had been produced by relatively literate cartoonists and writers who must have been familiar with the works of satirists like Lewis, James Thurber and Anderson. They are, in some sense, still mildly satirical, but all the barbs have been removed from the satire. As a part of the general availability of reading material for the semi-literate, they prepared the way for television – the *boob tube* ; one wonders whether those who first used the phrase were aware of Mencken's bitter characterization of *boobus Americanus*. The comic strip undoubtedly paved the way for the *situation comedy* or *sitcom* beginning in the 1950s in which 'typical Americans' made stupid mistakes but were never really malicious and somehow muddled through to the 'right' solution – that is, the one which most perfectly agreed with the values of family life and general conformity.

Nostalgia is a large part of what is packaged for popular, commercial entertainment. For example, door-to-door salesmen, almost completely obsolete by the 1980s (they have been replaced by telephone solicitors), are still satirized from time to time in *Blondie*. Only an occasional brave editorial writer dares attack *junk mail* (the term is first attested in 1954).[1] The term *sucker list* is available to describe those who have become victim of (now computerized) mass mailings, but the practice is apparently too important to mainstream business for anyone to risk satirizing it. Neither is there any reliable evidence as to its dating, although *sucker* as applied to an easy human victim is first listed in *OED* II from Toronto in 1838 and the term in the meaning 'a sponger, parasite' is called 'US *slang*'. (One might almost say here that the *OED* lacks a real sense of what the basic meaning in American slang is.) At any rate, the terms *sucker list* and *junk mail*, especially with the advantage that each may take from computerization, may describe what is really sacrosanct about twentieth-century American life.

Moving to the city often meant, also, moving north until fairly recently, when economic conditions have dictated movement of some northern corporations towards the *sun belt*. Urban growth was a feature primarily of New York, Pennsylvania, Massachusetts, Illinois and Ohio, where an overwhelming majority of the urban population lived in 1890; less than 8 per cent were in southern cities. By 1900 60 per cent of the residents of the North Atlantic states and 30 per cent of those in the Midwest were urban residents, contrasted with only 10 per cent in the South (Lingeman 1980: 327).

Immigrant groups, especially in the cities, had been arriving all along. It is commonplace that Irishmen, then Italians, then Jews, along with Polish and other European immigrants, flooded into cities like New York in the nineteenth century. For the Black population, movement out of the rural (and urban) South began on a large scale in about 1918 with the end of World War I, although the Black migration had begun in the 1880s.

World War I, which checked the influence of immigrants, created some labour shortages and motivated some industrialists to look to Southern Negroes as unskilled labourers. Although Blacks had been coming north for some time, the outbreak of the war produced a major quantitative difference (McKelvey 1969: 15–16). There was also the difference that Blacks did not fit the pattern of movement from the inner city to the suburbs like the other in-migrant groups.

The Blacks, however poor, did not conform to Brice's 'atoms of humanity' pattern, but formed a very real community with recognized leaders and a clear (developing) sense of its relationship to other communities in the cities and in the nation. Perhaps this is why Abrams (1965: 11) found that 'the influx of Negroes and other minorities into the cities . . . has added a dimension to the problem which cannot be reckoned with easily. The Negro concentration in central cities is changing [in the early 1960s] their social atmosphere. . .' De facto segregation contributed a large share to this 'new dimension'. Blacks were part of the pattern of movement into the cities, but they remained distinct in some ways.

'Negroes' – most of them, presumably, slaves – had formed 14 per cent of the total population at the time of the American Revolution and only 11 per cent in the early 1960s (Abrams 1965: 56). Their language, according to attestations, was much more different in the earlier period than in the latter. The greater attention to the language of the inner-city child, or to the Black English Vernacular, can, then, only have been the result of a different climate of opinion, not of raw linguistic differences. Greater contrast, especially in phonology, with Northern than with Southern dialects was one reason why the inner-city children's language attracted attention; unfamiliarity was another.

The inner-city conflicts had begun at least as early as the World War I migration, crowding (mostly White) old residents from the inner cities to those suburbs touted in the popular literature and culture. With the virtual halt to foreign immigration in the 1920s (Abrams 1965: 54), Blacks from the South were able to find employment opportunities in the Northern cities. Non-White population, 92 per cent of it Negro, outside the South grew sixfold between 1910 and the early 1960s and more than doubled between 1940 and the 1960s (Abrams 1965: 54). The standard example of inner-city change is, of course, Harlem with a Dutch

name becoming a locus of Black population and developing a
now long-term identification with the New York Black ghetto,
resistance movements, the Harlem Renaissance, the 'race' riots
of the 1960s, etc. The Black community's slavery, the Jim Crow
laws and segregation had been a harsher deterrent to incorpora-
tion into mainstream society than 'No Irish Need Apply'
advertisements had been to the Irish or the appellation *Christ
killer* (attested from 1941 but almost certain to have been used
earlier) for Jewish Americans.

In sports – one avenue of advancement open to national or
racial minorities – there had been a kind of progression. The Irish
had had their early period of dominance. In the 1880s a baseball
player of Irish extraction named Michael Joseph 'King' Kelly
innovated or popularized sliding into a base, and 'Slide, Kelly,
Slide' was a popular song with music and lyrics by the unrelated
John W. Kelly in 1889. The phrase was repeated by sandlot
players who knew nothing of its origin at least into the 1930s.
There were athletes of German ancestry like Honus Wagner and
George Herman 'Babe' Ruth. The Italian component was strong
enough in the game and among the fans that 'Bambino' as an
alternate nickname for the last needed no explanation. Joe
DiMaggio, Phil Rizzuto and other Italians found a place in
baseball in the period before World War II. At about the same
time, Henry B. 'Big Hank' Greenberg was a kind of symbol to
some Americans of Jewish background. Flexner (1982: 119)
shows how Irish ethnic pride entered into the names assumed by
boxers like 'Irish Bob' Cassidy . Irish baseball figures have
sometimes engaged in name changes, as when Philadelphia
Athletics manager Cornelius MacGillicuddy changed his name to
Connie Mack and managed to stay active in baseball from 1887 to
1950. Alleged need to make the name pronounceable to non-
members of the ethnic group, space-saving in cooperation with
headline writers for the sports pages, and other factors have been
offered as explanations of this particular type of assimilationism.
When Barney Ross (born Barnet Rasofsky) beat Jimmy McLarnin in May 1935 for the welterweight boxing title after having lost
to McLarnin in September 1934, sports writers emphasized the
ethnic pattern theme quite openly. Whatever the name changes
accomplished, they did not – and probably were not designed to –
fool anyone about the origins of the person involved. McLarnin
had won the title by beating Benny Leonard (born Benjamin
Lerner), and the names Benny, Bernard and Leonard are as
recognizably Jewish in the United States as Yehudi – indeed, to
the average *goy*, probably more so.[2]

When Ross lost to Henry Armstrong in May 1938, a new group had placed dominance on a new plane, with a champion of not one but three weight divisions. Armstrong had, for some obscure reason, changed his name from Jackson. It was not a step towards assimilation; Blacks had long since undergone name changes (Johnson being notoriously the one surname most taken over from the slaves' former masters) without its being of any help in their overcoming prejudice. When Joe Louis, undisputed heavyweight champion from 1937 to 1949, dropped the surname Barrow, the act may have reflected an attitude towards his improverished youth. When a Lithuanian surnamed Kukauskas had adopted the ring name (Jack) Sharkey, he (or his manager) had drawn upon the associations that both names had for boxing fans. *Mutatis mutandis*, it was probably the same process that made name changes routine among Hollywood 'stars' except at marriage.[3] For reasons a little less clearly related to boxing, Sidney Walker became Beau Jack, a lightweight champion in 1942. Cuban Kid Gavilan, who took over the gimmick of a 'bolo punch' from Filipino fighter Ceferino Garcia (Flexner 1982), was christened Gerardo Gonzales. Name changes could come easily to a public figure from a Spanish-speaking background, since 'Anglos' consistently overlooked the Hispanic custom of matronymic as well as patronymic identification.

Once past the *color line* (a Southern term during Reconstruction, from 1875, which was *raised* in 1878 but *drawn* in 1885 – and soon a familiar idiom in other sections of the country), Blacks made an impact on professional sports proportionate to the delay in their being allowed to compete with Whites. The Black impact on professional sports produced an unprecedented dominance by one ethnic group. Already Joe Louis and Jack Johnson, who had won the heavyweight championship in 1910, had made such an impact in boxing that the term *white hope*, for any 'Caucasian' male who appeared to be able to box, became a part of many Americans' vocabulary. After Robinson in baseball and a few others, Black talent exploded in professional and in college sports. Soon, by the 1980s, a White player on a professional basketball team was to become almost a rarity, as was a White runner among the leading ground gainers in professional football. The idea of a White heavyweight boxing champion became ludicrous. At just the time when television (with terms like *instant replay*) took over spectator sports and made them almost completely electronic, Blacks were the group dominating the activity. (Tennis and golf – and, as one Black comedian pointed out with wry humour, polo –

remained minor exceptions.) In baseball, the 'national pastime' with which Union soldiers had diverted themselves between Civil War battles, an especially significant crossing of the 'color line' occurred. A sports writer appropriately named Meany had designated the National (baseball) League as a 'new minor league' before Branch Rickey of the Brooklyn Dodgers managed to get Jackie Robinson past the colour barrier – which had been erected, insofar as the still primarily northern and eastern 'big leagues' were concerned, in the 1880s just as commercial profit came into the picture. The year was 1947, and a real change in race relationships began that year at least in the domain of sports.

Blacks may have been primarily associated with the South at the time, but the barriers to be broken down were ethnic rather than regional. Black Caribbean players like Roberto Clemente, from Puerto Rico to which the game had been imported from Cuba as early as 1894 (Huyke 1973), were also able to take advantage of the new racial tolerance. In a sense, no activity was as appropriate as this sport for the breakthrough of a propertyless group.

Not now regional, according to *DARE* I, but still very American in some usages were *big league* and *bush league*, both terms very much associated with baseball which spread metaphorically into other areas. *Bush league* is first attested by *DA* (neither *OED* II nor *DARE* I lists it) from 1909; *bush leaguer* from 1907 – a derivational chronology which one might expect to be reversed if historical dictionaries were perfect and human language a little simpler.[4] Ring Lardner's *You Know Me, Al*, subtitled *The Memoirs of a Busher*, preserves a definitive picture of the real meaning of the second compound in its depiction of an athletically talented but countrified, innocent but boorish 'busher' (a term starting in 1910 according to *DA*) that was strikingly opposed to the ballyhoo about athletic heroes which was being fed to Americans in newspaper sports sections. (Lardner's 'Champion' did the same for boxers.) The same has apparently never been done for football, and Ronald Reagan's portrayal of George 'Win One for the Gipper' Gipp, suitably White but active before racial factors came to the attention of sports fans, probably did not hurt his eventual campaign for the presidency.

Regional prejudices had been allowed to enter the terminology of sports in terms like *Texas leaguer*, a hit (single) consisting of a bloop fly ball that someone should have caught. The phrase may be obsolescent by now, since major league teams are now located in Houston (National) and Arlington (called 'Texas' in the official listing of the American League) in that state and players dependent offensively upon such hits or defensively unable to prevent them are no longer associated with that state or the old Texas League. In fact, *OED* II cites *Verbatim* 1977 that 'we are no longer besieged by such terms as "Texas leaguer"'. Of course, a Dallas–Forth Worth area that calls itself 'the Metroplex' would hardly encourage the continuation of such a disparaging term.

The increasingly spectator sports of the twentieth century have contributed figuratively to other domains of activity. Safire (1985) speculates on the origin of *('way) out in left field* and comments on *ballpark figure* ('rough estimate'), *keep one's eye on the ball* – which may just as well come from golf – ('be attentive to the task at hand'), *be [caught] off base* ('suffer the results of inattention or overambition'), *right off the bat* ('immediately') and *go to bat for* ('intercede for'), *play ball with* ('cooperate with, especially in a not fully respectable venture'), *be in there pitching* ('persevere') and *take a rain check* ('postpone an activity to a later date, without precise commitment as to the date involved'). These expressions are presumably twentieth-century in origin, although to my knowledge no one has cited historical data. Like any other occupation, baseball has a number of characteristic terms and expressions which are not known to the general public and hardly need figure in a treatment of American English.

Although the many who remained in the slums while the few made enormous sums with their talents (in entertainment as well as sports) inherited the term *ghetto* for the depressed areas in which they lived, neither the dominance of the talented few nor the continued poverty of the great masses matched the familiar American immigrant pattern. Here was not a recent immigrant group willing to undergo a little bit of delay and frustration in being assimilated; this was a community of people who had been denied assimilation for a period of time approaching three centuries. The Blacks competed with Hispanics for the unpleasant distinction of being the least assimilated large group of Americans.

A convenient cultural index of the differences in the communities, of the quasi-independent nature of the Black community, can be seen in popular musical culture. The great shift in the Black population in that general direction had brought jazzmen and Mississippi Delta bluesmen up the Mississippi River to Chicago and then across to New York. White groups like the Original Dixieland Jazz Band, Bix Beiderbecke, Bennie Goodman and even the Paul Whiteman orchestra – along with assimilating Blacks like W.C. Handy – brought an absorption of jazz and the blues into general American popular musical culture. Ravel and a few others wrote compositions which absorbed some of the features of jazz and the blues into European musical culture. It is now difficult to appreciate just how great the difference would have been in the 1920s. One index of that difference would be the verbal differences between blues lyrics with disguised but highly explicit sexual descriptions and the 'Victorian' nature of White popular music lyrics in the remnants of the genteel tradition (Dillard 1977: 23–44). Black patterns (jazz, the blues, the dozens, churches with fancy double-branching names and call-and-response preaching styles, etc.) and perhaps some Southern rural traits became part of the culture of the inner city. Other Blacks with a long-time history of residence in the North were more nearly assimilated, but evidences of a milder form of segregation and of cultural and linguistic differences can be found.

With the exception of an occasional successful Black business-man like George of *The Jeffersons* and a rare rendition of a 'hip' inner-city type on television, the Black population of the country is ignored in the media also. A mild form of ethnic slang often accompanies these concessions to the existence of Blacks. *Tokenism* and *token Black*, terms essentially of the 1960s, are recognized designations for such representations. The movie *Putney Swope* (1969) was one of the first of many satires on the process; in language, as usual, only a few exotic terms like *Johnson* ('penis') were presented. *Cotton Comes to Harlem* (1970) had ethnic kinesic differences as a critical factor in the plot; a Black character was capable of recognizing that certain masked robbers 'ran white'. The appropriate portmanteau *blaxploitation* was applied to such productions. Notably, the fact that inner city Blacks had critical and growing educational and economic problems was glossed over.

Although in-migration from the South was the immediate source of most of the dialect difference, there is evidence that Black dialect – which is attested earlier in the northern colonies than in the southern – in a reduced form had been around all along. Humorist James Thurber, born in Ohio but inseparably associated with New York City, *The New Yorker* and the suburban commuter lifestyle, wrote in the late 1930s of the phonology (without calling it that, of course) of Della, a 'colored woman' represented as being originally from New England with no Southern accent. Della did not, Thurber insisted, say /d/ for /ð/, nor did she omit /r/. Revealingly, Thurber pointed out that one might listen to her from an adjacent room without suspecting that Della was 'colored'. ('What Do You Mean It "Was" Brillig?' in Thurber 1937). Della's apparent pronunciation /riyvz/ for *wreathes* is part of the humour of Thurber's sketch. Thus, it can be said that she had one of the less salient phonological features of BEV (see Chapter 3 above; Holm 1980: 56) but not one of the stereotypable ones usually recognized in the popular press and in relatively urbane literature of the *New Yorker* variety. Della also apparently had some different feature distributions for some of her words, leading Thurber to the (good-naturedly humorous) conclusion that she was indulging in the equivalent of malapropism which he could only compare, as the title suggests, to portmanteaux of Lewis Carroll.

A few decades later, the observations that Thurber made would have been virtually taboo in the publications for which he wrote. The same factors resulted in the extreme care of the media to avoid racial comments and anything that could be called a racial slur. In sports, typically, radio and television announcers did their best to be colour blind, and the occasional one who slipped (as in an attempt to explain the Black dominance) could be subject to severe reprimand or even dismissal. But terms and kinesic acts like the 'High Five', celebrating an outstanding play by meeting the scorer's hand high above both heads with one's own open hand, came in with the Blacks. So did 'spiking' the ball (throwing it to the ground after a touchdown) and various sorts of dance-like activities ('shuffles') by one who had scored a touchdown. In basketball, various forms of 'slam dunks' were known to be characteristic of individual Black players; centre Darrell Dawkins of the Philadelphia 76ers reportedly had a dozen or so types of slam dunk with verbal designations ('Disgrace in your face') for each. Unmarked possessives like *Chicago ball* became the norm in both football and basketball from 'jock' (former athlete) sportscasters who, because of self-consciousness about reports of their having left or even graduated from college still functionally illiterate, were often given to hypercorrection (e.g. *Hubie and I's analysis*). Because of either Black or Southern (the latter also of low prestige on the networks) influence, the wide receiver (a player whose sole task on the field was to catch passes from the quarterback) ran a /rawt/, not a /ruwt/.

Outside sports, music and entertainment, the comparability to other immigrant groups was even weaker. Economically, the talented minority of Blacks did move into the higher brackets; the earnings of television personalities Bill Cosby and Oprah Winfrey are legendary. The vast majority, however, did not move into the middle class as had Irish, Italian and Jewish immigrants, but remained distressingly often below the 'poverty line', for which official figures are periodically given. Certain Hispanics seem to be caught up in the same syndrome; the success of José Ferrer and Geraldo Rivera has not correlated with a bettered lot for the average Puerto Rican in the United States.

The Blacks' language assimilation pattern (again, somewhat comparable to that of the Hispanics) did not match the familiar immigrant pattern: foreign language and broken English for the first generation, bilingualism with some tendency towards English dominance for the second, and English with some receptive control and occasional reluctant production of the 'old country' language for the third. Labov (1963, 1972b) has shown how ethnic groups were able at one time to exert a dominant influence over the dialect of at least some especially suited areas, but the vast majority of the Blacks who moved into the inner cities and who entered school systems with the Whites after the Supreme Court's desegregation decision of 1954 had a dialect as radically non-standard as it was lacking in the kind of legitimacy academic recognition could provide. 'Language deprivation' theory achieved a prominence in the 1960s that no one who had read any of the standard introductions to linguistics could have believed would ever be foisted off on any group. The educators of the inner cities of the North (especially New York, Washington, Detroit, Philadelphia) were noteworthy in their reactions when they were confronted with the results of school desegregation stemming from the federal mandate to desegregate, an effect which did not really begin to take place until the early 1960s. Nothing had prepared these educators for the great differences the Black children brought to the classroom; 'language deficit' was the sad conclusion many of them were led to adopt in the absence of any real insights, grammatical or historical, into the nature of BEV. Non-redundant pluralization, producing perfectly normal BEV sentences like

> Them three boy all got bicycles

led prominent psychological testers to jump to the conclusion that the 'concept of plurality' was lacking and that concept teaching was the basic task of the inner city teacher. Traditional textbooks featuring rural scenes and vocabulary were anything but helpful to these children, whose parents may have migrated from the rural South but who themselves had grown up thinking milk came from bottles or from plastic containers. Blacks had been present, of course, in New England, New York and the North in general ever since early colonial times.

West African languages had been substantially unavailable to Black Americans for two centuries or so. When the Black Pride movements of the 1960s sought a language to rally around, they tended to choose the historically irrelevant Swahili (reminding one vaguely of the Jamaican Ras Tafarians who looked to an Ethiopia from which none of their ancestors had come) or Arabic. Black Muslims became a force in the nation's politics for a time, and names like Malcolm X and Elijah Muhammed became familiar along with those like Muhammed Ali (Cassius Clay) and Kareem Abdul-Jabbar (Lew Alcindor) in the world of professional sports. Ali's demonstrative nature was probably responsible for the temporary vogue of *a.k.a.* ('also known as').

Ethnic factors were an important part, but only one part, of what made the cities something new in American dialect distribution. In spite of persistent 'ghettoization' (the term *barrio* was borrowed by 1939 as a euphemism for *Spanish-speaking slum*), mixing was much more commonplace in the cities than in the small towns and rural areas. Isogloss bundles, even individual isoglosses, could be brought to the cities only if the lines were drawn between apartments in the same building, rooms in the same apartment, and even beds in the same room.

New York City had long stood out among northern metropolises, with unmatched transit and commuter rail facilities already in place at the beginning of the post-war era (Bello 1958: 54). Crowding in the city has brought the removal of some businesses and other activities. Championship boxing matches, once routinely held at its Madison Square Garden (which, before two moves, was actually at Madison Square), now seem to take place somewhat more often in Las Vegas. A few movements to bring opera and other musical events live to the rest of the country, some of which grew tired of electronic representations of the 'Met' (Metropolitan Opera) and the New York Philharmonic, grew up. But what Black slang called the 'Big Apple' retained a unique place in American culture.

So much was New York city *sui generis* that one of the major works of modern dialectology, Labov's *Social Stratification of English in New York City* (1965/6), tended to restrict itself to an excellent treatment of class structure as a correlate of language usage and to ignore the importance of the Black in-migration. Labov at that time apparently considered that Blacks could be identified with working-class New Yorkers by social, non-ethnic features.

New York was, not however, perfectly typical of the inner city problem. Where Washington had 55 per cent Black population by the early 1960s, Detroit 29 per cent and Baltimore 35 per cent, New York had only 15 per cent (Abrams 1969: 54). One of the reasons for the relative limitation of Black in-migration into New York City was that Puerto Ricans 'began pouring in after 1940 and competed with the Negro for the available jobs' (Abrams 1965: 54). It was probably this working-class distribution that caused Labov *et al.* (1968) to announce 'Black and Puerto Rican English' in their title, although hardly dealing with Puerto Ricans at all in their linguistic investigation. The continuing work of Labov *et al.* 1968 and Labov 1972a, and eventually Labov's shift to Philadelphia and his work and that of his followers there mirror in a sense the growing awareness of the social/ethnic factor in America's dialects and in its language history.

Most of these developments began soon after World War II, in which segregated armed forces had been maintained. In the war itself, the big demographic change was the admission of women to the armed forces, in special acronymic groups of which the Navy WAVES was probably the most noteworthy name, with the Coast Guard SPARS and the Army WACS trailing. The Army women's group, however, probably promoted a greater number of puns on the grounds of the Army now being *wacky*. The German terms treated above and a few hybrid Japanese terms like *kamikaze* ('suicide') *pilot* seemed like permanent acquisitions at the time but by now have been virtually forgotten, like the slogans 'Remember Pearl Harbor' (from the attack of 7 December 1941) and 'V for Victory'.

The Vietnam War, in which field soldiers were drawn from the ranks of those who could not qualify for deferments as college students and thus *de facto* from Blacks and other minority groups, had perhaps little direct but much indirect influence. It has been reported that Black English was dominant in 'Nam'; White soldiers who wished to survive had to adopt at least some token features of Black language and/or kinesics. The conflict, generally embarrassing to Americans and with probably at least as much opposition as support from the populace of the country particularly from the educated – was long ignored in the media and Vietnam veterans tended to complain that they were forgotten men. More recently, however, television representations of the conflict have grown more frequent. Some representation of Black speech and cultural patterns – as many, probably, as a medium like television can handle – have made their way into televised representations of the war.

The linguistic consequences of urbanization have not, however, been limited to the Black population. Chinese food names, for example, and *Joss house* ('temple') were familiar urban phenomena of the first half of the twentieth century. The former – but not the latter – have tended to spread even into small-town America by the 1990s. American small town restaurants, where the doubtfully authentic *chop suey* stood alone in earlier decades, have *moo goo gai pan* as a fairly standard item now. Italian food terminology – even in small towns where there are virtually no Italians – has also tended to pervade small-town America, with *pizza* becoming so much an American dish that one of Al Capp's characters had to have it explained to him that pizza, and not pork and beans, was the national dish. Only in the eastern cities, perhaps, is *pizzeria* fully acceptable; the hinterlands tend to be uneasy about its possible connection to *pissoir*. *Pizza-ria* was noted in Waco, Texas in the 1960s and was still in use in at least one place in Columbus, Ohio in 1989. Primarily in the cities and towns, other names for food and drink concoctions tended to take on local forms, some of them rather temporary. What is generally known as a *milkshake* (including ice cream), for example, became a *cabinet* in Rhode Island and south-eastern Massachusetts, a *frappe* elsewhere in Massachusetts, and other special names elsewhere.

A Western term like *skid row*, originating in the logging industry as *skid road* (with the 'corruption' to its best-known contemporary form motivating an uncharacteristic explosion of purism from McCulloch 1958), is now generally associated primarily with the city. Abrams (1965: 47) uses the term several times on one page, always in connection with a section of the city associated with near-hopeless derelicts. He would not appear to have any awareness – and neither would the average American using it – of the logging associations of the term. Nor, for that matter, are most of those who know the Bowery as the archetypical skid row of New York City aware that the term had rural associations ('farm') among the early Dutch inhabitants.

The more recent type of suburbanization, sometimes called 'white flight', as a linguistic phenomenon has hardly been investigated at all. It is well known that 'flight' to the suburbs has taken many, especially Whites but some middle-class 'ethnics' also, away from the inner city, and it is generally assumed that those involved in the flight speak something more like the national standard English than do the ones who remain behind in the ghettos. The demographics are also fairly well known. According to Udall (1965: 160–1):

> Between 1950 and 1959, while our cities' populations increased by only 1.5 per cent, the population of our suburbs increased by 44 per cent. Even this flight to the suburbs – in part a protest against the erosion of the urban milieu – has had its element of irony, for the exodus has intensified our reliance on the automobile and the freeway as indispensable elements of modern life. More often than not the suburbanite's quest for open and serenity has been defeated by the processes of pell-mell growth.

The new suburbanites were more likely to be *dinks* (*double income, no kids*) as a matter of economic necessity and, because of the need for both husband and wife to work and of the decline of public transportation, a *two-car family*.

For just a little more irony, the automobile sometimes had to be *towed* like a ship by a tug, and by 1956 the *towaway zone* was part of the most inland American scene and vocabulary. Changes in the automobile itself have rendered *running board* obsolete along with other terms like *rumble seat*. And, as Atwood (1961: 117) pointed out, the cosmopolitan and international term *charivari* (*shivaree*) for a raucous wedding serenade was rural in distribution by the early 1960s, more urban youngsters preferring to decorate the car the newlyweds were to use with tin cans and *Just Married* signs. The automobile has become virtually the American symbol of internal mobility, but hardly of international expansion. It may be significant that airports, by nature more cosmopolitan, have names like Sky Harbor (Phoenix, Arizona) and Port Columbus (Columbus, Ohio).

One of the hardly suppressible factors in the movement to the suburbs has been that the problems of the inner-city schools can be evaded there. Families already successful in the mainstream tend to move to the suburbs, and the educational opportunities there facilitate assimilation to the mainstream for the children of suburbanites. There are complicating factors like the 'weekend hippies' who spent Saturday and Sunday in the inner city in the 1960s, the fashionable nature of rock and roll language among teenagers, and the attempted 'gentrification' of inner-city areas. (A recent television documentary distinguished between *inner city*, where the poverty of minority groups remains a problem, and *downtown*, where slum elements have allegedly been eliminated.) Nevertheless, it appears that the inner city is the locus of the least and the suburbs of the most standard variety of

American English. The well-educated products of those school systems also show some tendency towards international interests, foreign travel and awareness of foreign languages and dialects. For such people, British English may be less 'foreign' than the dialect spoken in the inner city.

The very awareness of American/British differences may have worked towards the resolution of some of those differences, particularly in an international community. Almost everyone now knows about American *apartment* and British *flat*; Svejcer (1978: 140) points out that (urban) Americans are likely to collocate the latter with adjectives like *little* and *cheap*. For Americans, anyway, the 'sexy' connotations of *The Apartment* (the title of a film released in 1960) could not possibly apply to *The Flat*. In the case of words like *drugstore* and *chemist's*, it has long been the case that, as in a true language-contact situation, the American talking to the Englishman has wanted to use *chemist's* and the Englishman to use *drugstore*. Much the same can be said for *hood/bonnet* (of an automobile), *truck/lorry* or *gasoline/petrol*. Americans hardly produce *trunk call* and *long distance call* has become familiar in England only recently, but almost anyone in either country would understand the other. *On one's own* ('alone' – sometimes even *on our own*, where two persons can be alone, 'with no one else around') is familiar to American watchers of BBC programmes on public television, although intuitively most find the locution a bit strange and must remember to adjust for the British meaning. J. K. Galbraith had hardly coined the phrase *affluent society* in his book of 1958 before British periodicals were using it. Most British would seem to have accepted the proposition that 'American English is good English'; hardly anyone in Britain now emulates the judgement of *Punch* of 1869 to 1871 (Thurber 1937: 51) that *reliable* (for example) was ' a new and unnecessary American adjective' which Britons should resist – whether or not the assumption about the historical provenience of the adjective is correct.

Although integration of the 'two streams of English', especially at the upper socio-economic levels, should not be over-emphasized, the attitude expressed in Alan Jay Lerner's (1956) *My Fair Lady* (Act I, Scene I) adaptation of Shaw's *Pygmalion* that 'In America, they haven't used it [English] for years' is apparently an antiquated sentiment. (Not fifty years ago, the idea was at least as prevalent in the United States as in England.) The argument that American English is 'good' English has also outlived its usefulness; there is really no more reason for Americans to defend their use of the language, and very few if any British maintain the contrary position. Television watchers, especially Public Broadcasting System fans, in the United States are constantly exposed to British-produced programmes such as *Monty Python's Flying Circus* and *Fawlty Towers*, in the latter of which the failure of a British hotel keeper to understand that an American requesting a *screwdriver* wanted a cocktail and not a tool was one of the less credible instances of humour. British groups like The Beatles and The Rolling Stones have long since been accepted as practitioners of the perhaps originally American popular musical type known as rock and roll, and they have long been imitated by native American groups.

Receptive control, at least, of many of the features of the English of different sides of the Atlantic has become fairly well established. If there is accommodation because of a desire to reach an international market, still diagnostic features of each national variety are well established in the passive repertory of the other. In the case of 'high tech[nology]' there is virtually no difference; a *hard copy* is familiar to computer-oriented Americans as much as to British people of the same type – and just as mysterious to the old-fashioned, who wonder why paper is 'hard' and a plastic disk is 'floppy'.

Nevertheless, there is not identity, even among the most urban and urbane of the American and British populations. In quite recent times much attention has been paid to 'the variable lack of deletion in independent clauses of what [Joos 1964]' calls *propredicates* (Butters 1983: 1) In a sequence like –

I saw her half an hour ago. You can't have done. (British)

– where a perhaps simplistic notion of an 'underlying' form would be

(1) I saw her half an hour ago. You can't have *seen her half an hour ago*.

the most usual American form by far would be

(2) . . .You can't have.

with the italicized portion of (1) above 'deleted'.
Both British and American, presumably, would have

(1a) You can't have done so.

Butters shows some use of forms like (1) by Americans (and a long pre-history of the structure in English), although frequency is shown to be much greater among the British.

Usages like *Do you have NP?* are felt to be more normal by

Americans than *Have you any* . . .? (Svejcer 1978: 89–90). *Had
you any* . . . ? seems more bizarre, and *Used you to* . . .? is
very limited among Americans, although it is used by some as a
'tonier' variant of *Did you use to* . . .? (Others are caught in the
middle somewhere and resort to circumlocutions like *Was it
(formerly) your custom to* . . .?) Probably the *in which* locution,
as in –

> . . . one of the qualities in which the father wanted the son
> to have . . .

– observable generally in Middle America (eastern Texas to
southern Ohio at least) would seem even more bizarre to the
British. Among those most likely to be influenced by current-day,
superficial re-anglicization, American English teachers who
'revere British usage' as many of the rest of us do not may still be
most likely to imitate British usage, whether it be the propredi-
cate discussed above or an expression like 'Sorry!' rather than
'Excuse me!' or 'Pardon me!' (Butters 1986: 60). It was a high
school Spanish (not English) teacher, in my memory from the
1930s, who insisted that *secret'ry* and *cemet'ry* were 'correct'.
Such considerations were once quite important to Americans of a
certain educational status; in recent years, however, a great deal
of argumentation in favour of the legitimacy of American English
has eliminated much of whatever influence such attitudes would
have had.
  Some of the current trends, like those of the feminist
movement which favours 'inclusive' language rather than the
masculine gender-dominated grammatical features which are
generally traced back to Proto-Indo-European, are no more
American than British. (One may well anticipate, however,
particularly violent American feminist reaction to the discussion
of the Dumb Dora syndrome above.) Attempts to introduce
lexical changes, like the substitution of *chairperson* for *chairman*,
have made some headway, although it is a fair bet that the
signature which contains the initials, the last name and the word
*chairperson* has a female department head as referent. The new
would-be genderless pronoun *s/he*, on the other hand, never had
any real chance of adoption. No more real influence seems to
have been exerted by Black awareness groups who wish to
counteract traditional English associations of dark colours with
evil and white with purity, innocence or the like.
  A number of usages can be easily observed as markers of one
or another kind of identification with a group. The pretentiously
'correct' *between you/he/she and I* has extended itself also into

academic usage, the unreconstructed vernacular speaker using more regularly *between me and you/him/her* alongside *It's me/us/him/her/them*. *Between you and I* seems fairly common even among college professors and rectors of Episcopal churches. Probably everyone has some sense of the artificiality of the use of the 'nominative' pronoun in the 'predicate complement' construction. Walt Kelly's Pogo, famous for

We have met the enemy and he is us

could not have used *we* as the final word any more than Oliver Hazard Perry, who provided the model phrase in his naval dispatch of 10 September 1813, could have substituted *our'n* for *ours*. The self-conscious correctness for which Pyles (1952) castigated Americans may be less pronounced in the 1990s, but a brief period with a group of English teachers can shake one's confidence in that kind of progress.

The changes in American English, as these pages have tried to show, have been complex and have resulted from complex factors. Nevertheless, they are normal historical changes. The various hypotheses of adstratum (substratum or superstratum) influence on language change or lack thereof do not appear to be resolved, for example, by considerations of the development of Black English or of any other American dialect. The theory of colonial 'lag', given prominence in Marckwardt (1958), reduced to a secondary function in Marckwardt/Dillard (rev. 1981) and thoroughly minimized in Dillard (1985; see also Görlach 1987), has appeared to be on the way out because of general studies of colonial languages, not because of the special nature of American English. It may well be that original impetus for that historical attitude was the need, no longer felt, to legitimize American English by proving that we used little or nothing that had not been previously used in England. Language contact has been emphasized more herein than any of those theories of change simply because the data I have been able to gather tend to support that theory more than any other.

The spread of English, and recently perhaps especially American English, to become an international language – 'the world's second language' in some presentations – can be accounted for rather easily in terms of military and socio-economic developments in the nineteenth and twentieth centuries and not by any special linguistic qualities of English in general or of American English in particular. Experiments designed to teach chimpanzees or other primates American Sign Language have been centred in the United States – and their lack of impressive accomplishment demonstrated there. Historically, grammatically and otherwise, the language in the long run demonstrates how Americans are normal members of the human race. Our language history unites us with Great Britain, it is true, and also with Europe; the contact varieties which have figured so much in our language history link us more than we had suspected with the so-called Third World. In the long run the linkage is simply with humanity throughout the entire world.

## Notes

1 *Junk* has a possibly maritime origin, meaning, from 1485, 'an old or inferior cable or rope'. A meaning first attested in 1762 – 'The salt meat used as food on long voyages, compared to pieces of rope' is semantically as close to *junk food* as anything else in the word's range of meanings. Thus, one might say, the history of Americanisms – in the broader sense adopted in this work – has come full circle, from sea to sea.

2 *Goy* and its plural *goyim* ('gentiles') are likely to be better known in urban areas with large Jewish populations than elsewhere, although the terms are well known to those who read magazines like *The New Yorker* and read or attend plays intended for Broadway production, as are terms like *maven* ('expert'), *goniff* ('robber' or 'shrewd person'), *shikse* ('gentile girl or woman') and others. More restricted in outsider use are *ghazó* and its plural *ghazé*, terms used by Roma ('Gypsies') for outsiders. Hancock (personal communication) estimates that there are some 1,200,000 who adhere to the cultural patterns of *Romaniya* (comparable to *Yiddishkeit* for Jews) in the United States.

3 For an excellent treatment of name changing in the process of assimilation, see Mencken's Supplement II (1967: 402–67).

4 Suburbanization and over-population have brought a virtual end to *sandlot* (first attested for baseball in San Francisco in 1890). *OED* II lists an occurrence as late as 1979 but in a context which may be reminiscing and even nostalgic. College athletes in recent years have tended to use the term *sandlot* in a deprecating sense. The American feeling for the *national pastime* (1920s and 1930s according to Flexner 1982: 35, who also notes that *national game*, referring to the rules under which the game was played rather than to the widespread nature of the sport, was used in 1856) has, however, led to the formation of the *little league* (not listed in the dictionaries, but the first such organization was founded in 1939 in Philadelphia according to Flexner 1982:44). Flexner says that by this date there were 15,000 such organizations.

# Bibliography

ABRAMS, CHARLES (1965) *The city is the frontier*. Harper & Row, New York.

ADAMS, ARTHUR T. (ed.) (1961) *The explorations of Pierre Esprit Radisson, from the original manuscript in the Bodleian Library and the British Museum*. Ross and Haines, Inc., Minneapolis.

ADAMS, CHARLES C. (1971) *Boontling: an American lingo*. University of Texas Press, Austin.

ADAMS, JOHN (1822) *Sketches taken during ten voyages in Africa, between the years 1786–1800, including observations on the country between Cape Palmas and the River Congo*. Hurst, Robinson & Co., London.

ADAMS, RAMON F. 1944/1968 *Western words, a dictionary of the American west*. University of Oklahoma Press, Norman.

ADLER, JACOB (1975) The etymology of Canuck. *American Speech* **50**: 159–9.

AKERMAN, JOE A, Jr (1976) *Florida cowman: a history of Florida cattle ranching*. Florida Cattlemen's Association, Kissimee, Florida.

ALBION, ROBERT G. (1939) *The rise of New York port*. Charles Scribner's Sons, New York.

ALEXANDER, HENRY (1928) The language of the Salem witchcraft trials. *American speech* **3**: 390–400.

ALLEN, HAROLD (1986) Primary dialect areas of the upper midwest. Reprinted from *Studies in honor of Charles C. Fries* in Allen and Levin (eds) 1986: 303–4.

ALLEN, HAROLD (1989a) New or old-fashioned? Informal awareness of chronological status. *American Speech* **64**: 3–11.

ALLEN, HAROLD (1989b) Response: Canadian raising in the upper midwest. *American Speech* **64** (1): 74–5.

ALLEN, HAROLD and LEVIN, MICHAEL D. (eds) (1986) *Dialect and Language* variation. Harcourt, Brace, Jovanovich, New York.

ALLEN WILLIAM FRANCIS (pseudonym Marcel) (1865) The Negro dialect. *The Nation* I: 744–5 (reprinted in Jackson 1967: 74–81).

ALLEYNE, MERVYN C. (1980) Comparative Afro-American. Karoma Press, Ann Arbor, Michigan.

ALLEYN, MERVYN C. (1989) Review of Suzanne Romaine, Pidgin and Creole Languages. *Journal of pidgin and creole languages* **4** (No. 20): 305–10.

ALVAREZ, NAZARIO MANUEL (1972) *La herencia lingüística de Canarias en Puerto Rico.* M. Pareja, Barcelona.

ANDREWS, CHARLES M, (1934) *The colonial period of American history.* Yale University Press, New Haven, Conn.

ANGOGO, RACHEL, HANCOCK, IAN F. (1980) English in Africa: emerging standards or diverging regionalisms. *English world–wide* **1**(1): 67–96.

ARNADE, CHARLES W. (1961) Cattle raising in Spanish Florida. *Agricultural History* XXXV: 116–24.

ASBURY, HERBERT (1938) *The Barbary Coast: an informal history of the San Francisco Underworld.* Garden City Publishing Co. Garden City, New York.

ATKINS, JOHN (1735) *A Voyage to Guinea, Brasil and the West Indies.* London.

ATWOOD, E. BAGBY (1950) *Grease* and *greasy* – a study of geographical variation. *Studies in English* **29**: 249–60. University of Texas Press, Austin.

ATWOOD, E. BOGBY (1953) *Survey of the verb forms in the eastern United States.* University of Michigan Press, Ann Arbor.

ATWOOD, E. BAGBY (1962) *The regional vocabulary of Texas.* University of Texas Press, Austin.

ATWOOD, E. BAGBY, BABINGTON, M. (1961) Lexical usage in southern Louisiana. *Publications of the American Dialect Society* XXXVI: 1–24.

AXTELL, JAMES (1988) *After Columbus: essays in the ethnohistory of colonial North America.* Oxford University Press, New York and Oxford.

BAILEY, BERYL LOFTMAN (1965) Toward a new perspective in Negro English dialectology. *American Speech* **40**: 171–7.

BAILEY, CHARLES-JAMES N. (1968) Is there a midland dialect of American English? ERIC ED 021240 (Education Resources Information Center, Bloomington, Indiana).

BAILEY, GUY B., BASSETT, MARVIN (1986) Invariant *be* in the lower South. In Montgomery and Bailey (eds): 158–70.

BAILEY, GUY B., MAYNOR NATALIE (1985) The present tense of BE in southern Black folk speech. *American Speech* **60** (3): 195–213.

BAILEY, GUY B., MAYNOR, NATALIE (1987) Decreolization? *Language in society* **16**: 449–7.

BAILEY, RICHARD A, GÖRLACH MANFRED (1982) *English as a world language.* University of Michigan Press, Ann Arbor.

BAILY, FRANCIS (1797) *Journal of a tour in unsettled parts of North America in 1796 and 1797,* Jack D. L. Holmes (ed.), Southern Illinois University Press, Carbondale and Edwardville, rpt 1969.

BAKKER, PETER (1987) A Basque nautical pidgin. *Journal of pidgin and creole languages* **2**: 1–30.

BALMER, RANDAL (1989) *A perfect babel of confusion: Dutch religion and English culture in the middle colonies*. Oxford University Press, New York and Oxford.

BARBAG-STOLL, ANNA (1983) *Social and linguistic history of Nigerian Pidgin English as spoken by the Yoruba with special reference to the English-derived lexicon*. Stauffenberg Verlag, Tübingen.

BARNARD, JOHN (1726) *Ashton's memorial: or, an authentick account of the strange adventures and signal deliverances of Mr. Philip Ashton*. Richard Ford and Samuel Chandler, London.

BARTLETT, JOHN RUSSELL (1859) *A glossary of words and phrases usually regarded as peculiar to the United States*. Little, Brown, Boston.

BEECHER, LYMAN, HARVEY, JOSEPH (1818) *Memoirs of Henry Obookiah, a native of Owyhee and a member of the foreign mission school, who died at Cornwall, Conn., February 27, 1818, aged 26 years*. Office of *The religious intelligencer*, New Haven, Conn.

BELL, MARGARET DWIGHT (1820), *A Journey to Ohio*, Yale University Press, New Haven, Conn.

BELLO, FRANCIS (1958) The city and the car. *Exploding Metropolis*, the editors of *Fortune*. Doubleday, Anchor Books.

BENES, PETER, BENES, JANE M. (eds) (1985) *American speech 1600 to the present*. Dublin Seminar for American Folklife, Boston, Mass.

BENTLEY, HAROLD W. (1934) *A dictionary of Spanish terms in English: with special reference to the American southwest. Studies in English and comparative literature* **175**. Columbia University, New York.

BERNARD, J.R.L.-B. (1969) On the uniformity of spoken Australian English. *Orbis* **18**: 62–73.

BICKERTON, DEREK (1982) *Roots of Language*. Karoma Press, Ann Arbor, Mich.

BICKERTON, DEREK, BYRNE, FRANCIS (1990) *Fi* and *fu* origins and functions in some Caribbean English-based creoles. *Lingua* **62**:97–120.

BLANTON, LINDA L. (1980) Southern Appalachia: social considerations of speech. In Dillard (1985): 73–90.

BLOOMFIELD, MORTON W. (1948) Canadian English and its relation to eighteenth century American speech. *Journal of English and Germanic philology* **47** 59–67.

BOLINGBROKE, HENRY (1799/1806) *A voyage to Demarary*. R. Phillips, London.

BOLTON, HERBERT E. (1921) Athanase de Mézières and the Texas–Louisiana frontier, 1768–80. Arthur H. Clark Co., Cleveland, Ohio.

BONEY, F.N. (1990) A British 'grand tour' of Crackerland: Basil and Margaret Hall view frontier Georgia in 1828. *Georgia historical quarterly* LXXIV, 2 (Summer): 277–92.

BOORSTIN, DANIEL J. (1973) The Americans. The democratic experience. Random House, New York.

BOSSU, JEAN BERNARD (1777) *Nouveaux voyages dans l'Amérique Septentrionale*. Changuion, Amsterdam.

BOUCICAULT, DION (1861) The octoroon: or, life in Louisiana.

BOWMAN, HAZEL L. (1948) Background materials for the study of Florida Spanish. University of Florida Master's thesis, unpublished, Gainesville.

BRADFORD, WILLIAM (1647) *Of Plimouth Plantation. 1620–1647*. Wright and Potter, Boston, rpt 1901.

BRANDT, ELIZABETH A., MacCRATE CHRISTOPHER (1979) *Multilingual variation or contact vernacular in the Southwest: 'Make like seem heap Injin'*, Amerindian Ethnolinguistics Symposium, XIII Congress of Americanists, Vancouver, British Columbia.

BRASCH, WALTER M. (1981) *Black English and the mass media*. University of Massachusetts Press, Amherst.

BRECKENRIDGE, HUGH HENRY (1792) *Modern chivalry: containing the adventures of Captain John Farrago and Teague O'Regan, his servant*. John McCullouch, Philadelphia.

BRINTON, DANIEL J. (1859) *Notes on the Florida Peninsula*. Philadelphia.

BROOKS, CLEANTH Jr (1935) *The relation of the Alabama–Georgia dialect to the provincial dialects of Great Britain*. LSU Press, Baton Rouge.

BROOKS, CLEANTH Jr (1953) Foreword to Still, James *The run for the Elbertas*. University of Kentucky Press, Lexington, Kentucky.

BRYANT, WILLIAM CULLEN (1850) *Letters of a traveller, or, notes of things seen in Europe and America*. Ben A. Putnam, New York.

BRYCE, JAMES (1921) *Modern democracies*. Macmillan, New York.

BUTTERS, RONALD (1983) Syntactic change in British English propredicates. Journal of English Linguistics 16: 1–7.

BUTTERS, RONALD (1986) Query: *sorry* and 'excuse me'. *American Speech* **61** (1): 60.

CARUSO, JOHN ANTHONY (1961) *The Great Lakes Frontier*. Bobbs Merrill, Indianapolis.

Camp meeting at Gray's Hill (1886) *The southern bivouac* (Vol. II). No. 1 (June): 232–4.

CARTER, HODDING (1963) *Doomed road of empire*. McGraw-Hill, New York.

CARVER, CRAIG M. (1987) *American regional dialects, word geography*. University of Michigan Press, Ann Arbor.

CASSIDY, FREDERIC G. *et al.* (1985) *Dictionary of American regional English*, Vol. I: Introduction and A–C. Belknap Press, Cambridge, Mass. and London.

CATLIN, GEORGE (1973) *Letters and notes on the manners, customs, and conditions of the North American Indians: written during eight years' travel (1832–1839) amongst the wildest tribes of Indians in North America*. II vols. Dover Publications, New York.

CHABOT, FREDERICK C. (1940) *Texas letters*. Yanaguan Society, San Antonio, Texas.

CHAMBERS, J.K. (1989) Canadian raising: blocking, fronting, etc. *American Speech* **64** (1): 75–88.

CHASE, GEORGE DAVIS (1942) Sea terms come ashore. *Maine bulletin* **44:** 8, 20 February.

CHAUDENSON, ROBERT (1974) *Le léxique du parler créole de la Réunion.* Librairie Honore-Champion, Paris.

CLAPIN, SYLVA (1902) *A new dictionary of Americanisms.* L. Weiss & Co., New York.

CLARK, THOMAS D. (1969) *Frontier America: the story of westward movement* (2nd edn). Charles Scribner's Sons, New York.

CLEMENS, SAMUEL L. (1872) *Roughing It.* Harper, New York, rpt 1949.

CLEMENS, SAMUEL L. (1917) *Life on the Mississippi.* Harper & Brothers, New York and London.

CLEVELAND, HENRY WHITNEY (1887) Old Scipio. *The Southern Bivouac* II: 672.

COMMAGER, HENRY STEELE, MORRIS, RICHARD B. (1958) *The spirit of seventy-six: the story of the American revolution as told by participants.* Bobbs-Merrill, Indianapolis.

COOPER, JAMES FENIMORE (1846) Redskins: or Indian and Injin. Burgess and Stringer, New York.

CORNE, CHRIS, BAKER, PHILIP (1982) *Ile de France creole, affinities and origins.* Karoma Press, Ann Arbor, Mich.

COROMINAS, JOAN (1972) *Tópica Hespérica.* Editorial Gredos, Madrid.

CRANE, EVA (1983) *The archaeology of beekeeping.* Cornell University Press, Ithaca, New York.

CRESSY, DAVID (1987) *Coming over: Migration and communication between England and New England in the seventeenth century.* Cambridge University Press, New York.

CROSBY, ALFRED W. Jr (1972) *The Columbian exchange: biological and cultural consequences of 1492.* Greenwood Publishing Company, Westport, Conn.

DACY, GEORGE R. (1940) *Four centuries of Florida ranching.* Britt Publishing Company, St Louis, Missouri.

DALBY, DAVID (1972) The African element in American English. In Kochman, Thomas (ed.), Rappin' and stylin' out: communication in urban Black America. University of Illinois Press, Urbana.

DALLAS, R.C. (1883) *History of the Maroons.* Strahan and Reese for Longman, London.

DANA, R.H. Jr (1840) *Two years before the mast, with authentic illustrations of the period and an introductory sketch of the author by his grandson H.W.L. Dana* Dodd, Mead, New York, rpt 1946.

DANA, R.H. Jr (1841) *The seaman's friend.* Charles C. Little & James Brown, and Benjamin Loving & Co., Boston, Mass.

DANIELS, JONATHAN (1962) *The Devil's Backbone: the story of the Natchez Trace.* McGraw-Hill, New York.

DANZIG, ALLISON, REICHLER, JOE (1959) *The history of baseball.* Prentice-Hall, Englewood Cliffs, NJ.

DARBY, WILLIAM (1821) *Memoir on the geography, and natural and civil history of Florida.* T.H. Palmer, Philadelphia.

DAY, RICHARD, SATO, CHARLENE (1980) Categories of transformations in second language acquisition. In Dillard, J.L. (ed.), *Perspectives on American English.* Mouton, The Hague.

D'COSTA, JEAN, LALLA, BARBARA (eds) (1989) *Voices in exile: Jamaican texts of the 18th and 19th centuries*. University of Alabama Press, Tuscaloosa.

DeCAMP, DAVID (1958) The pronunciation of English in San Francisco. *Orbis* VII: 372–91.

DeCAMP, DAVID (1971) Toward a generative analysis of a post-creole speech continuum. In Hymes, Dell (ed.), *Pidginization and creolization of languages*. Cambridge University Press, 349–70.

DeCAMP, DAVID, HANCOCK, IAN F. (eds) (1974) *Pidgins and creoles: current trends and prospects*. Georgetown University Press, Washington, DC.

D'ELOIA, SARAH G. (1973) Review of J.L. Dillard, Black English. *Journal of English linguistics* **7**: 87–106.

DeLEON, I. (1654) *Relation du voyage des François fait au Cap de Nord en Amérique*. Edme Pepingue, Paris.

DeQUILLE, DAN (1947) *The big bonanza*. Alfred A. Knopf, New York.

DeVOTO, BERNARD, (1947) *Across the wide Missouri*. Houghton Mifflin, Boston, Mass.

DeWOLF, GAELAN DODDS (1990) Social and grammatical differences in English usage in Canada. *American Speech* **65** (1): 3–32.

DICKENS, CHARLES (1957) *American notes*. Oxford University Press, New York and London.

DICKINSON, JONATHAN (1944) *Jonathan Dickinson's journal: or, God's protecting providence, being the narrative of a journey from Port Royal in Jamaica to Philadelphia between August 23, 1696, and April, 1697.*, ed. Evangeline Walker Andrews and Charles M. Andrews. Yale University Press, New Haven, Conn.

DICKINSON, SAM (1976) *'Hands' and hands*. Louisiana Folklife Quarterly.

DILLARD, J.L. (1971) The transitivizer and pidgin transmission. *Acta symbolica* II, No.1 (Spring): 44–5.

DILLARD, J.L. (1972) *Black English, its history and usage in the United States*. Random House, New York.

DILLARD, J.L. (1974) *Perspectives on Black English*. Mouton, The Hague.

DILLARD, J.L. (1975) *American talk*. Random House, New York.

DILLARD, J.L. (1977) *Lexicon of Black English*. Seabury Press, New York.

DILLARD, J.L. (1980) *Perspectives on American English*. Mouton, The Hague.

DILLARD, J.L. (1985) *Toward a social history of American English*. Berlin, Mouton/deGruyter.

DILLARD, MARGIE IVEY (1980) Larrupin': from nautical word to multiregionalism. In Dillard, J.L. (ed.), *Perspectives on American English*. Mouton, The Hague.

DILLARD, MARY L. (1987) Issues in reading and Black English revisited. ERIC document 270–950 Educational Resources Information Center Bloomington, Indiana.

DITCHY, J.K. (1932) *Les Acadiens et leur parler*. Baltimore, Johns Hopkins Press.

DOBSON, E.J. (1968) *English pronunciation, 1500–1700*. Clarendon Press, Oxford.

DORRILL, GEORGE (1986) A comparison of stressed vowels of Black and White speakers in the South. In Montgomery and Bailey (eds), *Language variety in the South*. University of Alabama Press, 149–57.

DORSON, RICHARD M. (1967) *Negro folklore from Benton Harbor, Michigan*. Fawcett Publications, Greenwich, CT.

DOUGLASS, FREDERICK (1855) *My bondage my freedom*. Johnson Publishing Company, Chicago, rpt. 1970.

DRECHSEL, EMANUEL (1976) 'Ha now me stomany that!' A summary of pidginization and creolization of North American Indian languages. *International journal of the sociology of language* 7: 63–82.

DRECHSEL, EMANUEL (1979) Mobilian jargon: linguistic, sociocultural, and historical aspects of an American Indian lingua franca. University of Wisconsin, Madison, unpublished dissertation.

DULLES, FOSTER RHEA (1930) *The old China trade*. AMS Press Boston, Mass.

DUNNING, JOHN (1976) *Tune in yesterday*. Prentice-Hall, Englewood Cliffs, NJ.

EDMONDS, A. (1984) *Let the good times roll: the complete Cajun handbook*. Avon, New York.

EDWARDS, JAY. (1974) African influence in the English of San Andres island. In DeCamp and Hancock (eds) 1974: 1–26.

EDWARDS, JONATHAN (1884) Memoirs of Mr. David Brainerd, *missionary to the Indians of North America* ed. James M. Sherwood, Funk and Wagnalls, New York.

EGNAL, MARC (1990) Review of Jack P. Greene, *Pursuits of happiness. Georgia historical quarterly* LXXIV (2): 293–5.

ELCOCK, W. D. (1940) The enigma of the lizard in the Aragonese dialect. *Modern language review* XXV: 4839–93.

ELIASON, NORMAN (1956) *Tarheel talk: a historical survey of the English of North Carolina to 1860*. University of North Carolina Press, Chapel Hill.

ELLIS, DAVID M., FROST, JAMES, SYRETT, HAROLD C., CARMAN, HARRY J. (1957) *A History of New York State*. Cornell University Press, Ithaca, New York.

FARMER, JOHN S. (1889) *Americanisms – old and new*. T. Poulter & Sons, London.

FASOLD, RALPH (1969) Tense and the form 'be' in Black English. *Language* 45: 763–76.

FASOLD, RALPH (1972) *Tense marking in Black English*. Center for Applied Linguistics, Arlington, VA.

FASOLD, RALPH (1981) The relationship between black and white speech in the South. *American Speech* 56: 163–89.

FAUSET, ARTHUR HUFF (1927) Negro folk tales from the South. *Journal of American folklore* 40: 213–303

FAYER, JOAN (n.d.) Written pidgins: implications for current pidgin theory, ms.

FEARON, HENRY BRADSHAW (1818) *Sketches of America: a narrative of a journey of five thousand miles through the eastern and western states of America*. Longman, Hurst, Reese, Orme & Brow, London.

FEATHERSTONHAUGH, G.W. (1818) *Excursions through the slave states, from Washington on the Potomac to the frontier of Mexico, with sketches of the popular manners and geological notices*. Harper & Brothers, New York.

FERGUSON, CHARLES A., HEATH, SHIRLEY BRICE (eds) (1981) *Language in the USA*. Cambridge University Press.

FISCHER, DAVID HACKETT (1965) *The revolution of American conservatism: the Federalist party in the era of Jeffersonian democracy*. Harper & Row, New York.

FLANIGAN, BEVERLY OLSON (1985) American Indian Pidgin English in early historical documents: evidence for pidgin transmission in the New World, unpublished ms.

FLEXNER, STUART BERG (1982) *Listening to America*. Simon & Schuster, New York.

FORBES, JACK D. (1967) *Nevada Indians speak*. University of Nevada Press, Reno.

FORDE, DARYLL (ed.) (1968) *Efik traders of old Calabar*. Oxford University Press, London.

FOREMAN, GRANT (1939) *Marcy and the gold seekers: the journal of Captain R.B. Marcy, with an account of the gold rush over the southern route*. University of Oklahoma Press, Norman.

FOX, JOHN (1909) *The Kentuckians. A Knight of the Cumberlands*. C. Scribners Sous, New York.

FRANCIS, W. NELSON (1954/1956) *The structure of American English*. Ronald Press, New York.

FRANKLIN, BENJAMIN (1787) *Writings*, Smythe (ed.) VIII: 606.

FRANKLIN, BENJAMIN (1789) Letter to Noah Webster of 16 December 1789. Gordon Williams, Washington, DC.

FRIEDERICI, GEORG (1926) *Hilfswörterbuch für den Amerikanisten*. Niemeyer, Halle.

FURNAS, J.C. (1969) *The Americans: a social history of the United States 1587–1910*. G. Putnam's Sons, New York.

GALVAN, MARY, TROIKE, RUDOLPH C. (1969) The East Texas dialect project, a pattern for education. Florida *FL Reporter* Spring/Summer 29–31, 152–3.

GENOVESE, EUGENE (1974) *Roll, Jordan, roll: the world the slaves made*. Pantheon Books, New York.

GILMAN, CAROLINE (1838) *Recollections of a southern matron*. Harper & Brothers, New York.

GILBERT, GLENN (1984) Review of McDavid, Raven I. Jr, O'Cain, Raymond K. *Linguistic Atlas of the Middle and South Atlantic States*, fascicles 1 and 2. University of Chicago Press, 1980. *Leuvense bijdragen* **73**: 407–15.

GILLAT, JOSEPH E. (1939) Lagniappe. *American Speech* **14**: 93–6.

GLIEB, FREDERICK (1950) *The baseball story*. G. Putnam's Sons, New York.

GODDARD, IVES (1977) Some early examples of American Indian Pidgin English from New England. *International journal of American linguistics* **43** (1): 37–41.

GODDARD, IVES (1978) A further note on pidgin English. *International journal of American linguistics* **44**: 73.

GÖRLACH, MANFRED (1987) Colonial lag? The alleged conservative character of American English and other 'colonial' varieties. *English world-wide* **8** (1): 41–60.

GOLDIN, HYMAN E., O'LEARY, FRANK, LIPSIUS, MORRIS (1950) *Dictionary of American underworld lingo*. Twayne Publishers, New York.

GOODMAN, MORRIS (1985) Review of Bickerton, Roots of language. *International journal of American linguistics* **51**: 109–37.

GRADE, PAUL (1892) Das Neger-Englisch an der westküste von Afrika. *Anglia* **14**: 362–93.

GREENE, LORENZO J. (1942) *The Negro in colonial New England, 1620–1776*. Kennikat Press, Inc., Port Washington, NY.

GREENE, JACK P. (1989) Review of Cressy David, *Coming over: migration and communication between England and New England in the seventeenth century*. *American historical review* **94**, (No. 3): 39–40.

GREENE, JACK. P. (1988) *Pursuits of happiness: the social development of early modern British colonies and the formation of American culture*. University of North Carolina Press, Chapel Hill.

GRIFFEN, CLYDE (1978) *Natives and newcomers*. Cambridge, Mass., Harvard University Press.

GREGG, JOSIAH (1844) *Commerce of the prairies*. H.G. Langley, New York.

GUITARTE, GUILLERMO L. (1983) Para una periodizaciùn de la historia del Español de America. *Siete estudios sobre el Espaûol de America*. Universidad Autónoma de México.

HACKETT, CHARLES W. (1931) *Pichado's treatise on the limitations of Louisiana and Texas*. University of Texas Press, Austin.

HAFEN, LeROY R. (ed.) (1982) *Ruxton of the Rockies*. University of Oklahoma Press, Norman.

HALL, CAPTAIN BASIL (1829) *Travels in North America in the years 1827 and 1828* (Vol. I of three). Edinburg, Cadell & Co., and London, Simpkin.

HALL, HOWARD JUDSON (ed.) Benjamin Edward Tompson, 1642–1714. First native poet of America, His poems. 1924.

HALL, ROBERT A. Jr (1966) *Pidgin and Creole languages*. Cornell University Press, Ithaca, New York.

HALL, ROBERT A. Jr (1944) Review of Edgar Sayer, *Pidgin English*. *Language* **20**: 171–4.

HAMILTON, MARILYN (1932) California gold rush English. *American speech* **7**: 423–33.

HAMILTON, DR ALEXANDER (1907) *Hamilton's Itinerarium: being a narrative of a journey from Annapolis, Maryland, through Delaware, Pennsylvania, New York, New Jersey, Connecticut, Rhode Island, Massachusetts, and New Hampshire from May to September, 1744.* Privately printed and distributed by Albert Bushnell Hart for William K. Bixby, St Louis.

HANCOCK, IAN F. (1971) *A study of the sources and development of the lexicon of Sierra Leone Krio.* University of London School of Oriental and African Languages, unpublished dissertation.

HANCOCK, IAN F. (1979) *English in St Helena: Creole features in an island speech. Society for Caribbean Studies,* Occasional Papers No. 11. University of the West Indies, St Augustine, Trinidad.

HANCOCK, IAN F. (1980) *The creole English of the Bracketville Afro-Seminoles.* In Dillard (1980): 305–33.

HANCOCK, IAN F. (1985) *The domestic hypothesis, diffusion and componentiality: an account of Atlantic anglophone creole origins.* Amsterdam conference on creole morphology, ms.

HARDER, KELSIE B. (1976) *Illustrated dictionary of place names*, United States and Canada. Van Nostrand, New York.

HARVEY, L.P., JONES R.O., WHINNOM, KEITH (1967) Lingua Franca in a vallancio by Encino. *Revue de littérature comparée* XLI: 572–9.

HARRIS, J. WILLAIM (1989/90) Portrait of a small slaveholder. *Georgia historical quarterly* LXXIV: 1–19

HARRIS, JOEL CHANDLER (1883) *Nights with Uncle Remus: myths and legends of the old plantation.* Houghton Mifflin & Co., Boston and New York.

HARRISON, J A. (1884) Negro English. *Anglia* 7: 232–79.

HEATH, SHIRLEY BRICE (1980) Standard English: biography of a symbol. In Shapen, Timothy, Williams, Joseph A. (eds), Standards and dialects in English. Winthrop Publishers, Cambridge, Mass.

HENRY, ALEXANDER (1809) *Travels and adventure in Canada.* Readex Microprint, New York, rpt 1966.

HERLEIN, J.D. (1718) *Beschryvinge van de volks-plantinge Zuriname: vertonende de opkomst dier zelver colonie, etc., mitsgaders een vertoog van de boschgrond, etc.* (2nd edn) Leeuwarden.

HERMAN, LEWIS HELMAR, HERMAN, MARGUERITE SHALETT (1947) *American dialects: a manual for actors, directors, and writers.* Theatre Arts Books, New York.

HIGBEE, EDWARD (1958) *American agriculture: geography, resources, conservation.* John Wiley & Sons, Inc., New York.

HIGHAM, JOHN (1968) Immigration. In Woodward C. Van (ed.), *The comparative approach to American history.* Basic Books, New York and London, 91–105.

HIRSHBERG, JEFFREY A. (1982) Review of Dillard, Lexicon of Black English. *American Speech* **57**: 3 (Spring): 52–73.

HOBART, BENJAMIN (1866) *History of the town of Abingdon, Plymouth County, Massachusetts.* Boston, Mass.

HOETINK, HARMANNUS (1974) Los Americanos de Samaná *Eme Eme. Estudios Dominicanos* **10**: 3–26.

HOLM, JOHN (1980) African features in white Bahamian English. *English world-wide* **1** (1): 45–65

HOLM, JOHN, SHILLING, ALLISON (1982) *Dictionary of Bahamian English.* Lexik House, Cold Spring, NY.

HOLM, JOHN (1988) *Pidgins and Creoles* (2 vols). Cambridge Language Surveys) Cambridge University Press

HOLMES, JACK D.L. (1965) *Payoso.* LSU Press, Baton Rouge

HOLMES, JACK D.L. (1967) Indigo in colonial Louisiana and the Floridas. *Louisiana history* **8**: 329–49

HORSMANDEN, DANIEL P. (1810) *The New York conspiracy, or a history of the Negro plot, with the journal of the proceedings against the conspirators at New York in the years 1741–2.* Southwick and Pelsue, New York.

HULBERT, ARCHER BUTLER (1929) *Frontiers, the genius of American nationality*, Boston.

HULBERT, ARCHER BUTLER (1931) *Forty-niners: the chronicle of the California trail.* Little, Brown, & C., Boston, Mass.

HUTTAR, GEORGE (n.d.) Epenthetic *-mi* in Ndjuka: a transitive marker? Ms.

HUYKE, EMILIO E. (1973) *El beisbol en Puerto Rico. IAlo!, mini- revista editata por la telefùnica de Puerto Rico*, Octubre.

INGRAHAM, JOSEPH HOLT (1835, 1966) *The Southwest by a yankee.* Readers Microprint, New York.

ISRAEL, KENNETH D. (1970) A geographical analysis of the cattle industry in southeastern Mississippi from its beginnings until 1860. University of Southern Mississippi, unpublished, dissertation.

JACKSON, BRUCE (1966) White dozens and bad sociology. *Journal of American folklore* **79**: 374–7.

JACKSON, BRUCE (ed.) (1967) *The Negro and his folklore in nineteenth-century periodicals.* University of Texas Press, Austin and London.

JAMISON, J. FRANKLIN (ed.) (1970) *Privateering and piracy in the colonial period: illustrative documents.* Augustus M. Kelley, New York.

JENSEN, ARTHUR R. (1981) *Straight talk about mental tests.* Free Press, New York.

JOHN, ELIZABETH A.J. (1983) Life in a Wichita village. *Chronicles of Oklahoma* **60** (Winter): 412–37.

JOHNSON, CHARLES SPURGEON (1934) *The shadow of the plantation.* University of Chicago Press, Chicago.

JOHNSON, MICHAEL P. (1989) Review of McWhiney 1988 in *Journal of Southern history* LV: 490.

JOOS, MARTIN (1964) *The English verb: form and meaning.* University of Wisconsin Press, Madison.

JORDAN, TERRY G. (1981) *Trails to Texas.* University of Nebraska Press.

JORDAN, TERRY G., KAUPS, MATTI (1989) *The American backwoods frontier: an ethnic and ecological interpretation*, Johns Hopkins University Press, Baltimore and London.

KAHANE, HENRY, KAHANE, RENNE (1986) *Graeca et Romanica scripta selecta. Vol. I: Romance and Mediterranean lexicology.* Aldolf M. Hakkert, Amsterdam.

KAHANE, HENRY, KAHANE, RENÉE, TIETZE, A. (1958) *The Lingua Franca in the Levant.* University of Illinois Press, Urbana.

KEMBLE, FRANCIS ANNE (1863) *Journal of a residence on a Georgia plantation in 1838–39.* Harper & Brothers, New York.

KETCHAM, RALPH (1974) *From colony to country: the revolution in American thought, 1750–1820.* Macmillan, New York and London

KIRKHAM, SAMUEL (1823) *A compendium of English grammar, accompanied by an appendix in familiar lectures; containing a new systematic mode of parsing; likewise exercises in false syntax, and a key to the exercises, designed for the use of private learners and schools.* Herald Press, Frederick-Town.

KIRHAM, SAMUEL (1829) *English grammar in familiar lectures accompanied by a compendium embracing a new systematick order of parsing, a new system of punctuation, exercises in false syntax, and a system of philosophical grammar in notes* (11th edn). Oliver Steele, New York.

KITTREDGE, GEORGE LYMAN (1904) *The old farmer and his almanac.* W. Ware & Co., Boston.

KNIFFEN, FRED B, GREGORY, HIRAM F, STOKES, GEORGE B. (1987) *The Historic Indians of Louisiana, from 1542 to the present.* LSU Press, Baton Rouge.

KNIGHT, HENRY C. (pseudonym Arthur Singleton) (1818, 1824) *Letters from the south and west.* Richardson and Lord, Boston.

KNIGHT, SARAH KEMBLE (1935) *The journal of Madam Knight, with an introductory note by George Parker Winship.* Peter Smith, New York.

KNIGHTS, PETER S. (1969) Population turnover, persistence and residental mobility in Boston, 1830–1860. In Thomstrom, Stephan, Sennet Richard (eds), *Nineteenth century cities, essays in the new history.* Yale University Press, New Haven and London.

KOEN, ALFONS L. (1976) *News from Molkai.* University Press of Hawaii.

KOCHMAN, THOMAS (ed.) (1972) *Rappin' and stylin' out: communication in urban Black America.* University of Illinois Press, Urbana.

KRAENZEL, CARL FREDERICK (1925) *The Great Plains.* University of Oklahoma Press, Norman.

KRAPP, GEORGE PHILIP (1925) *The English language in America* (2 vols). Frederick Publishing Co., New York.

KROCH, ANTHONY S. (1976) Toward a theory of social dialect variation. *Language in society* 7: 17–36.

KURATH, HANS (1949) *A word geography of the eastern United States.* University of Michigan Press, Ann Arbor.

KURATH, HANS (1972) *Studies in areal linguistics.* Indiana University Press, Bloomington and London.

KURATH, HANS, McDAVID, RAVEN I, Jr (1961) *The pronunciation of English in the Atlantic States.* University of Michigan Press, Ann Arbor.

LABOV, WILLIAM (1963) The social motivation of a sound change. *Word* **19**: 273–309.

LABOR, WILLIAM (1968) The reflection of social processes in linguistic structures. In Fishman Joshua, A. (ed.), *Readings in the sociology of language*. Mouton, The Hague–Paris.

LABOV, WILLIAM (1966) *The social stratification of English in New York City*. Center for Applied Linguistics, Washington.

LABOV, WILLIAM (1972a) *Language in the inner city*. University of Pennsylvania Press, Philadelphia.

LABOV, WILLIAM (1972b) *Sociolinguistic patterns*. University of Pennsylvania Press, Philadelphia.

LAIRD, CHARLTON (1970) *Language in America*. World Publishing Co., New York and Cleveland.

LAMBERT, WALLACE, TUCKER, RICHARD G. (1969) White and Negro listeners' reactions to various American–English dialects. *Social forces* **47** (June): 463–8.

LeCOMPTE, N.P. (1967) A word atlas of Lafourche Parish and Grand Isle, Louisiana. LSU, Baton Rouge. unpublished dissertation.

LEECHMAN, DOUGLAS, HALL, ROBERT A., Jr (1955) American Indian Pidgin English: attestations and grammatical peculiarities. *American Speech* **30**: 163–71.

LEITH, DICK (1983) *A social history of English*. Routledge & Kegan Paul, London and New York.

LeJEUNE, PAUL (1632) *Brieue relation du voyage de la Nouvelle France*. Sebastien Cramoisy, Paris.

L'ESCARBOT, MARK (1609) *Nova Francia: or the description of that part of New France which is one continent with Virginia*. Trans. into English by P. E., George Bishop, London.

LEWIS, RONALD L. (1989) From peasant to proletarian: the migration of southern Blacks to the central coalfields. *Journal of Southern history* LV (1): 77–102.

LICHTVELD, LOU (1951) *Woordenlijst van het Sranan-Tongo*. Bureau Volklectuur, Paramaribo.

LINCOLN, CHARLES H. (ed.) (1913) *Narrative of the Captivity of Mrs. Mary Rowlandson*. Barnes and Noble, New York, rpt 1959.

LINEBERRY, WILLIAM P. (1963) *The new states: Hawaii and Alaska*. H. W. Wilson Co., New York.

LINGEMAN, RICHARD (1980) *Small town America: a narrative history 1620–the present*. G. Putnam's Sons, New York.

LITTLEFIELD, DANIEL C. (1981) *Rice and slaves, ethnicity and the slave trade in colonial South Carolina*. Louisiana State University Press, Baton Rouge.

LLORENS, WASHINGTON (1968) Language of *germanía* in Puerto Rico *El habla popular de Puerto Rico* Cuaderno No. III.

LOFLIN, MARVIN D. (1967) A note on the deep structure of nonstandard English in Washington, DC. *Glossa* I: 26–32.

LOFLIN, MARVIN D. (1969) Negro nonstandard and standard English: same or different deep structure? *Orbis*. XVIII: 74–91.

LOFLIN, MARVIN D., SOBIN, NICHOLAS, DILLARD, J.L., (1969) Auxiliary structures and time adverbs in Black American English. *American Speech.* **48**: 22–36.

LOGGINS, VERNON (1931) *The Negro author: his development in America.* Columbia University Press, New York.

LOWERY, WOODBURY (1959) *The Spanish settlements within the present limits of the United States, Florida 1562–1574 with maps.* Russell & Russell, New York.

LUBBOCK, BASIL (1934) *Barlow's journal of his life at sea in king's ships, east and west Indian men and other merchantmen from 1659 to 1703, transcribed from the original manuscript.* Hurst & Blackett, Ltd, London.

LYONS, LARRY (1987) *The community in urban society.* Temple University Press, Philadelphia, Pa.

McCRUM, ROBERT, CRAN ,WILLIAM, MACNEIL, ROBERT, (1986) *The Story of English.* Viking, New York.

MACKAY, ALEXANDER (1850) *The western world, or travels in the United States in 1846–7.* R. Bently, London.

McCULLOCH, WALTER P. (1958) *Woods words: a comprehensive dictionary of logging terms.* Oregon Historical Society and Champoeg Press.

McDAVID, RAVEN I. Jr (1954/6) The dialects of American English. In Francis (ed.), *The structure of American English*: 480–543.

McDAVID, RAVEN I. Jr, O'CAIN, RAYMOND (1973) Sociolinguistics and linguistic geography. *Kansas journal of sociology* **9**: 1137–56.

McDAVID, RAVEN I. Jr, O'CAIN, RAYMOND (1980) Linguistic Atlas of the Middle and South Atlantic States. University of Chicago Press.

McKELVEY, BLAKE (1969) *The emergence of metropolitan America.* Rutgers University Press, New Brunswick.

McKELVEY, BLAKE (1971) *American urbanization: a comparative history.* Glencoe, IL.

McMASTER, JOHN BACK (1895) *A history of the people of the United States, from the Revolution to the Civil War* (4 vols). D. Appleton & Company, New York.

MADURO, ANTOINE J. (1961) *Spaanse documenten uit de jaren 1639 en 1640.* Drukkereij Sherpenheuvel, [Willemstad] Curaçao.

McWHINEY, GRADY (1988) *Cracker culture: Celtic ways in the old South.* University of Alabama Press, Tuscaloosa and London.

MAGNER, THOMAS F. (1976) The melting pot and language maintenance in South Slavic immigrant groups. *General linguistics* **16**: 59–67.

MALKIEL, YAKOV (1976) Changes in the European languages under a new set of sociolinguistic circumstances. In Chiappelli, Fredi (ed.), *First Images of America* II: 581–93. University of California Press, Berkeley.

MARCKWARDT, ALBERT H. (1957) Principal and subsidiary dialect areas in the north central states. *Publications of the American Dialect Society* 27 (April): 3–15.

MARCKWARDT, ALBERT H. (1958) *American English* (2nd edn). Oxford University Press (rev. J.L. Dillard, 1981).

MARRYAT, CAPTAIN FREDERICK (1960) *Diary in America.* Indiana University Press, Bloomington.

MARGRY, PIERRE (1875–86) *Découvertes et établissements des Français dans l'ouest et dans l'Amérique Septentrionale (1614–1754): mémoires et documents originaux.* Tomes I–VI, Paris.

MARTIN, SIDNEY WALTER (1944) *Florida during territorial days.* University of Georgia Press, Athens, Georgia.

MASON, JULIAN (1960) The etymology of buckaroo, *American Speech* 25: 51–5.

MATHEWS, MITFORD M, (1931) *The beginnings of American English.* University of Chicago Press.

MEALOR, W. THEODORE Jr, PRUNTY, MERLE C. (1976) *Open-range ranching in south Florida.* Association of American Geographers, *Annals* 66, 360–76.

MEINIG, D.W. (1986) *The shaping of America: a geographical perspective on 500 years of history.* Vol. I, Yale University Press, New Haven and London.

MELVILLE, HERMAN (1846) *Typee: a peep at Polynesian life.* Penguin Books, London, rpt 1972.

MELVILLE, HERMAN (1851) *Moby Dick.* Norton Critical edn, W.W. Norton, New York rpt 1967.

MENCKEN, H.L. (1919) *The American language.* Alfred A. Knopf, New York.

MENCKEN, H.L. (1921) *The American language* (2nd edn). Alfred A. Knopf, New York.

MENCKEN, H.L. (1923) *The American language* (3rd end). Alfred A. Knopf, New York.

MENCKEN, H.L. (1936) *The American language* (4th edn). Alfred A. Knopf, New York.

MENCKEN, H.L. (1945) *The American language* (Supplement 1). Alfred A. Knopf, New York.

MENCKEN, H.L. (1948) *The American language* (Supplement 2). Alfred A. Knopf, New York.

MENCKEN, H.L., McDAVID, RAVEN I. Jr, MAURER, DAVID (1963) *The American language.* Alfred A. Knopf, New York.

MEREDITH, MAMIE (1930) Language mixture in American place names, *American Speech* 5: 224–7.

MICHAUT, ANDRÉ (1804) *Voyage à l'ouest des monts Alleghenys du Kentucky et du Tenesée et retour à Charleston.* Imprimerie de Crapelet, Paris.

MILLER, ALFRED JACOB (1837) *The West of Alfred Jacob Miller.* University of Oklahoma Press, Norman.

MILLER, JOY L. (1972) *Be*, finite and absence: features of speech – Black and White. *Orbis* 21: 22–7.

MILLER, MARY RITA (1968) Attestations of American Indian Pidgin English in fiction and non-fiction. *American Speech* 42: 142–7.

MOBLEY, MILLY LOU (1938) *Me speak English.* Star–Bulletin, Inc., Honolulu.

MONTGOMERY, MICHAEL, BAILEY GUY (eds) (1986) *Language variety in the South: perspectives in Black and White*. University of Alabama Press, Tuscaloosa, Alabama.

MORA, JOSEPH JACINTO (1946) *Trail dust and saddle leather*. Charles Scribner's Sons, New York.

MORGAN, RALEIGH (1959) Structural sketch of St Martin Creole, *Anthropological Linguistics* **2** (1): 7–29.

MORGAN, RALEIGH (1964) St Martin creole and genetic relationships. In *Studies in honor of Charles C. Fries* ed. A. Marckwardt *et al*. University of Michigan Press, Ann Arbor.

MORGAN, RALEIGH (1972) L'ordre des mots dans le syntaxe du créole de Saint Martin, *Revue de la Louisiana/Louisiana review*.1: 65–81.

MORRIS, A.C. (1973) Names under the Florida sun. University of Florida, Gainesville, P.K. Yonge Collection MS.

MUFWENE, SALIKOKO (1989) Equivocal structures in some Gullah complex sentences. *American Speech* **64** (4): 304–26.

MUFWENE, SALIKOKO, GILMAN, CHARLES (1988) How African is Gullah and why? *American Speech* **62** (Summer): 120–39.

MULLIN, GERALD W. (1972) *Flight and rebellion: slave resistance in eighteenth-century Virginia*. Oxford University Press, New York.

MULLIN, MICHAEL (1989) Review of Sokel Mechal 1987, *The world they made together*. *Journal of Southern history* LV: 467–8.

MYERS, CAROL M. (1965) *Early New York State census records 1663–72* (2nd edn). RAM Publishers, Gardena, California.

NARO, ANTHONY J. (1978) A study in the origins of pidginization. *Language* **54** (2): 314–49.

NATHAN, HANS (1962) *Dan Emmett and the rise of early Negro minstrelsy*. University of Oklahoma Press, Norman.

NEEDLER, GEOFFREY D. (1967) Linguistic evidence from Alexander Hamilton's 'Itinerarium'. *American Speech* **42**.

NORMAN, ARTHUR M.Z. (1955) Bamboo English. *American Speech* **30**: 44–8

NUGENT, LADY MARIA (1966) *Lady Maria Nugent's journal of her residence in Jamaica from 1801 to 1835*. Institute of Jamaica, Kingston.

NWAVE XIV Panel Discussion 1987: Are Black and White vernaculars Diverging? *American Speech* **62** (1): 3–80.

OGDEN, GEORGE W. (1823) *Letters from the West* (Thwaites Vol. XIX). Melcher and Rodgers, New Bedford, Mass.

OLMSTED, FREDERICK LAW (1854) *A journey in the back country*. Corner House Publishers, Williamsburg, Mass. rpt 1972.

OLMSTED, FREDERICK LAW (1854) *The cotton kingdom*. Alfred A. Knopf, New York, rpt 1953.

ORKIN, MARK M. (1971) *Speaking Canadian English, an informal account of the English language in Canada*. Routledge & Kegan Paul, London.

OTTLEY, ROI, WEATHERBY, WILLIAM J. (1967) *The Negro in New York: an informal social history*. New York Public Library, New York.

ORBECK, ANDERS (1927) *Early New England pronunciation*. University of Michigan Press, Ann Arbor.

OWEN, CAPTAIN W.F.W, (1833) *Narrative of voyages to explore the shores of Africa, Arabia and Madagascar, performed in H.M. ships* Leven *and* Barracouta. (2 vols) J. & J. Harper, New York.

PADDOCK, HAROLD J. (1966) A dialect survey of Carbonear, Newfoundland. Memorial University of Newfoundland, unpublished thesis.

PAGE, THOMAS NELSON (1887) *In ol' Virginia; or, Marse Chan, and other stories.* Charles Scribner's Sons, New York.

PARKES, HENRY BAMFORD (1947/59) *The American Experience.* Random House/Vintage, New York.

PAYNE, L.W, Jr (1908–9) A word-list from east Alabama. *Dialect Notes* **3**: 279–328, 343–91.

PEDERSON, LEE *et al* . (1985) *Handbook of the Linguistic Atlas of the Gulf States* (Vol. I). University of Alabama Press, University, Alabama.

PEI, MARIO (1967) World pidgins. In *Talking your way around the world.* Harper & Row, New York.

PERLMAN, DOROTHY (1971) *The magic of honey.* Galahad Books, New York.

PHARR, ROBERT DEAN (1969) *The book of numbers.* Doubleday & Co., Garden City, New York.

PHILLIPS, PAUL C. (ed.) (1957) *Forty Years on the Frontier as seen in the Journals and Reminiscences of Granville Stuart, Gold-Miner, Trader, Merchant, Rancher and Politician* Glendale, California, The Arthur H. Clarke Co., Northwest Historical Series II.

PICKFORD GLENNA RUTH (1956) American linguistic geography: sociological appraisal. *Word* **12**: 211–29.

PIKE, ZEBULON (1966) *Sources of the Mississippi and the western Louisiana territory.* Readex microprint, New York.

PIPPIN, ROLAND, DILLARD J.L., JONES, JARRED (forthcoming) Preference for the lexical item /ant/ as a function of strength of ethnicity: a pilot project.

POLK, NOEL (ed.) (1989) *Natchez before 1830.* University of Mississippi Press, Jackson and London.

PONTILLO, JAMES JOHN (1975) Nautical terms in sixteenth-century American Spanish. SUNY Buffalo, unpublished dissertation.

POPLACH, SHANA, SANKOFF, DAVID (1987) The Philadelphia story in the Caribbean. *American Speech* **62**: 291–304.

PRINCE, J. DYNELY (1910) Jersey Dutch. *Dialect notes* III: 459–60.

PRINGLE, IAN (1983) The concept of dialect and the study of Canadian English. *Queens quarterly* **90**: 100–21.

PUTNAM, MARTHA S. (1987) Black sailors: Afro-American merchant seamen and whalemen prior to the Civil War. *Contributions to Afro-American and African Studies*, No. 103. Greenwood Press, New York, Westport, Conn. and London.

PYLES, THOMAS (1952) *Words and ways in American English.* Random House, New York.

QUINN, JANE (1975) *Minorcans in Florida, their history and heritage.* Mission Press, St Augustine, Florida.

RANDOLPH, EDWARD (1676) Report to the council of trade.*Documents relative to the colonial history of the state of New York procured in Holland, England and France by John Romeyn Brodhead, Esq.* III: 2. Weed, Parsons, & Co. Albany, rpt 1853.

RAMSEY, FREDERICK Jr, SMITH, CHARLES EDWARD (eds) (1939) *Jazzmen.* Harcourt, Brace & Co. New York.

RASICO, PHILIP D. (1986) The Spanish lexical base of old St Augustine, Mahonese: a missing link in Florida Spanish. *Hispania* 69: 267–77.

RASICO, PHILIP D. (1987) *Els Menorquins de la Florida: història, llengua i cultura.* Publicacions de l'Abadia de Montserrat, Montserrat.

RAYNAL, GILLAUME THOMAS FRANÇOIS (1780) *Histoire philosophique et politique des établissements.* Paris, chez Jean-Leonard Pellet.

READ, ALLEN WALKER (1933) British recognition of American speech in the eighteenth century. *Dialect notes* VI: 313–34.

READ, ALLEN WALKER (1937) Bilingualism in the middle colonies, 1725–75. *American Speech* 12: 93–9.

READ, ALLEN WALKER (1939) The speech of Negroes in colonial America. *Journal of Negro history* 24: 247–58.

READ, ALLEN WALKER (1941) English of Indians 1705–1745. *American speech* 16: 72–4.

READ, WILLIAM A. (1934) *Indian place names in Alabama.* LSU University Studies, No. 29, Baton Rouge.

READ, WILLIAM A. (1963) *Louisiana French.* Louisiana State University Press, Baton Rouge.

REDIKER, MARCUS (1987) *Between the devil and the deep blue sea: merchant seamen, pirates, and the Anglo-American maritime world, 1700–1750.* Cambridge University Press.

REED, CARROLL E. (1977) *Dialects of American English* (rev. edn). University of Massachusetts Press.

RICKFORD, JOHN (1985) Ethnicity as a sociolinguistic boundary. *American speech* 60: 245–90.

RICKFORD, JOHN (1986) Social contact and linguistic diffusion. *Language* 62: 245–90.

RISSANEN, MATTI (1985) Periphrastic *do* in early American English. *Journal of English linguistics* 18 (No. 2): 163–79.

ROBINSON, FAYETTE (1974) *The gold mines of California: two guide-books.* Promontory Press, New York.

ROLLINS, PHILIP ASHTON (1922) *The cowboy, his characteristics, his equipment, and his part in the development of the west.* Charles Scribner's Sons, New York.

ROTHSTEIN, MORTON (1989) 'The remotest corner': Natchez on the American frontier. In Polk 1989.

ROWLAND, DUNBAR, SANDERS, A,G., GALLOWAY, PATRICIA K. (eds) (1984) *Mississippi Provincial Archives 1729–1748.* LSU Press, Baton Rouge.

RUNYON, DAMON (1938) A call on the president. In Clark, Kin (ed.), *A treasury of Damon Runyon.* Random House, New York, 1958.

SAFIRE, WILLIAM (1985) Out in left field. In Thorn, John (ed.), *The armchair book of baseball*. Charles Scribner's Sons, New York.

SALA, MARIUS (coordinator) 1982 *El espaûol de América, Tomo I: Léxico*. Publicaciones del Instituto Caro y Cuervo, Bogotá, Colombia.

SALMON, VIVIAN (1966) Language planning in seventeenth-century England: its context and aims. In Bazell, C.E. *et al.* (eds), *In Memory of J.R. Firth*. Longman, London.

SANTAMARÍA, FRANCISCO JAVIER (1942) *Diccionario general de Américanismos*. P. Robredo, Méjico, D.F.

SAUER, CARL (1920) The geography of Missouri. *Geographic Society of Chicago Bulletin*, No. 7. University of Chicago Press.

SAUER, CARL MORRIS (1971) *Sixteenth century North America: the land and people as seen by Europeans*. University of California Press, Berkeley.

SAWYER, JANET B. (1959) Aloofness from Spanish influence in Texas English. *Word* **15**: 270–81.

SAYER, EDGAR SHEPHARD (1939/43) *Pidgin English*. The author, Toronto.

SCARGILL, M.H. (1977) *A short history of Canadian English*. Victoria, B.C.

SCHELE DE VERE, MAXIMILIAN (1872) *Americans: the English of the New World*. Charles Scribner & Co., New York.

SCHLEBECKER, JOHN T. (1975) *Whereby we thrive: a history of American farming 1607–1972*. Iowa State University Press, Ames.

SCHNEIDER, EDGAR W. (1983) The diachronic development of the Black English perfective auxiliary phrase. *Journal of English linguistics* **16**: 55–64.

SCHNEIDER, EDGAR W. (1989) Review of Dorill, G. T. Black and white speech in the southern United States. *Journal of pidgin and creole languages* **4** (2): 311–12.

SCHNEIDER, EDGAR W. (1981) *Morphologische und syntaktische variablen im amerikanischen Early Black English*. Peter Lang Verlag. (Trans. as *American earlier Black English, morphological and syntactic variables*. University of Alabama Press, Tuscaloosa and London, 1989.)

SCHNEIDER, G.D. (1966) *West African Pidgin-English: A descriptive linguistic analysis with texts and glossary from the Cameroon area*. Privately printed, Athens, Ohio.

SCHOEPF, JOHANN DAVID (1788) *Reise durch einige der mittlern und südlichen vereignigten nordamerikanischen Staaten. Johan Jacob Palm.* (Amerikanischen) (Vol. II). Trans. and ed. J. Morrison as *Travels in the Confederation (1783–1784)*. Bergman Publishers, New York, 1968.

SCHUCHARDT, HUGO (1909) Die lingua franca. *Zeitschrift für romanische philologie* XXXI: 441–61.

SCULL, HIDEON D. (ed.) (1943) *Voyages of Peter Esprit Radisson*. Peter Smith, New York.

ŞEN, ANNA LOUISE FRISINGER (1973) Dialect variation in early American English. *Journal of English linguistics* **12** 41–7.

SHELDON, GEORGE (1895–6) *A History of Deerfield, Massachusetts*. (Published privately), Deerfield.

SHIELDS, KENNETH Jr (1987) Germanisms in the English of eastern Pennsylvania. *Journal of English Linguistics* **20** (No. 2): 163–79.

SHIELDS, KENNETH Jr (1989) A note on the *greasy, greazy* isogloss in East–Central Pennsylvania. *American Speech* **64**: 280–4.

SINGLER, JOHN VICTOR (1989) Plural marking in Liberian Settler English, 1820–1980. *American Speech* **64** (1): 40–64.

SINGLER, JOHN VICTOR (forthcoming a) African influence upon Afro-American language varieties: a consideration of sociohistorical factors. In Mufwene, Salikoko (ed.), *Africanisms in Afro- American language varieties*. University of Chicago Press, Chicago.

SINGLER, JOHN VICTOR (forthcoming b) Copula variation in Liberian Settler English. In Edwards, Walter F., Winford, Donald (eds), *Verb phrase patterns in Black English and creole*. Wayne State University Press, Detroit.

SLAUGHTER, THOMAS P. (1986) *The whiskey rebellion, frontier epilogue to the American revolution*. Oxford University Press.

SLEDD, JAMES (1966) Breaking, umlaut, and the Southern drawl. *Language* **42**: 18–41.

SMITH, JAMES L. (1881) *Autobiography of James L. Smith*. Press of the Bulletin Co., Norwich, Conn.

SMITH, WILLIAM (1744) *A Voyage to Guinea*. J. Nourse, London.

Social Science Panel on the Significance of the Metropolitan Environment (1974) *Toward an understanding of metropolitan America*. Canfield Press, San Francisco, Calif.

SPAETH, SIGMUND (1948) *A history of popular music in America*. Random House, New York.

SPRAGUE, MARSHALL (1964) *The great gates: the story of the Rocky Mountain passes*. University of Nebraska Press, Lincoln and London.

SPRINGER, OTTO (1980) *The study of the English of the Pennsylvania Germans*. In Dillard (1980): 195–203

STEFÁNSSON, VILHJALMUR (1909) The Eskimo trade jargon of Herschel Island. *American anthropologist* **11**: 217–32.

STEWARD, AUSTIN (1857) *Twenty-two years a slave, and forty years a freeman*. William Alling, New York.

STEWARD, WILLIAM A. (1967) Sociolinguistic factors in the history of American Negro dialects. *Florida FL reporter* **5**: 1–7.

STEWART, WILLIAM A. (1968) Continuity and change in American Negro dialects. *Florida FL reporter* **6**: 3–14.

STEWART, WILLIAM A. (1969) Historical and structural bases of sociolinguistic variation: the copula in Black English. In Alatis, James E. (ed.), *Georgetown university round table on languages and linguistics*. Washington, DC.

STORY, G.M., KIRWIN, W.I., WIDDOWEN, J.D.A. (1982) *Dictionary of Newfoundland English*. University of Toronto Press, Toronto.

STUART, GRANVILLE (1925) *Forty years on the frontier*. Arthur H. Clark Co., Cleveland.

SVEJCER, ALEKSANDR D. (1978) *Standard English in the United States and England.* Mouton, The Hague.

TABBERT, RUSSELL (1989) The names Eskimo, Inuit, and Inupiag/Inupiat. *Names* **37**: 79–82.

TABBERT, RUSSELL (1990) Rare *whoming* pigeon sighted in the grove of academe. *American Speech* **65**: 164–5.

TANIGUCHI, JIRO (1972) *A grammatical analysis of artistic representation of Irish English, with a brief discussion of sounds and spellings.* Shinozaki Shorin, Tokyo.

TARPLEY, FRED (1970a) *One thousand and one Texas place names.* University of Texas Press, Austin.

TARPLEY, FRED (1970b) *From blinky to blue-john: a word atlas of northeast Texas.* The University Press, Wolfe City, Texas.

TAYLOR, ALLAN R. (1981) Indian lingua francas. In Ferguson and Heath, 180–6.

TAYLOR, DOUGLAS (1977) *Languages of the West Indies.* Johns Hopkins University Press, Baltimore and London.

THOMPSON, HENRY F. (1907) Maryland at the end of the seventeenth century. *Maryland historical magazine* II: 163.

THURBER, JAMES (1937) *My world and welcome to it.* Harcourt, Brace, Jovanovich, New York, rpt 1965.

THWAITES, REUBEN GOLD (1904–7) *Early western travels, 1748–1846.* The H. H. Clark Co., Cleveland.

TILLERY, CARLYLE (1950) *Red bone woman.* The John Day Co., New York.

TINSLEY, JIM BOB (1990) *Florida cow hunters: The life and times of Bone Mizell.* University of Central Florida Press, Orlando.

TJOSSEM, HERBERT KARL (1956) New England pronunciation before 1700. Yale University, unpublished dissertation.

TODD, LORETO K. (1974) *Pidgins and Creoles.* Routlege and Kegan Paul, London.

TOOLE, K. ROSS (1976) *The rape of the great plains: Northwest American cattle and coal.* Little, Brown, & Co., Boston, Mass.

TRAUGOTT, ELIZABETH CLOSS (1972) *The history of English syntax: a transformational approach to the history of English sentence structure.* Holt, Rinehart & Winston, New York.

TROXLER, CAROLE WATTERSON (1989) Refuge, resistance, and reward: the southern loyalists' claim on East Florida. *Journal of Southern History* LV (4): 563–96.

TSUZAKI, STANLEY M. (1971) Co-existent systems in language variation: the case of Hawaiian English. In Hymes, (ed.), *Pidginization and creolization of language.* Cambridge University Press.

TURNER, G.W. (1966) *The English Language in Australia and New Zealand.* Longman, London.

TURNER, LORENZO DOW (1949) *Africanisms in the Gullah dialect.* University of Chicago Press.

TURNER, MARTHA ANN (1972) *William Barret Travis: his sword and pen.* Texian Press, Waco, Texas.

TUTTLE, EDWARD F. (1976) Borrowing versus semantic shift: New World nomenclatures in Europe. In Chapelli Fredi (ed.), *First Images of America*, II: 595–614. University of California Press, Berkeley.

UDALL, STEWART L. (1965) *The quiet crisis*. Holt, Rinehart & Winston, New York.

VALKHOFF, MARIUS F. (1966) *Studies in Portuguese and Creole, with special reference . . . to South Africa*. Witwatersrand University Press, Johannesburg.

VAN DEN BARK, MELVIN (1931) Nebraska pioneer English. *American Speech* **6**: 237–41.

VANDERBILT, GERTRUDE L. (1881) *The social history of Flatbush, and manners and customs of the Dutch settlers in Kings County*, Grederick Loeser, Brooklyn, New York.

VAN LOON, L.G. (1938) *Crumbs from an old Dutch closet*. The Hague.

VER STEEG, CLARENCE L., HOFSTADTER, RICHARD (1958) *Great issues in American history*, rpt 1969. Random House, New York.

VIERECK, WOLFGANG (1980) The dialectal structure of British English: Lowman's evidence. *English world-wide: a journal of varieties of English* I: (1): 25–44.

VOORHOEVE, JAN (1973) Historical and linguistic evidence in favour of the relexification theory in the formation of creoles. *Language in society* **2**: 133–45.

WALSER, RICHARD (1955) Negro dialect in eighteenth-century drama. *American Speech* **30**: 270–6.

WARNER, IRIS (n.d.) *Old Crow Yukon perimeter of paradise*. Whitehorse, Canada, Star.

WATERMAN, JOHN H. (1966) *A history of the German language*. University of Washington Press, Seattle.

WEATHERFORD, JACK (1988) *Indian givers: how the Indians of the Americas transformed the world*. Crown Publishers, Inc., New York.

WEBB, WALTER PRESCOTT (1931) *The great plains*. Ginn & Co., New York.

WEBSTER, NOAH (1789) *Dissertation on the English language: with notes, historical and critical*, ed. Harry R. Warfel. Scholars' Facsimiles and Reprints, Gainesville, FL rpt. 1951.

WELLS, J. C. (1982) *Accents of English 3: Beyond the British Isles*. Cambridge University Press.

WENTWORTH, HAROLD, FLEXNER, STEWART BERG (1967) *Dictionary of American slang*. Thomas Y. Crowell, New York.

WERDEN, SIR JOHN (1676) Extract of a letter to Mr. Dyre the 30th of November 1676. *Documents relative to the colonial history of New York, procured in Holland, England, and France by John Romeyn Brodhead*, Esq. Weed, Parsons, and Co., Albany, rpt. 1853, III: 246.

WESEEN, MAURICE HALEY (1934) *A dictionary of American slang*. Thomas Y. Crowell, New York.

WHINNOM, KEITH (1956) *Spanish contact vernaculars in the Philippine Islands*. Hong Kong University Press, Hong Kong.

WHINNOM, KEITH (1965) The origin of the European-based pidgins and creoles. *Orbis* **14**: 509–27.

WILLARD, 'DOCTOR' (1829) Inland trade with Mexico. *Western Monthly Review* II: 197, 649. Rptd in Thwaite XVIII: 327.

WILLIAMS, GEORGE WASHINGTON (1883/1968) *History of the Negro race in America*. Arno Press rept, New York.

WILLIAMS, JOHN LEE (1837) *The territory of Florida: or, sketches of the topography, civil and natural history, of the country, the climate, and the Indian tribes, from the first discovery to the present time*. University of Florida Press, Gainesville, rpt 1962.

WINKS, ROBIN (1971) *The Blacks in Canada: a history*. Yale University Press, New Haven and London.

WINSLOW, OLA ELIZABETH (1968) *John Eliot, apostle to the Indians*, Houghton Mifflin, Boston, Mass.

WISE, CLAUDE M. (1973) Specimen of Louisiana French–English: or, Cajun dialect in phonetic transcription. *American Speech* **8**: 63–4.

WISTER, OWEN (1958) *Owen Wister out West: his journals and letters*, ed. Fanny Kemble Wister. University of Chicago Press.

WOLFRAM, WALT, DONA, CHRISTIAN (1976) *Appalachian speech*. Center for Applied Linguistics, Washington, DC.

WOOD, BETTY (1984) *Slavery in colonial Georgia, 1730–1775*. University of Georgia Press, Athens.

WOOD, GORDON R. (1971) *Vocabulary change: a study in varieties of regional words in eight of the Southern states*. Southern Illinois University Press, Carbondale and Edwardsville.

WOOD, PETER (1974) *Black majority: Negroes in colonial Carolina through the rebellion*. Alfred A. Knopf, New York.

WOOD, WILLIAM (1634) *New England's prospect*. Thomas Cotes, for John Bellamie, London.

WOODS, HOWARD (1979) A socio-dialectology survey of the English spoken in Ottawa: a study of sociological and stylistic variation in Canadian English. University of British Columbia, unpublished dissertation.

WOODWARD, W. ELLIOT (1864) *Records of Salem witchcraft, copied from the original documents* (Vols I and II), DaCapo Press rpt, New York.

WYETH, JOHN (1833) *Oregon: or, a short history of a long journey from the Atlantic Ocean to the region of the Pacific by land*. Printed for John B. Wyeth (Thwaites XXI), Cambridge, Mass.

YOAKUM, H. (1855) *History of Texas, from its first settlement in 1685 to its annexation to the United States in 1846*. Redfield, New York.

# Index

# Dialect Index

*(Note: References to dialects, especially, in this book are historically oriented. Materials indexed here do not necessarily apply to twentieth-century dialects spoken by similar populations or in the same areas.)*